Beyond Leveled Books

Karen Szymusiak
Franki Sibberson
Lisa Koch

Foreword by Sharon Taberski

Supporting Early and Transitional Readers in Grades K–5

Stenhouse Publishers
Portland, Maine

Stenhouse Publishers
www.stenhouse.com

Credits
Pages 76–77: "The Night Before Fishing Season Opens," from *Baseball, Snakes, and Summer Squash* by Donald Graves. Copyright © 1996. Reprinted by permission of Wordsong/Boyds Mills Press.

The following articles were originally published at Choice Literacy (www.choiceliteracy.com):
Pages 40–46: "Organizing Book Baskets: Letting Kids In On the Plan" by Katie DiCesare
Pages 132–135: "Nonfiction Books for Independent Reading: Moving Beyond Content Connections" by Franki Sibberson
Pages 139–142: "Comprehending Graphic Novels: A Primer for Teachers" by Mary Lee Hahn
Pages 144–146: "On Kidney Tables: Small Changes for Big Effects" by Karen Szymusiak
Pages 172–175: "Just Because They Can Doesn't Mean They Should" by Shari Frost

Library of Congress Cataloging-in-Publication Data
Szymusiak, Karen.
    Beyond leveled books : supporting early and transitional readers in grades K–5 / Karen Szymusiak, Franki Sibberson, Lisa Koch ; foreword by Sharon Taberski.—2nd ed.
    p. cm.
    Includes bibliographical references and index.
    ISBN 978-1-57110-714-5 (alk. paper)
    1. Reading (Elementary) 2. Children—Books and reading. 3. Individualized instruction. I. Sibberson, Franki. II. Koch, Lisa, 1968– III. Title.
    LB1573.45.S99 2008
    372.4—dc22
        2008027575

Cover design, interior design, and typesetting by Martha Drury

Manufactured in the United States of America on acid-free, recycled paper
14 13 12 11 10 09   9 8 7 6 5 4 3 2

To our families

Contents

List of Mini-Lessons

Foreword to the Second Edition

I would venture to say that there's not a teacher in our schools today who doesn't know about leveled books. We're under far too much pressure to move students through levels faster and faster, higher and higher. We're encouraged (advised, actually) to scour the leveled lists, to go online to search out levels, to sticker and label our books, and to tuck them safely into designated bins so that children are reading the right books—the ones at their level. If that's not scary enough, children often talk more about the levels they're on and the levels they want to read than about the books themselves. In this age of No Child Left Behind and the searing focus on increased achievement and test scores, levels have become an all-too-frequent gauge of how well we think kids are doing in the months before spring testing.

Leveling does have a place in our classrooms—a practical one. It can help match a child with a range of books he's likely to be able to read on his own and during guided reading, and it can play an important role in helping struggling readers become more proficient. But, as happens to a lot of good ideas in education, leveled books have turned into a dangerous national obsession. We know there's a lot more to teaching children to read than finding their levels and moving them upward. Children need to plateau in their reading. They need to consolidate their skills and strategies, to read widely and deeply, to increase their vocabulary, and to experience life and gain humor so that they have more knowledge and insight to bring to texts and consequently understand them better.

In this new edition of *Beyond Leveled Books*, Karen, Franki, and Lisa help us look beyond the levels, and beyond leveled books, to consider what else we might put into children's hands during reading time. They help us to see that, although we do want to match children with books they can read—books that support them as readers—this matching involves much more than percentages on reading assessments and numbered levels on texts. They bring us back to the reality that children are supported by books they love, books they crave, books about characters they admire, and books about topics that fascinate them. Kids, like adults, want to read books that move them—not to high levels but to tears, laughter, and wonder.

Beyond Leveled Books, Second Edition, provides ideas, suggestions, practical classroom advice, and articles from experts in the field about how we can deepen our understanding of the books in our classrooms. The authors show us how to organize our classroom libraries and give us expanded lists of books that support our youngest readers. They invite us to take a step back and examine our teaching, and then give us the tools we need to become more expansive and generous in how we look at readers and the books they read. What remains in this second edition is the strong focus on transitional readers in the intermediate grades. *Beyond Leveled Books* was one of the first books to focus on transitional readers, and, since the first edition appeared, the authors have continued teaching, learning, and expanding their wealth of knowledge. Several new lessons and ideas about teaching with series books and graphic novels are included, as well as new thoughts on supporting student book choice, and much more. The first edition helped us learn how to teach without buying into the old, and wrong, notion that kids in the intermediate grades already know how to read. This new edition provides us with a seamless look at how we can use leveling appropriately in the primary grades, and how we can continue to support, motivate, and teach transitional readers more effectively.

In essence, *Beyond Leveled Books* is about empowering teachers. It's about helping us understand that our job is more extensive and challenging—and more delightful, actually—than just moving children from level to level, faster and higher. It's about knowing about books ourselves so that we can motivate our youngest readers, our struggling readers, and our doing-just-fine readers to find joy and pleasure in reading so they'll choose to read even when they don't have to. That's our ultimate goal in the teaching of reading, and that's what this book can help you do—teach kids throughout the elementary years so they become lifelong readers.

Sharon Taberski

Foreword to the First Edition

Who among us hasn't heard the old adage that we learn to read from kindergarten through second grade and then read to learn from third grade on. This notion was pounded into the brains of so many teachers that we began to believe it, until that day of reckoning when we stepped into a fresh third-, fourth-, or fifth-grade classroom and faced a gaggle of enthusiastic, tousle-haired kids who were a far cry from using reading to learn. While some were actually engaged in reading, many were flitting from one book to another like butterflies to flowers, abandoning books helter-skelter after five or ten pages. Still others were dozing off while attempting to read the assigned chapter in the history textbook. And more than a few were staring out the window while their book lay undisturbed in front of them. Many of these children did not appear to be reading for content, sustaining comprehension, or lingering in books. Yet, based on what we had been taught, they were supposed to be reading to learn by this time.

Good readers don't stop learning to read in second grade and suddenly start reading to learn in third. Good readers never stop learning to read. I am a better reader today than I was yesterday and not as good as I will be tomorrow—and I survived my fiftieth birthday last year. Learning to read is a lifelong process. The more time we spend learning to read, the better we become at reading to learn. What bouncing, budding preadolescents need is more reading instruction, with methods and strategies to help them read for information, read to discern themes, read to enhance understanding, and read for enjoyment. What intermediate kids need is having their teachers read this terrific book by Franki Sibberson and Karen Szymusiak, educators extraordinaire.

In *Beyond Leveled Books* Franki and Karen shatter the learn to read/ read to learn myth into a kaleidoscope of practical shards of wisdom and insight about thoughtful reading instruction and practice. The many strategies and methods they describe are aimed directly at those vulnerable, transitional readers who run the risk of becoming stuck in the transitional stage if they do not receive the literacy instruction they deserve to become engaged readers who use reading to inform, understand, remember, and learn.

This is the first book I've come across that deals so naturally and directly with readers at the intermediate stage. Over the past few decades so many books have been written about emergent readers, so many resources have been aimed at early literacy, and so much staff development has been geared toward primary-grade reading instruction that the needs of intermediate-grade readers have often been relegated to the back burner. Not any more! Thanks to Franki and Karen, transitional readers will no longer be lost in the shuffle.

The authors define students at this stage as readers who have learned useful emergent reading strategies and who readily use decoding skills to decipher text. They are readers in transition between emergent and independent reading, who are capable decoders but who often have gaps in strategy use and understanding and who find it difficult to sustain comprehension over time. Transitional readers are not struggling readers. They are readers who have moved beyond the emergent stage and are beginning to encounter longer, more difficult text. Franki and Karen remind us that this is not the time to stop teaching reading. Rather, this is exactly the time to provide explicit instruction in a new set of strategies that will help readers at this stage understand and learn from more complex text, so that they will not become mired in the transitional stage, but will continue to develop as readers and move toward independence. The strategies, methods, and overall literacy practice described in this book are just what readers at this stage need to continue down the path to literacy.

Franki and Karen don't merely teach the content of a piece of text by focusing mainly on word level; they also look closely at "supports," the features and text elements that help transitional readers as they move toward independence. The section "Supportive Features of Text" in

Chapter 4 offers myriad examples of how to identify and use such supports. I am awed by how much the authors see in a text and how seriously they look at the writing and text elements to determine what they might teach. I found their discussion of the value of series books especially enlightening. I had never given the series genre its due; from now on I will think differently about the instructional usefulness of series books. In addition, considering supports when matching books with readers improves the chances of hooking transitional readers. As the authors write, "Bringing children and books together matters."

How I would love to be a child in one of Franki and Karen's classrooms! Clearly, they both are voracious readers and true book lovers. Their classrooms and schools burst with books of every genre and length. I am astounded by their knowledge of books. They seem to have read every new novel, picture book, and young adult trade book on the market. Whenever I see either of them, they have a passel of books to recommend—kids' books, adult nonfiction, poetry, and more. They understand that reading is about appetite and diet. They know that all readers have a broad spectrum of tastes, and they know their students well. They know them as people and as readers. They understand that interest plays a crucial role in engaging children in reading, and they strive to make books of every imaginable theme, genre, and topic available to all the students in their classrooms.

Franki and Karen are insatiably curious about kids' thinking. They spend time watching children, listening to them and studying their work to inform their instruction. They take notes of conversations, arrange opportunities for kids to talk to each other, and interview them to learn about their reading preferences and habits. This book abounds with methods for doing these things. I was struck by the practicality of many of the interview questions in Chapter 7, and I suspect kids would really love to answer them. The fact is, we cannot teach children if we don't know them. The authors understand this and take great pains to get to know their students' personalities, passions, quirks, and tastes in reading.

Every conversation I have with Franki and Karen leaves me thinking and wondering about how better to teach the children with whom I work. The authors are supremely thoughtful educators who never stop thinking about how to hone their own practice and strengthen their students' learning. Once again they've left me thinking, but this time about the ideas in their wonderful book. Franki and Karen have started a conversation about transitional readers that is long overdue. It is their sincere hope that teachers, staff developers, and educators of all types will continue this conversation long after they close this book. Kids in the intermediate stage were the focus of many literacy conversations when they were in kindergarten and first grade. Let's not forget them now. They deserve the same treatment they received when they were younger. The authors of this book want to fill teachers' hearts and minds with strategies for transitional readers in the same way we have been filled with information on emergent readers.

Early in the book, Ryan, a third grader, was asked about the book he was reading. He answered, "When it is closed, it looks dull. The real stuff is inside." When this book is closed, it looks great, thanks to Stenhouse; but Ryan is right when he says the real stuff is inside. Franki and Karen have loaded this book with the real stuff. You are in for a treat. Count on it!

Stephanie Harvey

Acknowledgments

Dorothy Parker once said, "I hate writing. I love having written." We love having written the second edition of this book. Along the way, the tasks of sitting down to write, formulating our thoughts, taking care of details, and meeting deadlines were at times frustrating. But not one of us would say that we hate writing. We simply hate the challenge of carving the time out of our busy lives. Once our hands are on the keyboard, we are hooked. Writing a second edition gave us the opportunity to rethink what we had written, add new ideas, update book lists, and be honestly reflective about our practice.

We are thrilled to have added several short pieces from some of our favorite writers. These people shared their perspectives on books and children. Kathy Collins, Diane DeFord, Katie DiCesare, Shari Frost, Mary Lee Hahn, Adria Klein, Loren Long, Lynn Salem, Josie Stewart, and Larry Swartz have important things to say that inform learning and teaching. We thank them for their contributions, their work in the field, and their support of this project from the beginning.

We are honored to have the foreword to this edition by Sharon Taberski. She has always been an advocate for children, and her work reminds us to stay true to our beliefs about learning and teaching. We appreciate her friendship over the years.

We consider it a privilege to be a part of the community at Stenhouse. Bill Varner and Philippa Stratton helped shape our vision for this second edition. Bill was incredibly patient as we forged ahead in the process. We appreciate the collaboration of everyone at Stenhouse that made this second edition possible.

Jen Allen gave us great feedback about where to go with our thinking early in the process. Her thoughts were insightful as always and helped us create a book that we hope makes a difference for students and teachers.

So many people were supportive of the first edition. We have always been fortunate to have people to think with and talk to about issues in literacy education: Tom Bates, Louise Borden, Cathi Elliott, Bob Griffith, Dr. Gloria Flaherty, Ralph Fletcher, Stephanie Harvey, Shelley Harwayne, Debbie Miller, Jill Reinhart, and Cris Tovani. Brenda Power worked tirelessly as editor on the first edition of this book. Without her expertise and patience, we would still be talking about writing. Her support with the first edition of the book and since then has been invaluable.

We are lucky to know Sally Oddi and the staff at Cover to Cover bookstore. Over the course of our careers, Cover to Cover is the place we go to find great books for our students. Sally knows books and children better than anyone we know.

The students and staff in the Dublin City Schools have always given us the chance to explore learning and teaching and to examine more effective instructional practice. After all, our work with children is the most important thing we do. We have always been lucky to learn with great colleagues as part of the Dublin City Schools.

Our families were so supportive as we took another look at *Beyond Leveled Books*. We have all learned the most about finding books we love from our children Zac Szymusiak and Amanda Blankenship, Alexa and Ana Sibberson, and Alec, Elle, and Kyle Koch. We appreciate the support and encouragement of our families.

Introduction

There are times in our lives when storytelling brings out a sense of truth that knocks us off our feet and shakes our perspective. What Lisa has written is the perfect introduction to a new edition of *Beyond Leveled Books*.

My Son Clark Kent

Lisa Koch

The day my son Alec was born I read him Jules Feiffer's *Bark, George* in the hospital. It was a gift from my cousin who taught me the importance of daily reading to instill a love for books. Each day after that, I read to him. He attended early learning classes where he discovered literacy in a preschool setting. He became familiar with Eric Carle, and *Chicka Chicka Boom Boom*. He yelled to the teacher, "Don't let the pigeon drive the bus!" And he continued to encourage George to bark as he reread his favorites and shared them with the other children in his class.

By the time kindergarten rolled around, he had dozens of books he loved. He begged to drive an hour to see Barbara Park, the author of the Junie B. Jones series. I waited with him in line for more than three hours just so she could "make his book special by writing her name inside of it."

I remember the days of kindergarten when he just couldn't wait to tell me what Junie B. had done in school that day. She was his friend, and he was a reader. I will never forget the day I drove four of his friends to a birthday party and they insisted on listening to the CD version of Junie B. instead of watching a movie. His entire class was in love with Junie B. and books.

Then first grade happened. Alec arrived in his first-grade classroom excited to learn. He was ready with backpack in hand, supplies in his box, and lunch in his bag. He was really ready!

Maybe he wasn't really ready, because each day he came home with a different ailment. He visited the nurse each day. His knees hurt, his stomach hurt, he was tackled on the playground and everything hurt. This went on for days as we tried to figure out why. One day he came home complaining that his eyes hurt. Alec does have eyes of different sizes and colors (a result of a premature birth). I took him to the doctor immediately. Okay, I took him to three different doctors who each said the same thing. "His vision is fine and his eyes are healthy." Alec still complained that his eyes hurt.

The Monday after the third and final visit, Alec bounded off the school bus with a solution! "Mom, I wore Collin's glasses in school today, and I could see better. My eyes didn't hurt, either. I think I need glasses." He was quite certain glasses would solve the problem.

Since I was sure he didn't need glasses just yet, I asked him to tell me more about Collin. "Collin wears glasses and he reads a level L," he said. "My teacher says if you read a level L, then you are a really good reader. I think I need glasses to read a level L."

Three doctors' visits and $678 later, I discovered Alec wanted glasses to read at level L.

As educators we know kids need just-right texts to scaffold their literacy skills. We are all familiar with Fountas and Pinnell and their system for teaching with leveled books. I agree that kids need time with just-right books or books they can read independently. But it is the teacher's job to place those books with care into the hands of children, and then, teach children to choose those books themselves.

Did I miss the seminar that instructed us to run out and get bins labeled from A to Z so students could blindly (or with glasses, it seems) make their way dutifully to the end of each bin?

My son, who read all the time in kindergarten, stopped reading for fun. Alec stopped reading for information, and he stopped reading to and with me.

Each evening he brought home two books in an envelope. Each had a sticker with a capital letter proudly displayed on the cover. That letter became our nightmare.

Getting Alec to read those books was like pulling teeth. He had left the world of great illustrations and colorful language and entered a world of texts with generic pencil drawings and meaningless phrasing.

I realize that very short texts will not have intricately developed settings, characters, and plots, but these books seemed comparable in interest to the long-discarded Dick and Jane readers. Alec had lost interest in the stories, which wasn't surprising. Our conversations about books changed. Instead of questions about characters, words, or what might happen next, he asked, "Mom, what level is this?" He looked at the covers of books at home, almost expecting to find a label, and then exclaimed, "It has to be, like, a level X!"

My heart was breaking. At age six my son was now reading for competition. His purpose in reading was to get to the top. He didn't understand or care about any other aspect of the reading experience.

I was devastated, and it became clear that I had to set up rehab. Books that even resembled those books in the lettered bins were forbidden at home. I needed Junie B., and I needed her now!

As I presented the newest Junie B. book to Alec, I saw it. It was the sparkle in his eye as he remembered his good friend Junie B. and realized these characters he loved were going on vacation in *Aloha Ha Ha*. We stayed up and read together until we'd finished the book. When it was over, we both fell asleep knowing he would have to take his books back to school and tell his teacher he hadn't read the books he had blindly chosen from his bin. He didn't read them because he didn't want to. He felt no ownership that comes with choice. He never browsed the bin, because he saw no variety in the books.

Teachers, please reorganize those bins. Divide your books by genre, author, series, topic, fiction, nonfiction, or favorites, but please stop with the bins of leveled texts with the A–Z or numbered labels.

Leveled books were intended to help teachers get just-right books into the hands of children. But please allow kids to choose in an authentic manner and allow them to fall in love with books again. The levels were never meant for the students to know.

Alec has been wearing glasses to school for the past four days as I write these words. They have no lenses in them, but he is sure they will help him get to level L. He wears his glasses and he's asked me to sign the note he has written:

Dear Mrs. T,
Please let Alec be a letter L.

chapter one

Challenging Leveled-Book Mania

Reading is devalued if the books we read are not worth the effort of reading—when what we read adds nothing of significance or importance to our lives. Reading should be life work, not just school work. Students can discover the many pleasures of reading when they are treated to books with authentic, rich language and convincing stories about life. Children can identify with Max when he is naughty and sent to his room in Maurice Sendak's Where the Wild Things Are. *They fly with him on his journey of imagination and return home to forgiveness and a hot supper.*

KATHY SHORT, LITERACY AS A WAY OF KNOWING

Some of the children's books we have collected over the years stand out as landmarks on our journey of teaching and learning. We must have read *The Napping House* (Wood 1984) hundreds of times to our children, who joined us in reciting this cumulative rhyme and enjoying the wonderfully amusing illustrations. We recall reading *Wilfrid Gordon McDonald Partridge* (Fox 1984) and encouraging our young learners to talk about their favorite memories. Together we explored the land of

Roxaboxen (McLerran 1991) and imagined worlds of our own. We read stories with universal themes like *Fireflies!* (Brinckloe 1985) and remembered when we had captured lightning bugs in jars on warm summer evenings. We could not forget the adventures of *The Very Hungry Caterpillar* (Carle 1981) or the rollicking family in *The Relatives Came* (Rylant 1985). We marveled at the beautiful language in *All the Places to Love* (MacLachlan 1994) and *Twilight Comes Twice* (Fletcher 1997). There were patterned texts like *Chicka Chicka Boom Boom* (Martin and Archambault 1989) and *Brown Bear, Brown Bear* (Martin 1992). There were books representing several versions of familiar stories like *Gingerbread Baby* (Brett 1999). Our classrooms were filled with high-quality books that almost guaranteed that our young readers would fall in love with reading.

Just as cartographers map the world, we were happy to be the architects of classrooms filled with wonderful children's literature. One could walk by any classroom and see the most-loved books propped up on the chalk ledge and hear wonderful stories being read to children. If you looked more closely, you could see children scattered around the room with treasures of books in their hands and eyes of wonder as they explored the pages of wonderful literature. Our students took their first steps toward reading in the pages of these authentic, superbly written books.

Anyone who has ever taught kindergarten or first grade knows just how exciting it is to watch five- and six-year-olds learn how to read. Children move from chanting along to a familiar and repetitive text to following along in a story read aloud to them. Before we know it, they are reading on their own.

Sometimes our students needed books that provided more obvious supports. Having access to books they could read independently was critical, so we were thrilled when The Wright Group and Rigby published the first leveled books. We remember the characters and stories that our children enjoyed. We came to love *Mrs. Wishy-Washy* (Cowley 1988), and we can still remember the words to *Dan, the Flying Man* (Cowley 1988). These leveled books had a valued role as a small part of our classroom library, where the best of children's literature still occupied center stage.

The leveled books that were first published focused on great stories matched with text that our newest readers could handle. Authors and publishers understood what our kindergarten and first-grade readers needed to grow. Books were created thoughtfully by publishers who had a strong understanding of this stage of reading development. These first leveled books built skill and confidence in our emerging readers, and promoted reading fluency.

Our emergent readers needed high-quality books that they could read independently, and these leveled books provided a foundation for us to teach strategies to them. It's important to understand the historical developments that have led us to leveled books. Understanding the development of published reading materials for children over the last century is important to consider. Diane DeFord and Adria Klein help us recognize the positive aspects of leveled books and caution us to think about how we are going to use them with our students.

Teacher Decision Making Is the Key to Choosing Among Leveled Books and Going Beyond

Diane DeFord and Adria Klein

Levels, Levels, Levels

In the prologue to Nila Banton Smith's newest edition of *American Reading Instruction* (2002), Richard Robinson quotes George Santayana, a turn-of-the-last-century writer, as saying, "Those who cannot remember the past are condemned to repeat it." With today's fast-changing educational trends, instant communication, and political mandates, this comment is even more pertinent. Current-day practices in reading education, such as the use of "little books," book rooms, leveled book lists, leveled book collections, leveled testing, and incentive reading systems based on leveling children's books, have historical roots that may inform us about effective practice.

These historical roots go back to the early 1800s when William H. McGuffey published McGuffey's Readers (1836–1844), "the first author to produce a clearly defined and carefully graded series consisting of one reader for each grade in the elementary school" (Smith 2002, 99). This series was popular until the last published edition in 1907, and it spawned a host of other reading series grade-level materials for readers. For the most part, basal reading materials emphasized high-frequency or phonetically regular words through the 1950s and 1960s, and these graded texts constituted a significant portion of the basal market (Smith 2002).

Materials began to change with new research in the '60s through the '80s to include natural language structures and high-quality stories for children. The first literature-based program was produced in the late 1980s for California (Hoffman 1998), and these materials caught on across the United

States. The popularity of grade-level texts waned as many publishers abandoned graded leveling procedures that emphasized carefully controlled vocabulary to meet the call for more authentic literature and natural language texts (Hoffman et al. 2006). Literature anthologies, as they were called, were still organized by grade level, but they depended on more features than the grade level of the passage as determined solely by readability formulas. An analysis by Hoffman et al. (1994) showed that approved programs in Texas in 1993 consisted almost entirely of literature-based materials. However, there has always been a market for materials to meet the needs of special populations (adult basic education, adolescent readers, English language learners, and others) and core reading programs that do not put struggling readers at a disadvantage.

The more recent use of leveled texts as "little books" that has dominated the market, and professional material about how to level trade books, has provided greater access to materials, but the influence of previous movements and emphases is still visible in today's books in the form of phonetically regular or decodable texts, predictable language structures, high-frequency vocabulary, and so on. There are several reasons why the shift occurred in favor of little books, leveled-book collections, and book rooms and has extended to leveled assessments. Criticisms of the literature anthology movement of the 1990s indicated that these materials were not meeting the needs of struggling readers (Hoffman et al. 1998), especially at the earliest stages of reading. Teachers wanted greater flexibility in matching student interests and abilities to good books at every level. There was also increased dissatisfaction with basal reading programs promoting a one-size-fits-all philosophy (Allington and Walmsley 1995). Consequently, many new resources for leveled books emerged. Some of these resources have helped teachers organize existing children's literature to better advantage, and some materials have been published just for the "leveled little book" market.

Matching Books to Readers

One early intervention program that had a real impact on this new direction was Reading Recovery (Pitcher and Fang 2007). Started in New Zealand in the 1970s (Clay 1985, 1993), Reading Recovery used a variety of leveled materials that teachers could draw upon from different publishers to make learning to read easier for those first graders at greatest risk of reading failure. When Reading Recovery was implemented in the United States in the early 1980s and it began to grow quickly (Pinnell, DeFord, and Lyons 1988), there was greater demand for these little books that provided leveled material. The Wright Group secured the rights to publish The Sunshine Books (1987), a collection of leveled little books that were originally published in New Zealand and Australia. Shortland Publications produced The Story Box (1981) and Jelly Beans (1985) that The Wright Group also distributed, and Rigby brought an Australian series, Literacy 2000 (1988), to the United States as well. Other publishers scrambled to produce or make available more books like these for instructional and assessment purposes. These books are assigned levels using a progression of difficulty from more simple to more complex and challenging texts (Brabham and Villaume 2002) that take language, story structures, and text features into account (Peterson 1991).

The idea of matching books to readers caught on, not only at kindergarten and first grade, but on through eighth grade. The Reading Recovery procedure for leveling materials was researched and described by Peterson (1988, 1991). This process takes into account students' background of experience and interest, familiar language structures, print conventions, match between and placement of picture and text, conceptual load, vocabulary (considering known and new), and strategies that readers are currently developing. These books were referred to as *predictable books* because of the way the story and the language led readers to actively predict as they read. The leveling process used in Reading Recovery was then adapted and expanded for classroom teachers by Fountas and Pinnell (1996, 1999, 2001, 2005), offering book recommendations for use in a guided reading framework. They recently launched a web page of more than 16,000 leveled-book titles. Their recommendations for leveling books include both published little books and children's literature up through eighth grade using an alphabetic system from A to Z. The emphasis behind these professional materials is on using materials to build strategic readers.

Although leveled books serve many important instructional purposes, especially helping to focus strategy instruction, they have also contributed to what many call "leveling mania" (Szymusiak and Sibberson 2001, 16). Lest leveled little books go the way of many other good ideas that bad things happen to (Hoffman 1998), or that by forgetting our past, we are condemned to just repeat it, we would like to suggest some notions that need careful consideration.

Positive Aspects of Leveling Books for Readers

- Readers make the most progress when books are not too easy or too difficult (Allington 2006). Texts should be easy enough to develop students' confidence and facilitate comprehension, but difficult enough to provide a challenge and require the reader to do some "reading work" (Clay 1991).

- Considering a just-right level helps readers read fluently and compre-hend better; thus they take on the traits and skills of better readers (Allington 2006; Rasinski 2003).
- Students who meet success in reading are more likely to persist, to read more with less off-task behavior, and to achieve more (Gambrell, Wilson, and Gantt 1981; Allington 2006).
- Acceleration in learning, or increased achievement, is possible for strug-gling readers when the text/reading level is matched (O'Connor et al. 2002).
- Groupings of books into levels can make it easier for teachers, parents, and children to select books to read. Having multiple ways of grouping materials, such as collections by favorite authors, genre, topics, and sea-sonal reading addresses the different ways readers read and the pur-poses for which they read on a daily basis. Keeping high-quality literature among the books read and displayed keeps the richness needed for broad conceptions of reading to develop and flourish (Pierce 1999). Watson (1997) suggests that the first questions we need to ask are "How appropriate are the stories to the lives of my kids? Will they be interested?" (638).
- Books that are used for instruction can be selected with emphasis on stu-dent needs at a certain point, but selections should be different for inde-pendent reading. The way in which the features of the text are used in the instructional setting may emphasize some aspects of the book but not others, allowing book titles to be used differently at other times.
- With the variety of books now available with these leveling features, schools can adapt a greater number of their book collections to support their particular students.

Cautions for Using Leveled Books for Readers

- Focusing solely on text difficulty limits students' choices, which can lead to boredom and resistance (Worthy and Sailors 2001). The books may be "easier to read" but lack relevance and significance in the lives of the children forced to read such a limited diet. For example, until recently, leveled books have consisted mostly of fiction, with few nonfic-tion books listed.
- When difficulty or reading level is the only criterion used for book selec-tion, students may have a skewed vision of the purposes of reading (Worthy and Sailors 2001) and of themselves as readers. They may not

select books they are interested in because those books aren't on the approved list. They may lose interest in reading because they have little or no choice in what they read, define themselves as a poor reader, engage in reading less often, and spiral further into a cycle of failure if they are reading at a "lower level" than their friends.

- Leveled lists may not contain the variety of genres and topics of interest to readers, or a broad base of types of reading (including newspapers, comics, graphic novels, magazines, and so on). Books that represent the cultural and linguistic diversity that children are interested in or identify with may not be on the lists. Lack of interesting and varied materials limits the world of the reader. We must educate each reader beyond an assigned level.

- Books within levels often vary widely (Pitcher and Fang 2007); sometimes an "appropriate book" in terms of interest is at a higher level than students might read for guided reading. Purpose and interest need to be part of some reading selections, without consideration for whether the book is to be used for guided reading. Different leveling progressions also make it difficult to compare and select books (Brabham and Villaume 2002).

- When putting the level on books, make the numerical or alphabetical rating as inconspicuous as possible. Foreground the content, topic, and author information. Helping readers understand what makes books appropriate for different purposes is important.

- Although leveling systems differ, the current one is still geared to students progressing normally through "grade levels." A different system is needed for upper-grade readers, adults, English language learners, and special populations so that their particular needs can be met.

Concluding Thoughts

There is clearly a need to provide students with extensive opportunities to read a variety of materials, with a significant number of instructional books meeting the interests and capabilities of every reader in the classroom. The challenges are many, but the benefits are clear: selecting books to support readers' abilities benefits teachers and children alike so long as teachers make decisions within and beyond leveled books based upon their understanding of students' interests and capabilities, meeting different purposes for reading.

Diane DeFord is the Swearingen Literacy Professor at the University of South Carolina. Adria Klein is professor emeritus at California State University, San Bernardino.

References

Allington, R. L. 2006. *What Really Matters for Struggling Readers: Designing Research-Based Programs.* New York: Pearson.

Allington, R. L., and S. A. Walmsley, eds. 1995. *No Quick Fix: Rethinking Literacy Programs in America's Elementary Schools.* New York: Teachers College Press.

Brabham, E. G., and S. K. Villaume. 2002. "Leveled Text: The Good News and the Bad News." *The Reading Teacher* 55: 438–441.

Clay, M. 1985. *The Early Detection of Reading Difficulties.* Portsmouth, NH: Heinemann.

———. 1991. *Becoming Literate: The Construction of Inner Control.* Auckland, New Zealand: Heinemann.

———. 1993. *Reading Recovery: A Guidebook for Teachers in Training.* Portsmouth, NH: Heinemann.

Fountas, I. C., and G. S. Pinnell. 1996. *Guided Reading: Good First Teaching for All Children.* Portsmouth, NH: Heinemann.

———. 1999. *Matching Books to Readers: Using Leveled Texts in Guided Reading, K–3.* Portsmouth, NH: Heinemann.

———. 2001. *Guiding Readers and Writers: Grades 3–6.* Portsmouth, NH: Heinemann.

———. 2005. *Leveled Books K–8: Matching Texts to Readers for Effective Teaching.* Portsmouth, NH: Heinemann.

Gambrell, L. B., R. M. Wilson, and W. N. Gantt. 1981. "Classroom Observations of Task-Attending Behaviors of Good and Poor Readers." *Journal of Educational Research* 74: 400–404.

Hill, S. 2001. "Questioning Text Levels." *Australian Journal of Language and Literacy* 24: 8–20.

Hoffman, J. 1998. "When Bad Things Happen to Good Ideas in Literacy Education: Professional Dilemmas, Personal Decisions, and Political Traps." *The Reading Teacher* 52: 102–112.

Hoffman, J. V., S. J. McCarthey, J. Abbott, C. Christian, L. Corman, M. Dressman, B. Elliot, D. Matheme, and D. Stahle 1994. "So What's New in the 'New' Basals." *Journal of Reading Behavior* 26: 47–73.

Hoffman, J., N. Roser, R. Salas, E. Patterson, and J. Pennington. 2006. *Text Leveling and Little Books in First Grade Reading.* Available online at http://www.ciera.org/library/reports/inquiry-1/index.html.

Hoffman, J., N. Roser, and J. Worthy. 1998. "Challenging the Assessment Context for Literacy Instruction in First Grade: A Collaborative Study." In *Assessing Reading: Theory and Practice,* ed. C. Harrison and T. Salinger. London: Routledge.

O'Connor, R. E., K. M. Bell, K. R. Harty, L. K. Larkin, S. M. Sackor, and N. Zigmond. 2002. "Teaching Reading to Poor Readers in the Intermediate Grades: A Comparison of Text Difficulty." *Journal of Educational Psychology* 94: 474–485.

Peterson, B. 1988. *Characteristics of Texts That Support Beginning Readers.* Unpublished doctoral dissertation, The Ohio State University.

———. 1991. "Selecting Books for Beginning Readers." In *Bridges to Literacy: Learning from Reading Recovery,* ed. D. E. DeFord, C. A. Lyons, and G. S. Pinnell. Portsmouth, NH: Heinemann.

Pierce, K. M. 1999. "'I Am a Level 3 Reader': Children's Perceptions of Themselves as Readers." *The New Advocate* 12: 359–375.

Pinnell, G. S., D. E. DeFord, and C. A. Lyons. 1988. *Reading Recovery: Early Intervention for At-Risk First Graders.* Arlington, VA: Educational Research Service.

Pitcher, B., and Z. Fang. 2007. "Can We Trust Leveled Texts? An Examination of Reliability and Quality from a Linguistic Perspective." *Literacy* 41: 43–51.

Rasinski, T. V. 2003. *The Fluent Reader: Oral Reading Strategies for Building Word Recognition, Fluency, and Comprehension.* New York: Scholastic.

Rog, L. J., and W. Burton. 2001/2002. "Matching Texts and Readers: Leveling Early Reading Materials for Assessment and Instruction." *The Reading Teacher* 55: 348–356.

Smith, N. B. 2002. *American Reading Instruction.* Newark, DE: International Reading Association.

Szymusiak, K., and F. Sibberson. 2001. *Beyond Leveled Books: Supporting Transitional Readers in Grades 2–5.* Portland, ME: Stenhouse.

Watson, D. 1997. "Beyond Decodable Texts: Supportive and Workable Literature." *Language Arts* 74: 635–643.

Worthy, J., and M. Sailors. 2001. "'That Book Isn't on My Level': Moving Beyond Text Difficulty in Personalizing Reading Choice." *New Advocate* 14: 229–239.

When *Matching Books to Readers: Using Leveled Books in Guided Reading, K–3* (Fountas and Pinnell 1999) was published, we couldn't wait to get our hands on it. This important tool for teachers helped us understand the text features that supported our readers at various levels of reading development. We could learn from this book about more effective ways to match our students to books that they could read successfully and independently. We were thrilled with this tool for teachers.

But along the way, this well-intentioned knowledge base gradually became a way to measure a reader's progress. Levels became more important than the features of books that could support or challenge a reader. Instead of a useful part of the information Fountas and Pinnell had so clearly identified for teachers, the levels became invisible badges that students wore to enter a not-so-invisible race. The goal had changed from recognizing books that support readers to moving up the levels to claim some sense of accomplishment. Children, parents, and some teachers began to focus on moving to higher levels instead of paying attention to what readers were doing and how particular books supported them.

We never intended for children to use levels to choose books. But across the country, teachers in the primary grades began sorting their entire classroom libraries into leveled baskets. It was important for teachers to understand why and how the books were leveled so they could use them as they worked with emergent and early readers. Unfortunately, once the books were placed in leveled baskets, they became a hierarchy of reading choices. Some students were limited to choosing books from certain baskets, and instead of the world of books being expanded for them, their choices suddenly became limited. This occurred in kindergarten, and first- and second-grade classrooms and clouded the notion of authentic reading.

Some of us remember a rather similar situation reading from the Science Research Associates (SRA) kits when reading meant getting to the next color level. Once we read a passage, we had to correctly answer a set of questions before we could move to the next color level of texts. There was pressure to keep up with our friends and those in our reading-ability groups. We learned to play the game. Yet reading at home was completely different. Reading became a pleasure when we could choose "real" books. There were definite differences in our purpose and our process for reading at school and reading at home. Even those of us who read from basal readers at school knew that reading meant doing pages in our workbooks after each story. Again this reading was much different from the reading we did at home, where reading meant diving into a story and getting to know the characters as though they were our friends. Reading at school was a game that some of us got very good at and others took great pains to survive. Reading at home was real.

Over the last few years, many of us have been on diets at one time or another. A diet is not one of our favorite things, but is something we do for our health and self-esteem. We've learned that for diets to last they need variety. We can't eat lettuce, grilled chicken, and oatmeal for months at a time. When we have been on diets without variety, we always end up deciding that maybe we'd rather just be a little plump. The journey without flavor and variety may not be worth the result of being thin.

We wonder if this is the same thing that our readers feel when they are given only a diet of leveled books. We wonder if, after months and months of leveled books as their only independent reading material, they feel like chronic dieters do. Maybe they watch other students in the room reading "real books" in the same way we watch our colleagues in the teachers' lounge eating brownies.

Children in elementary classrooms need to have choice in what they read if they are going to develop the skills to become lifelong readers. We are afraid that the use of leveled books in classrooms has created very inauthentic reading experiences for our students. We are worried about what has happened to classroom libraries across the country since we wrote *Beyond Leveled Books* years ago. When we rely solely on leveled books, what are we teaching our students about what it means to be a reader? What messages are we giving them about what good readers do? What are they learning about how to choose books?

As students move from being emergent readers to transitional readers and develop more competence in the older grades, a limited exposure to reading materials can be detrimental to their lives as readers. Children need to sustain a sense of discovery, develop an appreciation for the best of children's literature, and know that a wide world of reading awaits them.

Kathy Short tells us, "Choice is essential to learning. Through choice, learners are able to make connections to interests and experiences that are significant to them. They take ownership of their learning. When students can choose what they read and how they will respond to it, reading becomes a meaningful experience in their lives. In every classroom, we find children with a wide variety of interests, needs, and experiences. If all our students are going to find themselves in books and view the world from new perspectives, they need access to a wide variety of literature" (1997, 15).

In this second edition of *Beyond Leveled Books*, we once again reflect on our elementary classroom libraries and the ways we connect children to books. We have added a chapter on using leveled books with our youngest readers in kindergarten and first grade that includes new book lists. We consider the role of leveled books in the primary classroom and discuss the supports they offer our youngest readers as well as their limitations in encouraging a lifetime of reading. But we also remain concerned that limited access to books in the early grades can be a huge barrier to older readers.

Many companies are now publishing leveled books. We look at what features high-quality leveled texts have and which leveled texts fall short of supporting readers. We share some ideas for evaluating leveled books to find those that offer the strongest supports for our students.

We consider leveled books one tool for teachers to use as they plan reading experiences for their students. We think about what makes a just-right book and how teachers can help students develop the skills for choosing books. We expand our notion of developing literacy to include a variety of reading skills and behaviors we want our students to learn. We take a look at how we group children for instruction.

You will find many revised book lists throughout this second edition. They have been updated with the most recent titles available. Once again, we offer a chart of series books and the features that support transitional readers. We include some newly designed lessons that we have used to encourage young readers, and share several new routines for building a reading community.

An added feature of this second edition are the essays written by thoughtful educators who share our concerns about literacy development. Larry Swartz shares his thoughts on fiction for transitional boy readers. Mary Lee Hahn introduces us to graphic novels and how they help students develop critical reading skills. Shari Frost challenges us to think about the instructional decisions we make in the classroom. Kathy Collins helps us understand how choosing books can help students find just-right books as well as expand their world of reading.

We continue to challenge our thinking about leveled books. How can they support our early and transitional readers? What cautions should we consider when making the best instructional decisions for our students? Every decision is an important one. Let's think hard about the reading lives of our students. Allington (2006) reminds us, "In the end, no matter what procedure is used to attempt to put more appropriate books into the hands of students, it comes down to each kid and each book" (52).

chapter two

Expanding Our Definition of Just-Right Books in Our K–1 Classrooms

If we teach a child to read yet develop not the taste for reading, all our teaching is for naught. We shall have produced a nation of "illiterate literates"—those who know how to read, but do not read. The major purpose for teaching children to read is to help them become readers who readily turn to books for information and enjoyment.

CHARLOTTE HUCK, ELEMENTARY SCHOOL LANGUAGE ARTS

Franki's six-year-old daughter, Ana, has recently discovered the joy of gift certificates. After she received a gift certificate from Borders from her grandparents for Valentine's Day, Ana grasped the concept quickly: this little card entitled her to choose a book at the bookstore (although she called it a "gift ticket," which makes some sense, too). On her way to the bookstore, Ana was excited that she'd be able to choose something on her own. Needless to say, it was a longer trip than anticipated. Although Ana is a shopper at heart (she is Franki's daughter after all), this was her first experience with a gift certificate to a bookstore. She was "shopping for the perfect book."

Ana had always loved stories, and since she was at the end of her kindergarten year, print was just starting to make sense to her. She had several little books that she could read by herself, and she was quickly discovering that she could read some things without help. She was just beginning to see herself as a reader.

Ana went right to the children's section of the bookstore where young readers can touch and flip through books. After much browsing, Franki asked Ana to choose three books to look at further, trying to get her to narrow her search. Ana was hesitant to put some of the books back, so Franki wrote the titles on a piece of paper so she could remember them the next time she shopped or went to the library. Franki told Ana that she could go over to the comfy chairs to make her decision. In Ana's stack of three books, she had *Lilly's Big Day* (Henkes 2006) about a character she loved, *Best Best Friends* (Chodos-Irvine 2006) written by an author she loved, and *Put Me in the Zoo* (Lopshire 1960) because she realized while browsing that she could read it on her own.

Ana sat on the comfy chairs with her three books and looked at each book page by page. When she realized that she had enough money on her "gift ticket" to buy two of the books, she was thrilled. She decided to purchase *Best Best Friends* and *Put Me in the Zoo*. She added the third book to the list of "books for the next time."

Ana's shopping helped us rethink much about emerging readers and their choices of books. As teachers, we don't ever have the luxury of spending the amount of time Franki did with Ana to choose two books. We don't often get to witness the thinking behind choosing a book. Ana's thinking process was fascinating as she made sense of pictures and the sequence of the story. Her previewing taught Franki about her literacy development. Because she could not read the text in two of the books, she studied the pictures, deciding whether the story was one that she wanted to add to her collection. She verbalized to Franki and to herself what was happening as she turned each page. The conversation showed just how insightful Ana was in her thinking. We sometimes forget that picture reading is a big part of literacy development. Even though Ana couldn't read the text, she was continuing to grow as a reader by coming to the realization that the pictures supported what the text would later tell her.

After Franki's shopping trip with Ana, we began to think about just-right book bags. We began to worry that as our primary students are just learning to read, we may be giving them the wrong message about what "real reading" is. We have children who have loved books and stories from an early age. But now that text is starting to make sense to them, their book bags at school often contain only books that are "just right"—books at a level they can read on their own. We often use books like the ones Ana chose in our read-aloud or shared reading time, but when it comes to independent reading time, our students are often limited to those they can read independently. We need to consider the implications of such a limited selection of reading material.

When thinking about Ana's shopping choices, we know that all three of Ana's choices were just right for her own reading development but for different reasons.

Lilly's Big Day by Kevin Henkes
If we want children to fall in love with characters just like we fell in love with Nancy Drew and the Hardy Boys, they need access to books and time to read so they can really get to know the characters. Ana knows Lilly well from a previous book by Kevin Henkes. While previewing, she used what she knew about Lilly to predict what Lilly might do in this book. She was cheering for Lilly because she already knew and loved her. For students to have a lifelong love of reading, knowing and loving characters is critical.

Best Best Friends by Margaret Chodos-Irvine
Ana chose this book because she had recently seen an advertisement for it. Because *Ella Sarah Gets Dressed* (Chodos-Irvine 2003) is one of Ana's favorite books, Franki had pointed out the advertisement to Ana to let her know that the author had a new book coming soon. Ana was thrilled to find the new book on her trip to the bookstore. Knowing the author drew Ana to the book, but it was the story that appealed to her. It was about getting along with friends. Children need stories that help them make sense of life. This book did that for Ana.

Put Me in the Zoo by Robert Lopshire
Ana has a few Dr. Seuss books that she can read by herself. So as she shopped, she went to the Dr. Seuss section and was excited when she discovered that she could easily read the text in this particular book. This would be considered a just-right book at school.

Of course, it is critical that our new readers have time every day with text they can understand, deciphering all or most of the words on the page. But maybe it's time to expand our definition of just-right books. Maybe we need to include books that are good matches because they expand the reading lives of children and contribute to literacy development. If we limit just-right books to only those that can be read with nearly complete accuracy, what message are we giving our newest readers?

And what are we teaching our children about book choice? If readers are limited to books at a certain level, how will they ever learn to love characters like Lilly or to anticipate new books by favorite authors? How will they learn to choose books if they never have a chance to explore all of the options?

When we thought about Ana's upcoming year as a first grader, we didn't want her to think that she was reading only if she could say all of the words correctly. We wanted her to be able to browse for great books every day with the thoughtfulness and the skill that she used to choose her books at the bookstore.

What Ana did was the work of a thoughtful reader. How can we help students in our classrooms be prepared for a bookstore setting or a library if we expose them only to leveled texts? We are concerned that our students will not develop as readers if their choices are limited to leveled texts. If we allow them to choose only books from leveled baskets, how will they ever learn to choose books in a library or bookstore? With only limited leveled-book choices, how will our students discover great characters? How can they fall in love with all kinds of books if we limit their experiences to only those books we think they can handle? If we want our students to love to read and to read for authentic purposes throughout their lives, we need to think carefully about what books we make available to them.

Talking to Students

Since we wrote the first edition of *Beyond Leveled Books* in 2001, we have heard countless stories from teachers, parents, librarians, and children across the country about the effect of leveled books. What we have found over and over again is that when students read only leveled books, their definition of and purposes for reading change.

We talked to students in several kindergarten and first-grade classrooms. We consistently found major differences between students who were in strictly leveled-book classrooms and those who had a variety of books in their classroom libraries. Whereas students in the classrooms with a variety of books could name favorite books, favorite authors, and favorite topics for reading, students in the strictly leveled-book classrooms had difficulty thinking about their own reading. One student answered, "I love the 'H' books," whereas many other students had no comment at all. When we asked students to describe their favorite characters or authors, we were again faced with blank stares from those students who read only leveled books.

When we observed students browsing for books, those from the strictly leveled-book classrooms put very little thought into their selections. Some students just chose the first few books they encountered, and others admitted the "eeny, meeny, minie, moe" technique worked best for them. Hearing children say, "What difference does it make?" not only broke our hearts but led us to realize that level mania was detrimental to our youngest readers.

Again and again, students tell us that their goal as readers is to move to higher levels and to read chapter books. When we asked the students in our focus groups why they were in such a big hurry to read chapter books, one little boy replied, "Because they are the best. They are the highest level, and when you get to those, you are a good reader." Other students said that good readers get to the next level and get all of the words right in their reading tests.

As teachers, we don't intentionally set out to give students these messages about reading, but we can clearly see that when they have only a diet of leveled books and the goal is to "move to the next level," they develop literacy in very narrow ways. When levels are key, they don't learn to pay attention to authors they love, to read nonfiction topics that interest them, or to talk to others about characters they relate to. Instead, the entire focus is on text and print. There is much more to reading than getting the words right, and we need to help students develop a broader perspective of reading and all that it has to offer.

The Place of Leveled Books

Leveled texts for students in kindergarten and first grade are great instructional supports for teachers and provide useful insights about emerging readers. But the focus on leveled texts in the classrooms has gone too far. To some degree it is a result of the current political landscape that focuses on student achievement. An increase in the amount of testing, the standardization of curriculum, and the No Child Left Behind

Act have all put additional pressure on educators to create classrooms that look the same; the focus is on what is being taught and learned instead of on each individual child's unique strengths and challenges. It is time to move beyond leveled books, not only for our transitional readers, but for our emerging readers in kindergarten and first grade as well. The messages we send our youngest readers could stay with them throughout their school lives and beyond.

It is not uncommon to walk into kindergarten and first-grade classrooms that are filled with leveled books. There is no doubt that they provide a valuable support for early readers. Our concern is that many classroom libraries consist only of leveled books. In the name of supporting children in reading just-right books, baskets are organized by levels and many of our early and emergent readers are limited to choosing books from those baskets that match their assessed reading level.

We worry that we have forgotten that it takes a variety of books to contribute to students' growth as readers. Primary teachers have experienced the excitement when students first begin to read. The children are proud of their accomplishments and eager to read to anyone who will listen to them. We worry that when they are first learning to make sense of text, we lead them to believe that what we value is getting the words right and moving to the next level or basket of books. When classroom libraries and reading bags are filled with so many leveled books, we worry that children are missing out on the wonderful literature that can teach them much more about reading. It's like telling students that they aren't ready for real books. Their reading selections should also include texts that they want to simply browse, texts that represent a challenge, texts where the picture support may be the level they access now with hopes of reading the words later. A diet of only leveled texts can give students a distorted sense of what reading is all about. We need to remember that we added those first leveled books to our library years ago to fill a small gap in our classroom libraries. They were never intended to replace a broad range of reading material or to be the only material that students read on their own.

We would never fill an entire classroom library with only song books. We wouldn't encourage our students to read only familiar tales. They deserve to have a variety of high-quality books as they begin their lives as readers. Leveled books certainly contribute to students' reading lives. But if the choices our students have are limited to leveled texts, much of their growth as readers is stunted by a narrow view of what they can read.

Often teachers justify the leveled classroom library by suggesting that their students may choose any book when they visit the school library. Although this sounds valid, it is almost impossible to implement. How will our newest readers have the skills necessary to choose books by authors they love or books with characters they know if they've been given little support in their daily classroom practices? Teachers may say that students are introduced to authors and characters in their daily classroom read-aloud time, but students in leveled classrooms may be missing hundreds of author and character introductions compared with their nonleveled counterparts in just one year. Without these choices and experiences within the classroom we question how students can be expected to move to the real world prepared to make choices for reading, to recognize authors and characters, and to love to read.

If we want our newest readers to become well-rounded readers, we must provide opportunities for lots of reading in a variety of books. We also want them to respond to a purpose for reading. Will they choose a book because they love a familiar character or because they want to learn more about the place they may be going on vacation?

We have to look for high-quality children's literature that supports our students at this stage of reading development and make sure that the leveled books we have constitute only a small portion of the books available. High-quality children's literature must continue to be the core of our classroom libraries, and we have to expand our definitions of just-right books for all of our readers, even the ones at the earliest stages of reading development.

All Leveled Books Are Not Equal

Since the first leveled books were published, their quality has deteriorated. Fortunately, we still have some great companies producing engaging books like those first leveled books. However, every publishing company in the world seems to have joined the trend of creating their own leveled texts. The quality varies, and more often than not, the books do not provide the support that students need at this critical time in their reading lives. It is crucial for publishers of leveled books to know the needs of emergent readers. The publishers we trust are aware of the kinds of things that provide support to new readers, and it shows in their books.

Creating High-Quality Leveled Books for Beginning Readers

Lynn Salem and Josie Stewart

Leveled books are the perfect stepping-stones between shared board books and the ready-to-read series. These books provide the beginning reader the opportunity to do what all good readers do—read a book from beginning to end—on their just-right reading level. Guiding the child effectively to discover "the secrets" of the book and thus have a successful reading experience is a gift of the astute teacher. Providing the best book possible for a successful reading experience is the challenge of the publisher.

Seedling Publications was founded on our two passions: the passion for teaching beginning readers and the passion for picture books. These passions prompt the questions we ask in our selection and construction of a book as publishers and our use of little books as teachers: Is the book accessible to the beginning reader, yet does it have the qualities of a picture book? Does the book have features that make it worthy of the time children will spend with it? Does the language flow and sound natural? Does the book have an engaging story line and characters, a satisfying ending, and charming artwork that calls a child to return to it—a practice that builds fluency?

When we review a manuscript, we first pay attention to the story content. The story has to bring something new to the reader; we cannot afford a "so-what" experience for a child who is just discovering the wonder of learning to read. So when we find a ten-, twenty-, or thirty-word manuscript that is not contrived and has a surprise ending, we know it will produce a special book for a young reader.

An excellent little book invites the reader into the story, starting with a cover that provides a sneak preview of the concept and may even be the first event in the story. The cover can prepare the reader to engage in the story and provide a pathway for comprehending it. The title page illustration also can provide information about the story or may be the second event in the story. And just as the story begins before the first page, it doesn't end on the last page. Frequently, the story is extended or a "what if?" is presented on the back cover. Once again, this encourages the reader to stay engaged and go beyond the surface meaning. All kinds of support—the structure of the book, the conjuring up of past experience, the sneak preview—scaffolds beginning readers before they have even had to look at a word of the text.

Beyond the story content, we look carefully at the vocabulary and consider whether it is written in children's natural language. Are there words that children know that provide support or are anchors? Is there any repeated vocabulary? What vocabulary will be unfamiliar and how will it be supported? Is there a challenge in the reading, enough to build instruction around? Words that are unfamiliar to a child will call for support through pictures or the structure of the sentence(s). These vocabulary questions need to be addressed to create a good beginning-reading book and to guide teacher selection.

Pay close attention to where the key words are placed in the sentence. Notice if the pattern of the text is the same on each page or if the author moves the key words around so that even the most beginning of readers must do some reading work and self-monitoring. Word placement should be consistent—either on the bottom of the page or at the top of the page for the lowest-level books. Phrasing and page breaks are critical for high-quality little books. The best scenario is lines of text that break on a page in phrases that parallel how children speak. Fluent reading is promoted by familiar phrasing and carefully selected, natural vocabulary.

Higher-level books require the same scrutiny of text, structure, and illustrations. As story lines become more involved and picture support becomes less obvious, readers must sustain and analyze more information, particularly during a first reading of a text. In nonfiction, terminology begins to appear more often. The teacher's introduction and attentive guidance will help the young reader with more difficult concepts. Books that help build fluency are extremely important at the higher levels, too. All the features that make a book "readable" at a lower level apply at higher levels as well.

When constructing or choosing nonfiction, the book must be accessible to the beginning reader yet still provide new information. A nonfiction piece is not as beneficial if it provides only a list of information that the child most likely already knows. We look for a balance between well-known facts about the topic and a mix of new information. This is usually accomplished when the author approaches the topic from an interesting angle, such as focusing on one aspect of the topic or making comparisons that a child could easily relate to. For example, *The Elephant's Trunk* and *Monkey Tails* provide a different perspective on two well-known animals. Nonfiction can be an area of strength for the beginning reader and the second-language learner, particularly when the topic can be associated with some prior knowledge.

Careful field testing of the manuscript and illustrations with young readers of all levels of proficiency provides us with information we need to smooth out the rough spots in the text and illustrations. The same is true for teachers as they select books for a beginning reader. The level of the book is not as important as knowing the child and the level of support that this reader needs. Book selection is easier when you think about the content and structure of a book with your reader in mind.

Children gain experience from reading books with recurring characters. They draw on their familiarity with the character to succeed in reading a new book in the series. For example, Sherman, a lovable dog, and John and Lucy are all lively problem-solving characters in the Seedling books. Curiosity about a favorite character can motivate the beginning reader to meet challenges.

Creating books that are teaching and learning tools for children as well as visually appealing has provided us a great sense of accomplishment, particularly when we see the happiness on young readers' faces when they find success with one of our books. When children do what all good readers do—read a book from cover to cover and have a meaningful literary experience—we know we've reached our goal of helping children on their journey in literacy.

Lynn Salem and Josie Stewart are co-founders of Seedling Publications. Salem is a retired Reading Recovery teacher in Dublin, Ohio, currently writing books for children. Stewart is a kindergarten teacher in Dublin, Ohio.

A Classroom Library That Teaches Early Readers About What It Means to Be a Reader

Since we care so much about offering our students great children's literature, we are on a constant search for books that they can read independently. Then we need to help them recognize those books. If we want our students to choose books for independent reading, discover favorite authors, and reread favorite books, we need to make the classroom library inviting and accessible to them.

Organizing the Primary Classroom Library in Ways That Value More than Levels

We believe strongly that there are ways to support students beyond levels. We know that moving to new levels of independence is critical to these new readers. But we also know that they deserve more than that. We can organize our classroom libraries (including a limited section of leveled books) and still guarantee that students will make reading progress and develop the skills, attitudes, and behaviors of competent readers. The way we organize the classroom library, the books we feature, and the choices we give our youngest readers are all critical.

The way we display books for our children's independent reading time gives students insights about what we value in our classrooms. If all of our library space is organized into baskets by level, students will think that level is what matters. If chapter books are in a prominent section of our first-grade classroom, students will come to see that their goal as readers is to advance to chapter books. But if students see baskets of books organized by favorite authors, they begin to think about authors they enjoy and who they are becoming as readers. To assess our own classroom libraries we often look at them through the eyes of a child. What messages are we sending about what we value by the way we have organized our libraries?

Alongside leveled books, we often have books organized in the following baskets:

Favorite Authors
Interesting Nonfiction Topics
Favorite Book Characters
Song Books
Familiar Stories
Books We've Read Aloud

The variety of the baskets teaches our students what it is to be a reader. Just as older readers do, they begin to find authors they love. They begin to look forward to a new book featuring a favorite character. They learn to find a good nonfiction book when they are looking for information on a topic. Even if they cannot read every word in a book, it can be just right for other reasons that they value. When we think about building the whole reader, providing a variety of books allows us to support the whole child.

For example, one of the things that we want our readers to learn is the joy of reading about characters they love. This is especially important for beginning readers. When they find characters they love, they begin to know them well enough to make predictions about how they will think and act in the story. Young readers often develop a friendship with those characters and anticipate their next meeting in other books in the series. They develop a level of comfort as they depend on what they know about the character when they encounter a new book in the series.

FAVORITE BOOK CHARACTER BASKETS

Charlie and Lola by Lauren Child

I Absolutely Must Do Coloring Now or Painting or Drawing
I Am Not Sleepy and I Will Not Go to Bed
I Will Never Not Ever Eat a Tomato
Sizzles Is Completely Not Here
I'm Really Ever So Not Well
I've Won, No I've Won, No I've Won
Snow Is My Favorite and My Best
We Honestly Can Look After Your Dog
Whoops! But It Wasn't Me
My Wobbly Tooth Must Not Ever Never Fall Out
Boo! Made You Jump
I Am Too Absolutely Small for School
This Is Actually My Party
Can You Maybe Turn the Light On?
Say Cheese!
But Excuse Me That Is My Book
But I Am an Alligator
I Can Do Anything That's Everything All on My Own
You Can Be My Friend

David by David Shannon

No, David!
David Gets in Trouble
David Goes to School

Duck by Doreen Cronin and illustrator

Click, Clack, Moo: Cows That Type
Giggle, Giggle Quack
Vote for Duck
Click Clack Quackity Quack: An Alphabetical Adventure
Duck for President
Dooby Dooby Moo
Click Clack Splash Splash: A Counting Adventure

Duck and Goose by Tad Hills
Duck and Goose
Duck, Duck, Goose

Elephant and Piggie by Mo Willems
Mo Willems, author of *Don't Let the Pigeon Drive the Bus!* and *Knuffle Bunny*, has created a series for young readers. *My Friend Is Sad* and *Today I Will Fly!* were the first in the series. Both are the size of the traditional Dr. Suess books—small with lots of pages. Simple text and simple illustrations make them both perfect choices. Willems also uses talking bubbles.
My Friend Is Sad
Today I Will Fly!
I'm Invited to a Party
There's a Bird on Your Head

Fancy Nancy by Jane O'Connor and illustrator
Fancy Nancy
Fancy Nancy and the Posh Puppy
Fancy Nancy's Glamorous Gift
Fancy Nancy at the Museum
Fancy Nancy and the Boy from Paris
Fancy Nancy: Bonjour, Butterfly

Five Little Monkeys by Eileen Christelow
Five Little Monkeys Jumping on a Bed
Five Little Monkeys Sitting in a Tree
Five Little Monkeys Playing Hide-and-Seek
Five Little Monkeys Wash the Car
Five Little Monkeys Bake a Birthday Cake
Five Little Monkeys with Nothing to Do
Five Little Monkeys Go Shopping

Hondo and Fabian by Peter McCarty
Hondo and Fabian have very different days as a cat and a dog, but they end up side by side at night. Simple text and beautiful, supportive illustrations make this book a favorite for new readers to find success.
Hondo and Fabian
Fabian Escapes

Mercy Watson by Kate DiCamillo and illustrator
Mercy Watson Fights Crime
Mercy Watson, Princess in Disguise
Mercy Watson Goes for a Ride
Mercy Watson to the Rescue

Olivia by Ian Falconer
Olivia Forms a Band
Olivia Saves the Circus
Olivia and the Missing Toy
Olivia Helps with Christmas
Olivia's Opposites
Olivia Counts

Pigeon by Mo Willems
Don't Let the Pigeon Drive the Bus!
The Pigeon Finds a Hot Dog!

Scaredy Squirrel by Melanie Watt
Scaredy Squirrel
Scaredy Squirrel Makes a Friend

Stanley by Craig Frazier
Stanley Mows the Lawn
Stanley Goes Fishing
Stanley Goes for a Drive

Tacky by Helen Lester
Tacky the Penguin
Tacky in Trouble
Tacky and the Emperor
Tacky and the Winter Games
Three Cheers for Tacky

Mini-Lesson:

Using What We Know About Familiar Characters

Possible Anchor Texts:

Llama, Llama Red Pajama by Anna Dewdney or *Llama, Llama Mad at Mama* by Anna Dewdney

Why Teach It?

Readers of all ages love to read about characters they know and love. This is true for adult readers as well as children who are just learning to read. Understanding that knowing a character helps the reader think differently about future books that feature the character is important for young children to know to support their comprehension.

How We Teach It:

After reading the first book about a character, show children the cover of another book about the same character. Ask them to think about what they know about the character and to make predictions about what might happen in this next book based on the cover, title, and what they already know about the character. Chart their predictions. As you read, go back and see how well they were able to predict this character's actions.

Follow-Up:

Use different sets of books with favorite characters. Before reading each one, add new things you know about the character to a class chart. Keep an eye out for new books about favorite characters so that this talk becomes part of the natural conversation around books and characters.

SOME POSSIBILITIES FOR BOOK BASKETS FOR THE K–2 CLASSROOM LIBRARY

Longer Picture Books

Walt Disney's Cinderella by Cynthia Rylant
Rachel Field's Hitty: Her First Hundred Years by Rosemary Wells
Aladdin and the Enchanted Lamp by Philip Pullman
Hanne's Quest by Olivier Dunrea

Picture Books About Interesting People

You Forgot Your Skirt, Amelia Bloomer by Shana Corey
Molly Bannaky by Alice McGill
John, Paul, George, and Ben by Lane Smith
When Marian Sang by Pam Nunoz Ryan
Jesse Owens: Fastest Man Alive by Carole Boston Weatherford
Young Thomas Edison by Michael Dooling

New Versions of Old Favorites

The Princess and the Pea by Lauren Child
The Little Red Hen (Makes a Pizza) by Philemon Sturges

Goldilocks and the Three Bears by Caralyn Buehner
Out of the Egg by Tina Matthews
Jack and the Beanstalk by E. Nesbit

Favorite-Author Baskets

Byron Barton
Eric Carle
Mem Fox
Kevin Henkes
Robert Neubecker
Todd Parr
David Shannon
Nancy Tafuri
Melanie Watt
Mo Willems
Audrey Wood

BOOKS WE LOVE FOR KINDERGARTEN AND FIRST-GRADE CLASSROOM LIBRARIES: BOOKS TO HAVE ALONGSIDE LEVELED BOOKS

These are the books we have recently added to our libraries—books that our youngest readers can read on their own—not because of a "level," but because of the engaging story and great supports. We have added these to our older favorites like *Silly Sally* by Audrey Wood and *Time for Bed* by Mem Fox. We chose them for many different reasons, but we believe that young readers can engage in each one independently and consider themselves readers of many things. If we were to administer a running record, we're not sure they could read every book at an "independent" or "instructional" level, but we are confident there are little books that will serve that purpose. These books support new readers in the same ways that leveled books do: they are age appropriate and feature predictability and repeated phrases. The books below are just right for young readers because they offer predictability and variety during this critical time of their reading lives.

Apples and Oranges: Going Bananas with Pairs by Sara Pinto
This is a book about how two things are and aren't alike. The concept is odd, but the text and illustrations are so predictable

and supportive that early readers love it because they can read some fairly complicated sentences. The book is great for discussion as well and could lead to some fun with writing.

A Cat and a Dog by Claire Masurel
Cat and Dog do not think they could possibly be friends until they take the time to get to know each other—a great lesson at any age. Simple text and supportive illustrations make this book great for new readers. Young readers also like it because they get to growl!

A Good Day by Kevin Henkes
A bad day changes for Bird, Dog, Fox, and Squirrel, offering a lesson in point of view. Simple text and supportive illustrations make this story a great one for early readers. The conversation works especially well on those days when everyone seems to be struggling with something.

Bark, George by Jules Feiffer
George's mother takes him to the vet because he will not bark. The vet finds that George has swallowed all kinds of other animals. Readers of all ages will enjoy the surprise ending. This text is supportive through repetition.

Big Sister, Little Sister by Leuyen Pham
Big sisters are more experienced at just about everything except being the little sister. Repetitive phrasing and a consistent font are used to support new readers.

Bounce by Doreen Cronin
This is an enjoyable book about bouncing. The rhyme scheme is easy to pick up on, and the pictures are supportive.

Bus Stop, Bus Go! by Daniel Kirk
Tommy brings his hamster on the bus ride to school and of course, it escapes. *Bus Stop, Bus Go!* repeats, and the dialogue is expressed in bubbles.

Butterfly Butterfly: A Book of Colors by Peter Horacek
This story, about a girl and a butterfly, has few words on each page, large print, colorful illustrations, a predictable pattern with matching pictures, and a surprise ending.

Charlene Loves to Make Noise by Barbara Bottner
Charlene is shy at school and gets embarrassed easily, but when she is at home, she plays the drums and loves to make noise. She promises herself she will not be shy "tomorrow." Almost every sentence in this book starts with the name *Charlene*. The text is simple yet offers character depth and support to new readers. It's good for classroom conversation as well.

Chickens to the Rescue by John Himmelman
Whenever there is a problem on the Greenstalk farm, there is no need to worry. Chickens to the rescue! Young readers "crack up" over this one! It's got the days of the week, supportive illustrations, repetitive text, and a surprise ending—what more could any reader want?

Clip-Clop! by Nicola Smee
Cat, Dog, Pig, and Duck all want a ride on Horse's back. He swings them until they fly into the haystack. Worried, he asks if they are all right, and he is relieved when they all yell, "AGAIN!" This is a simple book with a sense of story. It offers dialogue, cumulative text—of which we haven't seen a lot in recent years—and repetitive phrasing as well as a strong conversation piece with Horse's reaction to the possibility of hurting his friends.

Dear Zoo by Rod Campbell
The perfect pet may be difficult to find when the request is written to the zoo. The story is about a child who writes to the zoo for a pet. Each page starts with, "So they sent me a . . ." At the bottom of each page is the reason why the child sends each animal back until finally the perfect pet arrives. This book is good on many levels. It has simple images placed on white backgrounds. It demonstrates a sense of story with an introduction, problem, and solution. There is great use of adjectives, and illustrations are labeled. *Dear Zoo* introduces the concept of letter writing. The message is that persistence pays.

Do Lions Live on Lily Pads? by Melanie Walsh
Lions don't live on lily pads, frogs do. This question-and-answer book is great support for both fluency and comprehension. The text is simple and clear, and the illustrations are bold.

Dog's Colorful Day by Emma Dodd
Dog starts his day white with one black dot but ends with ten colorful dots. His adventures are chronicled through expressive language, bold text, and distinct color choices. Plus, readers practice spelling numbers along the way and have as much fun as Dog does!

Ella Sarah Gets Dressed by Margaret Chodos-Irvine
This is a repetitive story about a little girl who doesn't like others choosing her clothes.

Emily's Balloon by Komako Sakai
This is a story every child can relate to: losing a helium-filled balloon. It's a wonderful story with simple sentences and matching illustrations.

First the Egg by Laura Vaccaro Seeger
Which came first, the chicken or the egg? This is a simple nonfiction book for early readers to contemplate questions and see how the process progresses. Readers love the cutout pages and looking to see what comes next. Text and illustrations complement each other to support fluency and comprehension.

Gossie and Gertie by Olivier Dunrea
Gossie and Gertie are best friends. The lesson here is that they can be best friends but still do their own thing. It's a simple story with a great message for our youngest audiences. Repetitive phrasing and use of dialogue makes this one great on many levels.

Grumpy Bird by Jeremy Tankard
Bird is so grumpy he just wants to walk. When Bird realizes his friends have all joined him and are following his every move, he decides it is kind of fun. Bold illustrations and a surprise ending make this one a hit.

Hippo! No, Rhino by Jeff Newman
What happens when Rhino gets the wrong sign at the zoo? This predictable text is easily read with few words and is a great story.

Hoptoad by Jane Yolen
Everyone cheers as Toad tries to get across the road without getting run over by a truck. This book has few words but the story

is clear, as is the reader's enthusiasm. Don't worry—the toad makes it. Young readers get nervous every time.

How Do You Make a Baby Smile? By Philemon Sturges
Animals and an older sister do what they can to make their babies smile. This simple story brings out the tricks of those older siblings.

How to Be by Lisa Brown
Great descriptive words and simple sentences describe how to be a spider, a bear, a monkey, a snake, a turtle, a dog, and a person.

Hurry! Hurry! by Eve Bunting
The illustrations along with two words on each page are perfect for young readers. The two words (*Hurry! Hurry!*) let the reader know to look for an exciting ending to this barnyard story.

In My New Yellow Shirt by Eileen Spinelli
A yellow shirt might not seem like the greatest birthday gift unless it comes with some imagination. Each sentence begins with "In my new yellow shirt . . ."

I'm the Biggest Thing in the Ocean by Kevin Sherry
Squid thinks he is bigger than everything else in the ocean until he is eaten by a whale. Then he is bigger than everything in the whale. Teachers will want to capture readers' expressions when they realize Squid has been eaten; they laugh and laugh. This book will be a classroom favorite! We promise. The text, pictures, and font support readers on all levels.

Kitten's First Full Moon by Kevin Henkes
Kitten just can't get to that bowl of milk that happens to be the first full moon she has ever seen. After many attempts she returns home to a nice bowl of milk. The phrase "Still there was a bowl of milk just waiting" is repeated. Illustrations are in black and white and very cute.

Lemons Are Not Red by Laura Vaccaro Seeger
New readers can get this by the third page. The text reads, "Lemons are not RED. Lemons are YELLOW. Apples are RED." This continues through different natural objects. The art-

work is beautiful, and young readers pore over the book because they can read it right away.

Llama, Llama Mad at Mama by Anna Dewdney
Llama gets mad when shopping with Mama. This amusing tale is told in a rhythmic rhyme that all children will enjoy.

Llama, Llama Red Pajama by Anna Dewdney
This is one of those great rhyming books kids can read because they've heard it over and over. It begs to be read again and again. When Mama puts Llama to bed, he begins to worry and fuss until she assures him that she is always near. This familiar bedtime ritual is told with humor that young children will enjoy.

Love You When You Whine by Emily Jenkins
This book reassures children that we love them when they whine, when they won't eat dinner, and more. Each page has one line of text that matches the picture.

Maybe a Bear Ate It! by Robie H. Harris
What do you do when you can't find your book? PANIC! This is a great story about misplacing something so valuable only the worst thoughts come to mind. "Maybe a bear ate it!" The text and illustrations support this adorable book where the character ends with every teacher's dream line: "I love my book."

Move Over, Rover! by Karen Beaumont
It is raining outside, but Rover is dry in his doghouse until all his friends come to seek shelter, saying, "Move over, Rover." What they don't know is that Skunk was there first! Young readers love to share this book because of the smelly surprise at the end. This is a cumulative text offering substantial support for both fluency and comprehension.

My Car by Byron Barton
Sam tells about his car and his journey to work as a bus driver. The text is bold and matches the bright illustrations. New readers love the first page announcing, "I am Sam."

New Socks by Bob Shea
Leon gets new socks that seem to make him fairly confident. Young readers love Leon. He is a bright yellow bird with glasses

and new giant orange socks. Leon's personality keeps them reading over and over.

Not a Box by Antoinette Portis
A small bunny is using a box for lots of imaginary play. Each page is repetitive and simple. The pictures provide great support for the reader. *Not a Stick* by the same author is just as charming.

Orange Pear Apple Bear by Emily Gravett
This entire story is told using the four words *orange, pear, apple, bear*. The use of language and illustration is amazing.

Ready, Set, Skip! by Jane O'Connor
This is a book about the process of learning something new. It uses dialogue between two people, rhyme, a sense of story, and accomplishment. It is also very funny that the main character thinks her mother is far too old to be able to skip.

Silly Sally by Audrey Wood
In this all-time favorite, "Silly Sally went to town walking backwards upside down." If ever a book begged to be read over and over and couldn't help but be memorized and "read" aloud, this is it. It's great for character recognition, rhyming, and patterns, and the placement of text is perfect.

Sleepyhead by Karma Wilson
This book about bedtime has a rhyming, repetitive text that delights young readers.

Taking a Bath with the Dog and Other Things That Make Me Happy by Scott Menchin
This book is about a child who is trying to decide what would cheer her up. She asks around to find out what cheers others up. Each two-page spread starts with the question, "What makes you happy?" New readers supported by repetitive phrasing and illustrations will quickly be reading this on their own.

Thank You Bear by Greg Foley
Bear finds a box he thinks is perfect for Mouse. Before he can give it to Mouse, his friends make him question his decision.

When Mouse sees the box he crawls inside and says, "What a perfect box. Thank you, Bear." The simple text and charming story beg to be reread.

The Cow Who Clucked by Denise Fleming
Cow goes looking for his lost "moo." The animals on the farm use their own animal sounds to let Cow know they did not take Cow's moo. The text is repetitive to support young readers.

The Deep Blue Sea: A Book of Colors by Audrey Wood
In this perfect cumulative text by Audrey Wood, color words are in matching fonts to support readers as they make their way through this amusing story.

The OK Book by Amy Krouse Rosenthal
Readers come to understand that they can try to learn and do many things without always being perfect. Children like to read this book not only because the little man is a stick figure that looks like the word *OK* but because the text is simple.

Tip Tip Dig Dig by Emma Garcia
In this colorful, predictable book about trucks and all the wonderful things they can do, pictures offer support for simple text.

What! Cried Granny: An Almost Bedtime Story by Kate Lum
Patrick is having his first sleepover at Granny's house when they realize she doesn't have the items necessary for the occasion. Not to worry, Granny has what it takes to fix the situation. This is a story full of dialogue, irony, and humor.

What Will Fat Cat Sit On? by Jan Thomas
This is an inviting story with hilarious illustrations, as the farm animals try to get Fat Cat to sit anywhere but on them. The predictable text begs for reader interaction.

Where Is the Green Sheep? by Mem Fox
This is a favorite book with repetitive text. As with all of Mem Fox's books, the rhythm and simplicity make it perfect for new readers.

Whose Chick Are You? by Nancy Tafuri
The egg hatches, but who does the chick belong to? Goose? Duck? Hen? Bird? Or Swan? Repetitive phrasing and charming illustrations make this a hit with young readers.

Why Do I Have to Eat Off the Floor? by Chris Hornsey
A dog asks his child owner why he can't do all the things that she is allowed to do. Simple sentences and great humor make this one a perfect match for young children.

Wow! City! / Wow! America!/ Wow! School! by Robert Neubecker
The illustrations in these oversized books keep readers interested. At the bottom of each two-page spread is the word "Wow!" and a word that names an object or location. Children will be fascinated by the illustrations and will quickly learn to read the simple text.

Organizing Book Baskets: Letting Kids In On the Plan

Katie DiCesare

I happily spend my days with first graders. I love to guide them as they discover, read, and tell stories. I am curious about kids. What does reading look like in the classroom? What motivates kids to read? What kinds of books support kids learning to read? I feel an overwhelming responsibility to meet the needs of first-grade readers. I want them to have success reading words, understanding their reading, and linking it to their lives. But most of all, I want them to love reading. Here are some of the ways I organize books, and have my students help me organize books, to promote that love of reading.

Beginning with "My Stack"

The first thing I do to prepare for my students each day is collect the books I will be sharing with them. I start by finding books that will support my discussion or mini-lesson for my reading and writing workshop. I find books that will help my students explore math ideas. I find books that will help us think about science, social studies, or health concepts. It's my favorite part of the day because I can't wait to observe how these books will support them as learners. As I choose books to use for teaching, I am thinking about my students. I think about how Angela will light up when I show her *Here Comes Spring and Summer and Autumn and Winter* (Murphy 2000). I am hopeful that it will help her generate ideas for the book about seasons that she is writing. I know she will enjoy the delightful pictures and the simple text. I imagine Jeremy devouring books like *Mercy Watson to the Rescue* in the Mercy Watson series by Kate DiCamillo. He loves to read series books and enjoys good pictures and interesting characters. I think about how Astrid will probably not stop asking me for *Here's a Little Poem* (Yolen and Peters 2007) after I reread some of our favorites. She loves to reread and go back to her favorites because she feels safe and successful.

My stack is my guide for the day. The children look forward to what is new, old, and different. They know that what I read aloud and what we read together will instantly be part of our classroom library.

Our classroom library contains many different kinds of books because kids need practice with different kinds of reading (and isn't it just more fun to get your hands on different things?). First graders need practice reading picture books, song books, rhyming books, nursery rhymes and fairy tales, author books (getting to know many books by the same author), nonfiction books, poetry, and leveled books.

Collaborating with Students to Develop Basket Themes

One of the first baskets we add to the library is one we call the Good Books for Picture Reading basket. These "picture reading books" are those read-aloud books that the kids enjoy and will want to revisit on their own but don't quite have the tools yet to read independently. Picture reading is also one of the first strategies I want students to practice as they begin to decipher words on the page. I encourage them to retell the story in their own words as they use the pictures as a guide.

After we think more about what picture reading is, we think about books that make sense to have in this basket. This year, books like *Unlovable* (Yaccarino 2002), *Caps for Sale* (Slobodkina 1968), *Ruthie and the (Not So) Teeny Tiny Lie* (Rankin 2007), and *Harry the Dirty Dog* (Zion 1956) are in this basket. I love how this basket provides a scaffold for students who begin to grab and read these books independently.

Another important basket that we create is labeled We Can Read. After we read titles like *I'm the Biggest Thing in the Ocean* (Sherry 2007), *Tanka Tanka Skunk!* (Webb 2003), *What Will Fat Cat Sit On?* (Thomas 2007), *Mary Wore Her Red Dress* (Peek 1985), and *Where Is the Green Sheep?* (Fox 2004), we begin thinking about why these are books "we can all read." This year students came up with things we noticed: there are just a few words on each page, the words repeat, there are words we know (like color words), the pictures match the words, and we like the stories! I posted their thinking about the basket, and we have continued to add books with similar features to the basket throughout the year.

The Rhyming basket was added after I realized (through reading a number of rhyming books aloud) that my students were struggling with oral cloze. I took this opportunity to suggest that we add a basket for rhyming books to our library. We had many discussions about how rhyming words sound and what they look like in different stories. We added favorites to our Rhyming basket like *Oh, A-Hunting We Will Go* (Langstaff 1991), *Is Your Mama a Llama?* (Guarino 1989), and *Llama, Llama Red Pajama* (Dewdney 2005). As students began to develop an understanding for rhyming words, they noticed that we could put many of the nursery-rhyme books and some song books in this basket. We discussed that for organizational purposes it might be difficult to find the books we needed if all three baskets were combined. (I loved that they were thinking about books!)

Song books are an immediate favorite for primary kids. We talk about creating a Song basket and why a book would fit in it. *The Wheels on the Race Car* (Zane 2005), *Ten in the Bed* (Dale 2006), *Over in the Meadow* (Keats 1999), *A Tisket, A Tasket* (Fitzgerald 2003), and *The Lady with the Alligator Purse* (Wescott 1988) are a few my students enjoy. Once I sing and read them, the students join in and want to do the same. I have many copies of these song books because they are so popular.

The Fairy Tale basket becomes a favorite for first graders because the books are repetitive and predictable. I want them to know these classic tales.

These books delight children with inventive words and engaging illustrations that encourage picture reading.

I like starting with Byron Barton's version of the fairy tales. His simple text and bright pictures support picture reading for my early kids, and simple text invites my transitional kids. We add to the basket quite a bit throughout the first month and then of course throughout the year. I like to find many versions of different fairy tales to add to this basket; they add variety and immediately start conversations about comparing and contrasting. Some of their favorites are *The Gingerbread Man* (Aylesworth 1988), *Somebody and the Three Blairs* (Tolhurst 1990), *The Little Red Hen* (Barton 1993), and *Out of the Egg* (Matthews 2007). Often, students will check out a fairy tale in our school library and add it to our basket.

Seedling Publications has a series of Nursery Rhyme Lap books that I use quite a bit for introducing strategies for reading words. These Nursery Rhyme books are bigger than a picture book but not quite as large as your typical Big Book. The first page of each book contains a complete nursery rhyme. The actual story is an extension of the nursery rhyme and is simply written like a leveled book. I love how the books meet the needs of different readers. I like how the words are large enough for choral reading. The kids love the stories because of the simple text, great pictures, and the anticipation of the back cover. They leave the reader thinking and predicting. They leave me with opportunities for shared or interactive writing at the end of the book. We keep the stack of them against the wall with the label "Nursery Rhyme Stories."

The Nonfiction baskets include many topics, such as ocean animals, weather, and seasons. We spend time searching through the already organized but untitled baskets of books. Students work with partners to decide on a label that describes the books in the baskets. We share our discoveries, and the partners introduce their baskets to the other students and then put them in our library.

Poetry is something that we read all year, so I think it is appropriate to keep a pretty little Poetry basket in our room. Poetry books like *Little Dog Poems* (George 1999), *Calendar* (Livingston 2007), *Poems for the Very Young* (Rosen 1993), and *Here's a Little Poem* (Yolen and Peters 2007) never stay long in our basket.

Other Areas in the Classroom Library

One area that I have already set up when students arrive in late summer is the author baskets, where I feature many books by the same author. The baskets also have a label and picture of the author on them. Audrey Wood, Mem Fox, Eric Carle, and Kevin Henkes books are just a few of the favorites I start the year reading aloud to my students.

These baskets of books are organized by favorite authors.

These stories become some of the first ones students begin selecting for reading workshop. The baskets also help me connect my students to real authors. I use the author baskets as a way of developing writer identity during writing workshop and later use them as a study for mentor authors. Another area I have organized and set up is the smaller leveled book baskets. In the past, I have put a letter that matches the level for each book to its basket. But the kids ended up paying too much attention to the level instead of the actual book. They got lost in who was reading at what level instead of getting lost in the book. I decided not to put a number or letter that corresponds to a level on the books and baskets.

This year, I just put colored dots on the individual books and then on the corresponding baskets, thanks to an idea I read about in *Growing Readers* by Kathy Collins. If I need a leveled book for a student or know students who would benefit from leveled practice, I can grab the color basket that matches that reader or group of readers.

Titles that we are using as models in writing workshop are always put on the book display. These are the only books I ask my students not to keep in their own book bins. They are always available to read, but I ask that they be put back on the display shelf so that I have access to them for workshop discussion.

Here, a dot system is used to organize leveled books.

The books displayed here help students learn about writer's craft, such as the use of punctuation.

The Power of Collaborative Organization

Debbie Miller points out that "charts, student work, and the organization of books and materials reflect the teaching and learning in your classroom." To me, this means we work with kids to establish our space. We collaborate with the students to think about and set up our library space. Together, we explore our school library and discuss what we notice. We compare it with the parts of our library that are already set up. We come up with new ideas for our class library, creating book baskets and discussing why and where certain books are sorted, and then label the baskets with our thinking.

There is a sensation that I am unable to describe . . . maybe the coziness that you feel when you walk into a space you've crafted. There is an appreciation of the just-right colors, soft lighting, a comfy cushion, and open space. It is a comfortable and safe feeling where you know you are at home. That's what it feels like in our library space.

Katie DeCesare is a first-grade teacher in Dublin, Ohio.

References

Collins, Kathy. 2004. *Growing Readers: Units of Study in the Primary Classroom.* Portland, ME: Stenhouse.

Miller, Debbie. "Inviting Students to Organize Books and Materials." Choice Literacy. http://www.choiceliteracy.com/members/login.cfm?hpage=157.cfm.

How Do Levels Affect Our Strongest Readers in Kindergarten and First Grade?

In the first edition of this book we focused on the transitional readers in grades two through five. Since that time, we have had questions and concerns from teachers about those students who reach that "transitional" stage of reading before second grade.

When Franki's oldest daughter, Alexa, was in the first grade, she was in the "20+ basket." This meant that during reading time, she could read books at level 20 and above. This was above average for a beginning first grader. But Alexa was not happy. Her favorite book, *Cookie's Week* (Ward 1988), was in one of the lower-level baskets, so she had to read that one at home. There were definitely great books in the 20+ basket, and she had a wonderful teacher who supported her reading from the start. But Alexa also wanted to reread old favorites.

In our work around the country, we have heard countless stories from school librarians who are not allowed to buy books that are not leveled by some district-approved system. We have heard about very young children who tell relatives at holiday parties that they are "a level L," and public librarians who are asked to give children only books that are at a certain level of reading.

There is a continuing fascination with and focus on levels. We worry that our early readers are no longer reading high-quality picture books and are being limited to reading leveled books. We get so excited that students are moving ahead that we often forget that there are many great picture books that can improve and enrich their lives as readers.

The publishers of children's literature have recently brought out great, supportive early chapter books. Children are able to read books like *Henry and Mudge* (Rylant 1987) and *Mr. Putter and Tabby* (Rylant 1997) in their early years of reading. However, it seems that as soon as students begin to like Henry and Mudge, they are hooked on chapter books and no longer read picture books. It is our responsibility to ensure that students are reading a variety of texts. We are big fans of Henry and Mudge books. We love Henry and his dog. We love Cynthia Rylant, and we love the stories. We know they provide great supports and are a great first chapter-book series for primary students. They are brilliantly written, wonderful stories in an easy chapter-book format.

What worries us is that Henry and Mudge books (as well as the others that fall into this category) have become a coming-of-age genre. Parents of first graders get teary-eyed when their child brings home a chapter book. In their minds, this is an important step, and we agree. Every step in a child's literacy development deserves a celebration.

Parents are thrilled to see their students reading a chapter book, and they begin to expect that all books the child reads will look and feel more like chapter books. They don't always understand what we do about supports in texts. We often spend some time at parent-teacher conferences opening copies of Henry and Mudge books alongside a favorite picture book by Jan Brett. We do not intend for parents to see one book as better than the other. Instead we want to have them rethink this idea of chapter books. They are not necessarily more difficult than picture books. In fact, if you read a page of a Henry and Mudge book and a page of Jan Brett's *Trouble with Trolls*, you will see a difference. The page in Brett's book has far more words, contains words that are more difficult to read and understand, and has a more complex sentence structure. We can do the same thing with *Henry and Mudge: The First Book* by Cynthia Rylant and *Lilly's Big Day* by Kevin Henkes.

> *Henry had no brothers*
> *and no sisters.*
> *"I want a brother,"*
> *he told his parents.*
> *"Sorry," they said.*
> *Henry had no friends*
> *on his street.* (25)

> *"One day Lilly's teacher, Mr. Slinger, announced to the class*
> *that he was going to marry Ms. Shotwell, the school nurse.*
> *Lilly's heart leaped. She had always wanted to be a flower girl.*
> *"It will be the biggest day of my life," said Mr. Slinger.*
> *"Mine, too," whispered Lilly.* (49)

The problem is that many of these young readers leave picture books behind once they read their first chapter book. In doing so, they miss out on many great stories, much rich vocabulary, and many messages about the world. We know many third and fourth graders who have never heard the story of the Gingerbread Boy or the Little Red Hen. When parents see the examples above, they often realize that picture books should not be discarded once students can read early chapter books.

Our concern extends to the students in second through fifth grades as they become transitional readers. If our youngest readers assimilate a distorted sense of reading, it will affect their development as they approach the transitional stage of reading development. If they abandon wonderful children's literature and adopt a limited perspective of reading, they take on invisible barriers to developing into fully competent readers.

Many of our second and third graders, especially those who have grown up on a diet of leveled books, come into these middle elementary grades hoping to move beyond picture books to chapter books. They see chapter books as more sophisticated and grown-up. As teachers, we know that many picture books are appropriate for transitional readers. And we know that many of these are actually better for transitional readers than for beginning readers. It is our role to help place value on picture books and to help our transitional readers understand that fatter chapter books are not necessarily better than picture books.

In his book *Choice Words: How Our Language Affects Children's Learning*, Peter Johnston talks about the importance of identity. He says, "Building an identity means coming to see in ourselves the characteristics of particular categories (and roles) of people and developing a sense of what it feels like to be that sort of person and belong in certain social spaces" (2004, 23).

We hope that each of our students fulfills the role of reader in our classroom and in life. We create reading communities and classroom libraries so they can recognize the characteristics of competent readers and develop identities as thoughtful, lifelong readers.

chapter three

Understanding Transitional Readers

Teaching children to read and providing them with something worthwhile to read is not a job for the faint of heart in this world. But I'll keep at it, and I won't be alone. You'll come too. We're fortunate, you know. Too many people in this world spend their lives doing work that doesn't really matter in the great scheme of things, but bringing children and books together does matter.

And we get to do it.

KATHERINE PATERSON, "BACK FROM IBBY"

Teaching is an endless search for ways to make learning meaningful and purposeful for students. Teachers work long and hard to help readers become more independent, and they create engaging learning spaces for their students because bringing children and books together does matter.

We appreciate the opportunities we have to bring books and children together. We encourage conversations in our reading workshops that support our students in recognizing who they are as readers. We think about the needs of our early readers in the primary grades and set out to expand our notion of matching books to transitional readers. Transitional readers begin to encounter a variety of texts that offer new challenges for them as readers. We recognize how unique transitional readers can be, and we are fascinated by the diversity of our students' reading habits and needs.

Jonathan read and understood everything he was given to read. But he read only to complete assignments and rarely enjoyed his books. He would read with little passion and then move on to another book. Jonathan read because he was expected to read.

Mollie loved to read. She read and reread books that her teachers and parents had shared with her, but she would never pick up a book that was unfamiliar to her.

Kimberly enjoyed reading a variety of books in every genre. After she finished reading a book, however, she would spend days looking for another one to read. She was seldom able to choose a book on her own.

Maddie read fluently and enjoyed hearing stories read aloud. She loved to discuss books and the characters in them. But from talking to Maddie about the stories she read, it was obvious that she did not pick up the meaning that the author intended. She often missed important points that affected her understanding of the story.

Anthony had favorite authors and series. He especially liked the Horrible Harry series by Suzy Kline. He understood his reading each day and was able to retell it in detail immediately afterward. But when he picked up his book the next day, he struggled to recall what had previously happened in the story.

Chelsea loved the Bailey School Kids books by Debbie Dadey and was not interested in reading anything else. She enjoyed the characters and the stories and had been reading them exclusively for months.

Eddie was an artist. Each day during reading time, he pored over a stack of picture books. He looked carefully at each picture and studied the art. Only occasionally would he skim the text.

These children were well on their way to becoming independent readers. However, they had reached a critical point in their development and needed their teachers to engage them in learning experiences that would support them in new ways. They were in the transitional stage of reading. Because the needs of students like them are so different, we need to look beyond levels when choosing books for instruction and when helping students choose books for independent reading.

Every child moves through a transitional stage of learning to read. Although transitional readers are most likely to be found in grades two through five, we know that they are in all levels of elementary and middle school. Transitional readers have moved beyond the beginning stages of reading development. Most of them have the necessary decoding skills and strategies in place for successful reading and are able to integrate different cueing systems to construct meaning.

Transitional readers are not struggling readers. They have become competent at using many of the skills learned in the earlier stages of reading development; they simply need new strategies to read more complex texts and move toward independence. If the classroom lacks more sophisticated reading experiences, readers can stall in this transitional stage. In short, transitional readers are competent readers who need the support of thoughtful and purposeful instruction.

Rethinking Reading Instruction

There was a time when we never considered the transitional reader. We made major assumptions about those students who appeared to read because they were able to decode. We believed that students would naturally make connections between classroom activities and their own independent reading. As children move from picture books to longer chapter books, they need a great deal of support. We often assumed that all of the skills learned in emergent and early stages of reading would magically transfer to books with fewer pictures, longer text, and more complicated information.

We easily, and all too quickly, made the switch from learning to read to reading to learn and failed to offer our students a support system for continued growth as readers. We slipped into a faster, faster, and higher, higher mode of reading instruction regardless of our students' comprehension, fluency, response, and interest. We didn't expect them to use reading behaviors beyond decoding and minimal comprehension. We often pushed them into longer, more difficult texts without understanding why they were not accurately and easily constructing the meaning of what they read.

We now realize that the strategies that work well with emergent readers aren't necessarily the strategies that can help transitional readers become independent. As books become more difficult, they often have more depth. More and more upper-elementary teachers are trying to extend the teaching techniques that have been successful in the primary grades to their intermediate classrooms. But because transitional readers need to expand their strategies in different ways, this doesn't always work.

In an *Education Week* editorial, "Beyond the Good Start Mentality," Stanley Pogrow (2000) explained the problem. He wrote, "Students beyond second grade have not had sufficient prior experience in having discussions with adults about ideas, and therefore have no cultural sense of strategic understanding. I refer to them as 'students who do not understand understanding,' a problem that results from a lack of sophisticated conversation in the home—and in school. These students do benefit from structured and aligned approaches in the early grades. But when the curriculum gets more integrative and open-ended in the third grade, primary reliance on these same structured and aligned approaches actually retards learning. Something else is needed . . . we must move toward much more specialized, focused, and sophisticated forms of help" (44).

We could consider transitional readers "the great pretenders." Unless we look closely at what they are doing as readers and listen well to what they have to tell us, we may not realize that they are not growing as readers.

For years, we have worked with readers in grades two through five, and nearly all of them have mastered phonics and decoding skills. Yet we cannot consider them independent readers for a variety of reasons. We cannot continue to support them in the same ways we did when they were learning to make sense of print. We need to build on the foundation they have and support them in very different ways. If we continue to focus only on the strategies that were helpful to them at the early stages of reading, we will not give them the support they need to become thoughtful, independent readers. Without the right support, they will remain transitional readers for far too long. These readers are on the edge of independence. We need to focus our teaching in ways that move them beyond the transitional stage and help them learn more complex strategies of reading.

We need to reconsider reading instruction and design strategies that will help transitional readers move toward independence. Some of these children think that reading is an activity one does at school, something that makes their teacher happy and their parents proud. For them, reading becomes mechanical, constructing meaning becomes less important, and as a result, reading no longer offers the excitement it once had. These students need to be hooked again and be given opportunities to think about reading in a different, more complex way.

Defining the Transitional Reader

It is difficult to describe a single set of characteristics for transitional readers because each student has a unique reading profile. All are competent at many things but have gaps that indicate they still need support to make sense of many texts.

To better understand transitional readers, consider the continuum of how children develop reading skills over time. Emergent readers have not yet learned many strategies for understanding print. They have minimal decoding skills and often rely on pictures for most of the information they get from books. Early readers rely less on pictures. They are beginning to recognize high-frequency words automatically as they read, and they can read familiar texts with fluency.

Transitional readers understand and can readily use decoding skills to decipher texts. They have many strengths as readers and a great variety of weaknesses. In her book *On Solid Ground*, Sharon Taberski (2000) defines transitional readers as children who

- can recognize many words, even those considered "difficult" or content related;
- integrate meaning, syntax, and phonics fairly consistently;
- have a variety of ways to figure out unfamiliar words;
- can generally read independent-level text with fluency, expression, and proper phrasing;
- are beginning to handle longer, more complex text with short chapters and more interesting characters;
- can summarize texts they've read;
- are growing more aware of story and text structures.

The problem with considering stages and phases of reading ability after students have passed through the emergent level of reading is that the process becomes enormously complicated because of students' individual differences. Trying to place young readers on a continuum of development doesn't necessarily make it any easier to plan instruction, as Regie Routman (2000) writes:

> *I find the terminology used to describe readers and the developmental stages they go through very confusing. Oftentimes, it depends on the particular text or developmental continuum you are working with.*

> *Words such as* emergent, experimental, developing, early, *and*
> beginning *can have similar meanings. So can* transitional, expand-
> ing, *and* self-extending. *As well,* fluent, independent, advanced,
> *and* proficient *can carry comparable meanings. It all depends on who
> is using the term, what continuum is being utilized, and what context
> is being described.*
>
> *Part of the problem, as I see it, is that readers don't fit into neat cat-
> egories that can be described by a single word. Continuums and devel-
> opmental charts do provide a useful overview, common patterns, typical
> behaviors, recommended teaching focuses, and a helpful language for
> thinking about groups of readers. However, at best these frameworks
> can only serve as a guide for our teaching. As professionals we must focus
> on the real readers in front of us and respond to the actual behaviors we
> observe.* (108–109)

The goal for teachers is to move students from the transitional phase
of reading development to independent or self-regulating reading. At
this stage students have a wide range of abilities for analyzing complex
texts, dealing with unfamiliar material, and selecting appropriate and varied texts for reading. Through close observation, teachers of transitional
readers realize that their students have major gaps in both their use of
strategies and their understanding of reading. Although the gaps vary
from student to student, many show up frequently in any group of transitional readers. We want to be clear that we don't think that these gaps
are necessarily weaknesses. They are just areas in which the child is not
yet independent.

The teaching profession has carefully cataloged the stages, phases,
and needs of young readers who are just learning to read. There are clear
developmental and instructional guidelines for working with emergent
and early readers. In this book we intend to provide guidelines for helping students who have moved beyond the emergent and early phases of
learning to read. Though these readers' needs may be more subtle and
harder to define, there are specific, concrete strategies teachers can use
to help them develop new reading skills.

We worry about a rush of new leveled books on instructing upper-
elementary students that give teachers more of what is seen in the primary grades—leveled-book instruction and decoding skills. We are
concerned that even though each reader is unique, teachers will be forced
to use scripted programs to teach reading. Although our book is not
intended to provide a definitive guide for teaching transitional readers,

we hope it can begin an alternative conversation in the profession—one that emphasizes practical, thoughtful instruction that uses real books that support real readers as part of a classroom community.

A Close Look at a Transitional Reader

Although a strong foundation for early reading is critical, the different types of learning opportunities provided at the transitional stage are equally important. The unique abilities and needs of transitional readers represent a natural progression of learning to read. These readers are at an exciting stage. They have learned how to decode and make meaning of many texts. They are ready to face new challenges.

Franki's daughter Alexa had enjoyed reading all her life. As a transitional reader, she could understand difficult texts. Her favorite books had always tended to be nonfiction texts dealing with history and inventions. Her favorite author was Laura Ingalls Wilder. She read Laura Ingalls Wilder picture books, biographies and photo journals about the writer, and any magazine articles she could find about her. Alexa searched the Internet and spent hours looking at photographs of Wilder's homes. But, as a transitional reader, Alexa had never been able to read an entire novel by Wilder.

Alexa had trouble finishing any novel. Her bedroom, home, and classroom were filled with great books. But it seemed that every time Alexa read to the middle of a chapter book, she found another book that looked a bit more interesting. So she abandoned the first book and started the next. She lost interest over the time it took her to complete a longer book.

Alexa was in this stage for nearly eighteen months. Needless to say, Franki was beginning to worry. She had to keep reminding herself that all children go through this stage of reading development. The teacher in her knew she needed to support Alexa with the same level of commitment and excitement that she did when Alexa was just learning to read. But she also knew Alexa could stall in her development as a reader if thoughtful teaching and family support were not in place.

We know that students like Alexa can continue to grow as readers. But she needed explicit instruction and support from teachers who understood her needs. Parents and peers also had a role to play in helping her acquire the ability to sustain interest and comprehension through longer and more complex texts. We discuss in detail in later chapters specific strategies teachers and families can use to help readers like Alexa.

Because Alexa and other transitional readers can easily decode text at or above their grade level and answer simple comprehension questions on standardized tests, their deficiencies as readers often aren't easily recognized or addressed. In addition, because texts become more sophisticated as students move up through the grades, these students will need additional skills as readers to tackle increasingly complex books.

Characteristics of the Transitional Reader

In our work with transitional readers, we have found certain characteristics that are common to many. We have identified six areas of skill development that most often require explicit instruction and support from teachers.

Learning to Select Appropriate Books

Transitional readers often struggle with recognizing books that are appropriate to read independently. They often choose books that are either too easy or too hard. They tend to choose books on the basis of an inviting cover or a topic of interest to them.

These can be good reasons for selecting books, but without a more sophisticated awareness of a variety of strategies for choosing books, transitional readers sometimes spend a long time picking a book and often waste time reading books that turn out to be inappropriate, given their skills or interests. Teachers often see these transitional readers wandering aimlessly in front of the bookcases. Or they may notice that these students make frequent trips to the bookcases and baskets because they have failed to make a good choice and quickly return for another book.

Part of our instruction with these readers needs to be spent in teaching them ways to select a book that is a good fit at a certain time. Students need their own strategies for selecting books that will help them throughout their lives as readers.

Sustaining Comprehension

Difficulty in sustaining comprehension for a longer text is another common characteristic. These students struggle with monitoring their comprehension, so when faced with reading a longer text, they often lose comprehension as they continue to read. Because their monitoring strategies are not as sophisticated as the books they are reading, they often push forward, continuing to read the text (decoding the words), but never stopping to think about what they are reading. They frequently get to the end of a chapter and cannot recollect what they have just read.

Sustaining comprehension over an extended period of time can also challenge transitional readers. They may struggle to remember what they read the day before, so they need a set of strategies for remembering. This is often an issue for students who are just starting to move from single-story texts to short chapter books.

Maintaining Interest over an Entire Book

Early or emergent readers take up books that are simple and brief. As children move into longer texts, they need to develop persistence in their reading. Only then can they maintain interest in a text long enough to complete it and understand what they have read.

Understanding Many Genres

Transitional readers may enjoy feeling comfortable in their reading and may therefore be reluctant to explore new genres. They revisit books they have read before, they read books that the teacher has shared with the class in a read-aloud, and they may limit their choice of books to those that are similar to the ones they have already read. If these transitional readers are going to move to a higher level of independence, they need experience with a variety of genres, texts, and authors.

Because each genre has unique features, transitional readers need strategies for making sense of any text. They cannot make the leap to independence until they have thoroughly explored a variety of genres and learned a wide range of reading strategies for each.

Decoding and Fluency Skills

Many transitional readers are skilled at decoding but still need to develop more sophistication as they read texts with more complex vocabulary. They are ready to look more closely at the structure of words and patterns in language. Although many of them have developed decoding skills, they may need to become more fluent in their reading. Very few of the transitional readers we encountered had decoding problems that got in the way of their reading. But as texts become more complex, children need instruction to support their fluency.

Using Text Features

As transitional readers move from simple books to a wider range of reading material, they encounter texts with new structures and features and often lack the strategies they need to make sense of them. As plots become more complicated, the number of characters increases, and issues of changing time and place become more prevalent in the books they are reading, transitional readers struggle with comprehension. As they encounter nonfiction texts, they struggle with the variety of ways content is presented (text, graphs, pictures, tables, charts) and how to find relevant information.

Some transitional readers lack skills in only one of the categories just described, but that one problem may be serious enough to stop their growth as readers. Many transitional readers have needs in multiple categories and will need a wide range of instructional and support activities to continue to develop as readers. All transitional readers need to build their own identity as readers.

Thoughtful Teaching

The reading process is complex. And yet in some schools across America educators are being pressured to find the right list of leveled books, the best program, or the lockstep teacher manual that maps the journey for the reader and the teacher. In our efforts to monitor student progress, we use measures that sort children into reading haves and have-nots, and we attempt to structure learning to promote progress. Often the very structures we invent limit the possibilities for our young readers—draw boundaries around their learning experiences—and shrink reading down to an activity they do in school, rather than a meaningful, thoughtful part of their daily lives. Our efforts to improve reading instruction too often tighten the parameters, limit growth, and give children an artificial perspective of what reading is all about.

Because readers have unique needs, books may be difficult for a variety of reasons. When we think about the six areas of focus, most of the time, growth in reading is not necessarily dependent on reading level.

Children who have difficulty with stamina and working through an entire book may have that difficulty with an easy book or a harder book. For a child who can't choose books, learning about authors and genres is more important for building a lifetime of reading skills than going over to the leveled baskets and choosing a book at random.

Reading can't be distilled to a reading level, a basket of books, or a test performance. We can't shrink reading down to answering comprehension questions about a text. We can't define reading by the books that the teacher has chosen for the student to read. We can't teach reading with meaningless activities to be done after a text is read. We can't define reading by what students are asked to do on a standardized test. And we can't expect students to learn to read if they spend their time rotating from center to center. Often schools negate many of the less tangible, less easily measured characteristics of a successful reader. But many of the skills transitional readers need to develop aren't easily measured.

The complexity of the reading process makes every reader unique, and our instruction must acknowledge this complexity. Although we do not provide recipes in this book for meeting all the needs of transitional readers, we can explain how we have learned to link our classroom observations with skills instruction. Thoughtful teaching comes from a perspective that looks at individual children, that peeks into their learning lives and draws energy from the uniqueness of each of them. Thoughtful teaching is responsive teaching; it comes from observing each learner. Teachers have a deep-seated respect for students as people. Children are exciting human beings who will rise to the challenges of new learning when they are respected and provided with an environment that encourages them to discover what they know and explore what they have yet to learn.

Transitional readers will not move forward without explicit, thoughtful instruction. We need to offer them learning experiences that provide a lifeline as they take their first steps toward truly independent reading, model for them the reading behaviors we want them to develop, provide opportunities for practice, and fill our classrooms with conversations that make a difference.

Six of Franki's third-grade students were reading *A Taste of Blackberries* by Doris Buchanan Smith. In the story, Jamie, the main character's best friend, has died. A sentence in the book explicitly tells the reader that he died. In a follow-up discussion, Franki discovered that three of the students believed Jamie was dead, whereas the other three were convinced that he was still alive. During the conversation, one of the students found the line on page 33 of the text where one of the characters says, "Jamie is dead, darling." Another student, however, pointed out that Jamie appears in scenes in the book after that line of dialogue, so he assumed that Jamie was still alive because he was still mentioned in the book.

Franki, who was leading the conversation, realized that these students had not picked up the clues that would make it clear to them that the scene where Jamie appears after his death is a flashback. It reminded Franki that transitional readers sometimes miss the subtle (and not so subtle) clues embedded within the text. Franki used this opportunity to teach these students about flashbacks, but she also wanted them to recognize when they needed to go back into the text when their reading didn't make sense. The conversation helped these students clarify, defend, and revise their thinking. Franki used the insights she learned from her experience with this group of students to design additional small-group instruction on recognizing flashbacks (see the following mini-lesson).

Mini-Lesson:

Recognizing Flashbacks

Possible Anchor Texts:

The Summer My Father Was Ten by Pat Brisson, *Mr. Putter and Tabby Fly the Plane* by Cynthia Rylant, or *The Sunsets of Miss Olivia Wiggins* by Lester Laminack

Why Teach It?

Authors often use flashbacks to tell a story. In many books, like *A Taste of Blackberries* by Doris Buchanan Smith, the reader must be able to infer that the author has gone back in time. Children often lose their understanding of the text when the time or place of the story is changed. They sometimes need explicit instruction that helps them identify the clues the author gives to let readers know they are in a flashback scene. Such clues include a change in font, illustrations, or key phrases such as *he remembered*.

To help students discover a variety of clues that authors use, teachers can share the three picture books mentioned above with their students.

How We Teach It:

Each book is short and can be read in one sitting. After each book, have students focus on those pages where the flashback begins and

Follow-Up: ends. Identify clues the author provides, and put them on a comparative chart.

When students discover other books that contain flashbacks, they can share them with the class on a bulletin board or in a special place in the classroom. On a copy of the page from the book students can highlight the words that helped them recognize that a flashback occurred.

Thoughtful teaching is an endless cycle of teaching and learning enriched by what we know about our students. With each new day, we enter the lives of our students, and they share with us. If we listen well, and if we watch with careful eyes, our teaching will become stronger and the cycle will continue.

When asked about the book he was reading, Ryan, a third grader, said, "When it is closed, it looks dull. The real stuff is inside." Ryan had learned that books are treasures to be discovered—you have to jump inside to get to the real stuff. And so it is with teaching. When we close our minds, our eyes, and our ears to the real stuff inside every child, our teaching is dull. It's only when we take the time to discover the real stuff in every child that our teaching becomes powerful and the learning becomes a lasting treasure. The complexity of reading and the uniqueness of young readers should send us on a persistent search for thoughtful instruction.

Because using a leveled system of books with transitional readers is often counterproductive to the goals we are trying to accomplish, we spend the next chapters examining other ways to think about book choice for these readers. We look closely at the limits of levels as well as the challenges and supports that books at these levels provide.

Is There Life After Captain Underpants? Fiction for Transitional Boy Readers

Larry Swartz

My nephew Matthew, age eight, has passed through reading books in a series about Flat Stanley, Cam Jansen, and The Magic School Bus and during a recent phone conversation announced, "Uncle Larry, I'm now ready for *Captain Underpants!*" A week later, at a family gathering, I noticed that Matthew had crawled under a table to read the third book in the Dav Pilkey series as the adults gathered around and chatted. Like many boys, my nephew enjoys a funny, adventurous read, and like many young readers— boys and girls—he is caught up in collecting books in a series and reading more about characters that he has come to admire. Getting young readers hooked into chapter-book series is a stepping-stone to first novels. The familiarity of the characters, the comfort of an author's style, and the enjoyment of a genre such as mystery, adventure, fantasy, or humor hold strong appeal for many young readers. For boys in particular, reading chapter-book series is a significant experience in their reading lives and one of the strongest opportunities for immersing them in the world of fiction.

Many boys from second to fourth grade want books that are short and that they can complete over a brief period of time. They need a book with a good story in which they can become immersed so that they continue to read it completely. Because they take the guesswork out of choosing something to read, books in a series are easily accessible to young boy readers. Many boys enjoy not only the challenge of reading series titles in sequential order (at last count, The Magic Tree House series continues to number thirty-eight) but also being part of a community of reading what their friends are reading.

During the transitional years, boys and girls gain reading power through their experience with books. When boys learn to read a series of sequential chapters that create a complete story, they are given a chance to anticipate and predict—the major operations in reading. Chapter books mark a reading plateau because young readers are able to sustain their interest over several chapters, making sense of plot and characters as the information builds up. As the incidents and images in the books grow one upon the other, the children build a large framework for understanding that may be carried over to future novel reading. A wide range of reading abilities are represented in the transitional years. Yet the common need for these children is to read widely and often. A large selection of books is necessary for those who are moving into independent reading but may not have much security with print, who need high motivation accompanied by material that is accessible. The frequency of illustrations, the chapter length, and the size of the font are some features of chapter books that help give the children success, preparing them for first novels and beyond where text dominates illustration, chapters are not titled or numbered, and books become thicker.

Well-intentioned educators and parents hope that these young readers who enjoy chapter books and first novels will continue this reading passion as they encounter longer novels.

If we recognize that boys enjoy reading books in a series, we might also have to admit that much of this reading occurs outside of school. We need to conquer the myth that "boys do not like to read" that is getting a lot of attention. Boys like to read. Any discussion of boys and reading recognizes that boys are immersed in all kinds of reading. We can neither ignore the pleasure many boys get from information texts nor disregard the world of technology that is an important part of boys' reading lives. In many cases, however, boys do not like to read what they are presented with in our classrooms. Many novels that young males will be required to read in future years do not seem to engage them because of the issues and emotions, language and style that contribute to the quality of the novel but don't connect to the world of many boys. David Booth, author of *Even Hockey Players Read* (2000), advises that when teachers offer a rich and varied mix of books (including fiction) and are mindful of boys' reading preferences, they go a long way toward building engaging and inviting reading environments for boys.

Research tells us that those boys who learn to read later than girls can't catch up with reading novels and extended forms of narrative fiction. Yet, in today's language programs, many teachers give priority to this type of literacy activity. By and large, teachers provide children with fiction as the staple ingredient of their programs, and we tend to judge readers on their ability to read and respond to more extended fiction. Teachers may be delighted by the boys who read nothing but fiction, but the aim for all of our students should be a healthy balance where they become literate in a full range of reading materials.

We need to consider how schools select their novels and to care about what boys think about what they are made to read. When boys and girls read the same adventure novels, they may take different things from them. Girls for the most part, respond to the feelings of the characters and how their personalities are shaped by life events and relationships; boys enjoy the action and find that any sections that offer description and reflection detract from the story. Girls may read books with boy protagonists, but boys may have problems reading books about girls, often based on anxiety about their gender images.

I was visiting a bookstore one Sunday afternoon and noticed that a grandmother was willing to buy her grandson a batch of books. He was drawn to the shelf displaying series titles. She pulled one book off the shelf and said, "This looks like a good series." But she quickly noticed that the cover featured a girl and her horse. "Boys don't read those kind of books!" she informed him.

"Why not?" I asked myself. I wonder if we are perpetuating a stereotype by suggesting that some books are for single-sex audiences. I know, however, that boys do judge a book by its cover. Would boys choose to read series about Junie B., The Babysitters Club, or The Amazing Days of Abby Hayes? Some would (in private). Today's publishing industry produces a vast range of fiction that would be considered "boy books" (see list below), books that appeal to boys' particular tastes and interests. What is a good book for a boy?* What kind of book? What kind of boy?

There are differences between girl and boy readers. Many girls read more fiction than boys. Girls and boys choose to read different kinds of material on different topics. Girls achieve higher reading scores than boys. Girls tend to comprehend narrative texts better than boys do. With respect to attitude, boys generally provide lower estimations of their reading abilities than girls do and value reading as an activity less than girls do. Boys have much less interest in leisure reading than girls do, and are more likely to read for utilitarian purposes than girls are.

What is the life for boy readers after Captain Underpants? Will Matthew go on to read and get pleasure from books with both female and male protagonists such as *Sarah, Plain and Tall* by Patricia MacLachlan, *Bridge to Terabithia* by Katherine Paterson, or *Eggs* by Jerry Spinelli? When Matthew becomes an adult, will he, despite what current statistics inform us about men's tastes, choose to read fiction? As teachers, we have sincere interests in laying the yellow-brick reading roads of our students, step by step, book by book, page by page. If we discover the real reading interests of boys, our classroom programs will then need to accommodate their preferences and needs. Like the girls they sit beside in our classrooms, boys need to make choices in their literacy lives and develop a sense of ownership of their reading selves. When we understand and accept the differences of boy and girl readers, we can review our own reading environments and consider whether we discourage certain kinds of reading as unsuitable for classroom reading (often books that appeal to boys) or whether we guide students on the reading paths where they can meet titles and authors they might, or might not, meet on their own.

---

*A good book for a boy, according to James Maloney, author of *Boys and Books* (2000), is one he wants to read.

Boys like to read . . .

- **books that are funny**
  The Giggler Treatment (series) by Roddy Doyle
  My Weird School (series) by Dan Gutman
  The Adventures of Captain Underpants (series) by Dav Pilkey
- **books that appeal to a sense of mischief**
  Further Adventures of Eddie Dickens (series) by Philip Ardagh
  Jake Drake (series) by Andrew Clements
  How to Eat Fried Worms by Thomas Rockwell
- **books that focus more on plot and action than description**
  Survivor (trilogy) by Gordon Kormon
  Andrew Lost (series) by J. C. Greenburg
  The Magic Tree House (series) by Mary Pope Osbourne
- **books that invite them to solve problems along with the characters**
  Joe Sherlock, Kid Detective (series) Dave Keane
  A to Z Mysteries (series) by Ron Roy
  Marvin Redpost (series) by Louis Sachar
- **sequels that sustain engagement and invite them to discover what's up
  with characters they've come to care about**
  The Mouse and the Motorcycle (trilogy) by Beverly Cleary
  Tales of a Fourth Grade Nothing by Judy Blume
  Shredderman: Secret Identity by Wendelin Van Draanen
- **books that are visual**
  Bone (series) by Jeff Smith
  Travels of Thelonious: The Fog Mound by Susan Schade
  Geronimo Stilton (series) by Geronimo Stilton
- **books that describe other worlds, other times**
  The Secrets of Droon (series) by Tony Abbott
  The Time Warp Trio (series) by Jon Scieszka and Lane Smith
  The Spiderwick Chronicles (series) by Holly Black and Tony DiTerlizzi
- **books that reflect their image of themselves**
  Operation: Dump the Chump by Barbara Park
  Love That Dog by Sharon Creech
  Dexter the Tough by Margaret Peterson Haddix
- **books that their friends like to read: popular authors**
  Andrew Clements
  Roald Dahl
  Andy Griffiths
  Dav Pilkey
  Louis Sachar

Wonderland –?
Lemony Snicket
Golden Compass

Jon Scieszka
Lemony Snicket
Jerry Spinelli
Geronimo Stilton
R. L. Stine

Novels and the Transitional Boy Reader: Ten Essentials

1. Most boys prefer novels with only male characters.
2. Most boys prefer novels written by male authors.
3. If we offer boys great novels in our classrooms, they will grow to read novels as adults.
4. We always need to let boys choose the novels they are going to read.
5. Most boys choose novels that their friends like to read.
6. The novels we introduce in our language arts programs should be enjoyed by both boys and girls.
7. Being fixated on an author, genre, or series is a good thing for boys.
8. The majority of our elementary classrooms are led by women teachers. Boys need to observe men reading novels to get hooked on fiction.
9. If boys don't like to read novels, that's OK.
10. Complete this sentence: The best book for a boy is . . .

Larry Swartz has been an educator for over thirty years and is currently an instructor at the Ontario Institute for Studies in Education at the University of Toronto. He is the author of a number of teacher resources including The New Dramathemes, The Novel Experience, *and* Good Books Matter.

References

Booth, David. 2000. *Even Hockey Players Read.* Markham, ON: Pembroke.
Maloney, James. 2000. *Boys and Books: Building a Culture of Reading Around Our Boys.* Sydney, Australia: ABC Books.

chapter four

When Levels and Learning Clash: Moving from Levels to Supports in Designing Instruction

Knowing my books and my children, and making a match between them, is one of the most important things I do—and one of the most demanding. It is exacting work that has led me to adjust my priorities in how I use my planning and class time.

SHARON TABERSKI, ON SOLID GROUND

Independent reading is the anchor for our reading workshops. We also know that read-aloud, whole-class mini-lessons, small-group work, and individual conferring are important parts of our reading day. As teachers, we need to know books well. When we do, we find that we are better able to help students choose books, find appropriate books for read-aloud, and choose books for mini-lessons. When we know books, we are better equipped to help our students become independent readers. As Richard Allington (2001) reminds us, "Kids not only need to read a lot but they also need lots of books they can read right at their fingertips. They also need access to books that entice them, attract them to reading" (68).

Many teachers rely on a system of leveled books to match students with texts that meet their instructional levels. The recent practice of "leveling" books in the first years of reading instruction has become a standard component of literacy instruction (see Fountas and Pinnell 1996), and leveled books can be an enormously helpful tool. However, we must remember that they are just one tool among others, and that teaching for transitional readers requires multiple considerations beyond a text level if instruction is to be effective. If we know that children are unique and the reading process is complex, why would we limit our ability to match children with books by relying on a leveled list created by a person or a company that doesn't know us or our children?

When students' reading diet is exclusively a leveled one, their purpose for reading disappears. They read for us. They become eager to reach the next level instead of being eager to learn more from what they are reading. In our haste to put skills instruction back into reading programs, we may have forgotten what we know about teaching children to read. We have abandoned the important lessons we learned about real reading, real books, and real children.

We know leveling mania has gone too far when some teachers refuse to stock their classroom libraries with any books that haven't been leveled; and, responding to market pressure, publishers seem to be coming out with different ways to level books. When we see books like *A Wrinkle in Time* by Madeline L'Engle on a leveled book list, we wonder when all books will be assigned an arbitrary level. But we're most distressed by stories from a librarian friend who is bewildered when teachers come into the library and ask for "a book on hamsters for my third-grade class project that has to be level M."

Regie Routman (2000) cautions teachers:

Some schools have witnessed a leveling craze that has extended through grades three through five. Some teachers have grown accustomed to selecting books based on leveling guidance, and feel that they cannot conduct guided reading groups without it. But leveling books in these grades is neither a good nor appropriate use of teacher time. . . . What is most important for selecting books for middle-elementary-grade students is that the content and story line are developmentally appropriate, interesting, and relevant as well as accessible. Additionally, consider that complexity of plot, time sequence, character development, and the author's writing style all play a role in determining a book's difficulty. Once the child is reading well . . . levels can actually be limiting factors, because they don't take into account students' varying interests, back-ground knowledge, and motivation. (84)

This seems to align with where we are as a society these days. The faster-faster mentality is visible in many areas of our lives. Students competing in sports and other events have become more common. We have even seen ads for caffeinated soap—to get your day started before your morning coffee! Although we can't do much about these big issues, we can't allow these trends to affect our children as they learn to read. It is too important, and we can't afford to sacrifice what we lose by moving higher and faster.

As children move beyond the early stages of reading, we should provide books that support them in moving toward more independent reading and complex comprehension skills rather than moving them higher and higher, and faster and faster, through advanced levels. Transitional readers need to broaden their reading strategies and improve their comprehension instead of simply reading books that are leveled higher than the last book they read. When we consider the skills transitional readers need, we worry that sometimes teachers are expected to concentrate on moving children to the next level rather than helping them learn and use the strategies they really need. This transitional stage of reading provides the perfect opportunity for children to take more ownership of their reading. As teachers we have to be careful that we don't take too much control and ownership of our students' reading. Our students need the chance to do it for themselves.

We have heard countless stories of students lost when asked to choose a book for independent reading time. Kathy Collins shares a story about a student in her classroom that demonstrates the need for many strategies for choosing books and why it is important for teachers to know books by more than just level.

Supporting Student Book Choice

Kathy Collins

"Wow, look at all these books and stuff," Angelica said to her line partner as I led my first-grade class into the maze of metal shelving that filled our school lobby. This temporary installation meant one thing: it was the

PTA's Annual Spring Book Fair, and it was my class's thirty-minute time slot for shopping.

My students made their way among the aisles of books like a horde of sale-seekers at the mall the morning after Thanksgiving. They were chatty and excited as they flipped through books, eager to show their friends what they had found. I was moving with them among the shelves, valiantly trying to lure them from the Harry Potter gadgets, the mini-chemistry sets, the beading kits, and the American Girl journals and toward the shelves that were full of the kinds of texts they could read. It was at this point that I noticed Daniel. I watched for a minute as he walked around the book fair with his hands in his pockets. He just stared at the shelves, not touching anything, not talking to anybody.

I watched Daniel struggle to find a book. He zigzagged through the maze of metal shelving, and when the fourth-grade class showed up to take our place at the book fair, I rushed him to pick something. "I don't know what to pick," Daniel said, almost in tears as he folded and unfolded the five-dollar bill he had pulled from his pocket. By now, the rest of my students were finished shopping and sitting along a wall in the hallway, growing louder by the second as they surveyed each other's books and pencil toppers while the fourth graders were chomping at the bit to get into the book fair. I told Daniel we had to leave, but I promised him that our student teacher would bring him back to the fair later that afternoon.

I remember feeling surprised that it was so hard for Daniel to find a book. In our classroom, my students shopped each week for their just-right books from the classroom library, and Daniel always seemed at ease. But then I realized the significance of what had happened. Daniel didn't know how to find a book for himself. When faced with all the choices of the book fair, he was overwhelmed. It was then that I understood: Daniel was dependent on the constraints of the leveled portion of our classroom library for guidance when choosing books. When faced with books that weren't housed in a leveled-book basket and that had no colored dot sticker in the top right corner that indicated the level, Daniel was paralyzed. He had no sense of reading identity outside of his reading level.

I knew that outside school Daniel didn't go to the public library and that it was unlikely that he went to bookstores. The only real "shopping for books" experience he ever had was shopping in our classroom, but this occurred in a very structured and stylized sort of way: his book choice was regulated by level, by the numbers of books he could shop for, and by the day of the week he could shop, and all of this was regulated by me. Daniel was a dot-driven reader, and I was a dot-driven teacher.

In retrospect, I realize that it would have been helpful to Daniel, and to others like him, if I had shown them how to find books anywhere, not just in the safety of our classroom library, and if I had helped them cultivate a reading identity that was more than a reading level.

In the case of choosing books, there are several ways we can acclimate students to the real world of nonleveled bookstores and public libraries. First we should determine our students' just-right reading levels and show them where to find those just-right books in the classroom, making sure the structures are in place and expectations are understood so they have lots of time to read and talk about their books each day. Then it makes sense to give them opportunities to explore the library to find other things to read, to role-play and to explore as readers, to make their own way as readers, for even a little bit of time. This doesn't have to interfere with work we're doing in reading workshop or contradict our emphasis on just-right reading, nor does it need to feel like yet another thing that we need to squeeze into our already tight schedules.

Perhaps it's as simple and informal as offering ten or fifteen minutes of library time after lunch or first thing in the morning. This free library time may sound sort of "loosey goosey" and lacking rigor, but it doesn't have to be wasted time for students or downtime for teachers. In fact, this is a rich opportunity for teachers to better understand their readers and for readers to better understand themselves.

When students are left to their own devices and impulses in the classroom library, there is much for us to see and learn. As we watch Tonya and Vanessa lying side by side flipping through *My Father's Dragon* (Gannett 1948), the read-aloud chapter book we're in the middle of, we can choose to confer with them, teaching to raise the level of what they are doing as they look at the sketches throughout the chapters. We could teach them that looking ahead at the sketches can help them predict what might happen, or we can teach them that they can study the sketches to learn more about Elmer or the other characters, or we can encourage them to dramatize the sketches to support their envisioning abilities. Or, instead of a reading-conference type of interaction, we can choose to have a real conversation with Daniel and Tony, like a perfect partner would, as they sit side by side reading the *Adventures of Polo* (Faller 2006), which they pulled from the basket of comic book–like texts the students have created and filled. Or better yet, we can simply watch our students and eavesdrop on them to see what they do and say, with whom they align, and how they make use of their time with texts when they are free-range readers. I would argue that all of this is worthwhile data to collect and that it adds information to our accumulated knowledge about our readers. These observations are important data, even though there aren't numbers, statistics, rubrics, or school rankings attached.

A couple of years ago, I listened to Ellin Keene present at Teachers College, and she shared a story about a very shy, introverted first grader lying on the floor reading a book about outer space. The book was too hard for the child to read conventionally, which Ellen mentioned almost in passing because that wasn't the point of the story. The significance of this anecdote was how the child merged his interest in space with classroom reading to imagine a project, and how his huge self-initiated art and science project about the planets and outer space helped integrate him into the social world, the inner space, of the classroom.

Although I can't remember many details exactly, I do remember that after Ellin spoke, we, the audience, were walking out into our smaller study group sections. I heard many people voice concerns about the fact that the child she had described was not reading a just-right book. It was hard to get past this fact, I admit, especially with the emphasis on just-right reading.

But you know what? Isn't there more to being a reader than reading just-right books? After all, don't we call kindergartners readers before they have one-to-one match, sight words, and leveled books in their possession?

I worry that if our kids are limited to just-right books 100 percent of the time in our classrooms, they may not learn the possibilities and promise of reading nor will they easily develop their own goals and plans as readers that are more personal than moving to the next reading level.

I do want to make clear that I'm not, in any way, suggesting that we unlevel the leveled portion of our classroom libraries, or that we call on parent volunteers or former students to come in to school over the summer to scrape off the colored dots we've dutifully affixed on the top right corners of our books. Not at all. Instead, what I am saying is that there are tangible benefits when we find ways to let kids pursue their own interests in reading, allowing them to look at the books they want to read and giving them opportunities to play at reading as they explore books, invent projects, or simply read with someone they would never have the chance to read alongside during reading workshop. This seems important. I think Daniel would agree.

Kathy Collins works at the Teachers College Reading and Writing Project, Columbia University, and is a staff developer and consultant. She is the author of Growing Readers: Units of Study in the Primary Classroom *(2004) and* Reading for Real: Teach Students to Read with Power, Intention, and Joy in K–3 Classrooms *(2008).*

From Levels to Supports

We look at books with an eye toward instructing transitional readers in specific areas. As teachers, we know that levels provide a helpful tool for us, but we never share levels with the students. Instead of focusing on levels, we look for supports in various books that can be used to teach skills these readers lack. We define supports as those text elements that readers can use to build or clarify understanding. For example, in the previous chapter, Franki realized that some of her students didn't understand flashbacks. In planning instruction, Franki needed to find appropriate books with features that could help her students understand how flashbacks work. She selected *The Sunsets of Miss Olivia Wiggins* by Lester Laminack because that book uses font changes to signify time change. She also chose *Mr. Putter and Tabby Fly the Plane* by Cynthia Rylant because it uses key words to indicate flashbacks. Franki wasn't much concerned about the reading level of these books. Although it was important for her to consider whether her fourth graders could easily understand the content, it was more important for her to think about how the books could be used to help her students understand flashbacks when they encountered them in the future.

Books we use in teaching transitional readers have a variety of specific supports for instruction. Transitional readers benefit from teaching that helps them understand how to identify and understand the features of texts that are different from or more sophisticated than those they are already familiar with. We carefully choose books that will help our students use the text supports they contain to strengthen understanding in their own reading. We consider these books "anchor books" (Harvey and Goudvis 2007).

We know our books not merely by a listed level, but by the supports that they provide. We share information about these text supports with our students so they can become more independent in recognizing and using these supports to help them comprehend. We want them to consider many things as they choose books, such as topic of interest, author, mood, and difficulty of text.

An example of a text we use with transitional readers that has easy words but hard concepts is Donald Graves's poem "The Night Before Fishing Season Opens." The concept of time is crucial for understanding many texts, and students often need to be taught how to look for clues that will help them make inferences about time.

Mini-Lesson:

Possible Anchor Text:

Inferring from the Text in a Poem

"The Night Before Fishing Season Opens" by Donald Graves
(from *Baseball, Snakes, and Summer Squash*)

The Night Before Fishing Season Opens

After supper, Dad helps
George and me check supplies:
creel, bait tin, worms, pole,
rubber boots, not used
since last summer.
I see orange-bellied trout
dancing on the brook bank.

8:00 P.M.
Lay out my clothes
and wait for dawn;
burrowed into my pillow
hoping for sleep;
beneath the waterfall,
a pool boils
with hungry trout.

9:00 P.M.
Flip my pillow
to the cool side.
Cast my line
under the bridge, feel
the rat-a-tat of trout bites,
a quick jerk to set the hook.
I play the brookie to shore,
catch the speckled flash
of color before I swing
him to the bank.

9:40 P.M.
I imagine Mother's call
and smell the bacon;
bounce to the floor
and one by one I put on the clothes

from the neat pile
on the chair:
trousers, shirt, jacket.
I sit down, slip on my long socks;
reach for my boots.

Why Teach It? As students encounter more complex text, they are often expected to infer setting and other important elements. In many poems and novels, the author begins without explicitly telling the reader when or where the story is taking place. It is important for transitional readers to begin to use the clues in the text to determine setting.

How We Teach It: Share the poem with students. It is helpful for every student to have a copy or to enlarge the poem so that everyone in the class can read it. After the reading of the poem, think aloud and say, "The poem is called 'The Night Before Fishing Season Opens,' but I thought there were places in the poem where they were fishing. I wonder if this is really the night before fishing season begins. I think I'll read through it again to see if I can figure it out."

As you continue to think aloud, mention the following words and phrases that make it clear that the poem is truly about the night before fishing season begins.

8:00 P.M. . . .
burrowed into my pillow
hoping for sleep;

9:00 P.M.
Flip my pillow
to the cool side . . .

9:40 P.M.
I imagine Mother's call . . .

Follow-Up: Read other poems in the collection, such as "The Winner" or "First Baseball Glove," and think aloud as you read the text to the class.

The concept of text supports is particularly helpful in looking at books that are relatively simple to read or that have repetitive text patterns or phrases. When we first began to teach children in the intermediate grades, we thought that series books for young readers were all very similar. We categorized them as "beginning chapter books" and didn't differentiate among them. We assumed that if students simply read these books, they would get the support they needed to move toward more independent reading.

As we worked with the books and the children, however, we realized that there was a wide range of different supports among the "beginning chapter books" in our classroom library. We also took another look at the picture books that we had previously thought were too easy for our readers. We found that these books often contained wonderfully specific instructional features to use with transitional readers.

The next lesson is one we often use with transitional readers: using picture books to explain the concept of background knowledge. Students will find that using their background knowledge about familiar fairy tales can help them build comprehension.

Mini-Lesson: Using Background Knowledge

Possible Anchor Texts:

Dear Peter Rabbit by Alma Flor Ada, *The True Story of the Three Little Pigs!* by Jon Scieszka, or *Previously* by Allan Ahlberg

Why Teach It?

Students need to understand how critical background or prior knowledge is to comprehending text. As they continue to read about topics both familiar and unfamiliar to them, understanding the meaning of background knowledge and the role it plays in constructing meaning will help them learn how they can use it in their own reading.

How We Teach It:

Read the book aloud to your students. In the Ada book, for example, the story unfolds as various storybook characters exchange letters about a housewarming party hosted by the three little pigs. After reading the book, ask students to brainstorm things they knew about the characters that helped them understand the story. Encourage the students to refer to the stories they know as they discuss the present book. For example, students will realize that when Goldilocks writes, "There was a little girl in the forest all dressed in red and she was talking to a wolf," she is referring to Little Red Riding Hood on her way to her grandmother's house.

Follow-Up: Learning to use background knowledge is an important tool in understanding text. This lesson can be used as an anchor for future discussions on background knowledge.

Supportive Features of Text

There are many supports found in books that should be considered when matching transitional readers to texts. The more we know about certain books, the better we can support students as they learn to choose books that are right for them. Recognizing these supports helps us make sound instructional decisions. Knowing which books might be a match for the students in a classroom helps us choose good books for our classroom libraries and set up the library in ways that invite students to find these books. Once teachers become familiar with them, they can better help their students recognize and use them.

Students are so accustomed to reading books that clearly set up the story on the first page or two of the book that sometimes they find it difficult to make the transition to stories that take pages to unfold. It is helpful to model the kind of thinking strategies that are needed to build comprehension when readers have to suspend thoughts and questions until they find evidence in the text.

Text Setup

The way text is placed on the page can provide a great deal of support for transitional readers. Often books at this level are set with large type, generous spacing between lines, and wide margins. Many books contain only one sentence or phrase per line, the line breaks suggesting the pauses of spoken language. This arrangement of text promotes fluent reading. It supports the reader enough so that reading speed does not get in the way of comprehension. The level of text support of course varies from book to book. Some books, such as the Henry and Mudge series by Cynthia Rylant, provide a great deal of support. Sentences are usually short, and lines always break at the end of a sentence. Longer sentences are separated at appropriate pauses. For example, in the book *Henry and Mudge: The First Book*, the following sentence breaks at the comma to encourage the natural pause that should occur:

Mudge had floppy ears,
not pointed. (10)

Other books, such as those in the Junie B. Jones series by Barbara
Park, assume that readers know to pause at appropriate spots without support: margins are smaller; text is set with a uniform line length, with words
broken at the end of a line; and pages don't always end with a period.

Hooks

Early chapter books often contain features designed to hook the readers'
interest and help them begin piecing together bits of information. For
example, the back cover might contain a story summary, excerpts from
reviews, enticing blurbs from other authors, and mention of awards the
book received. Maps, a dedication, and a list of other books written by
the author also serve to entice the reader. The cover, the title, and the
chapter titles can help readers predict what the book might be about.

If we teach students how to preview on their own, they can use the
strategy to choose books and to aid comprehension. All of these features
help transitional readers gain as much information as they can before
reading the book. These supports lay the foundation for readers to construct meaning and unfold the more complex plots, characters, and story
lines of chapter books. For example, in *The Van Gogh Cafe*, Cynthia
Rylant hooks the reader at the end of each chapter with a sentence that
leads into the next chapter: each chapter title is taken from a word or
phrase contained in the last sentence of the previous chapter. For example, one chapter ends with the following sentence:

And besides, someone with a deeper secret is about to arrive at the Van
Gogh Cafe. Someone tall and sad and elegant. Someone who could be a
star . . . (29)

The chapter that follows is called "The Star."

Illustrations

At the early stages of reading development, children rely heavily on pictures to help them comprehend the text. We often assume that children
can move easily from picture books to chapter books when in fact they
continue to rely heavily on pictures and may have few strategies for

understanding text that stands alone. Being aware of how much support pictures provide for transitional readers plays an important part in matching children with books.

We always look at the illustrations in books to determine how they support the text. Many early chapter books contain a short paragraph and an illustration on each page. The Minnie and Moo series by Denys Cazet, for example, has pictures and limited text on every page. Many of the pictures illustrate even the smallest details in the text. Such illustrations provide a great deal of support for the reader. In other books, the pictures may still be connected to the text, but very little meaning or plot can be determined from merely looking at them, and often the pictures are not on the same page as the text they are illustrating. This is the case, for example, in *Little House in the Big Woods* by Laura Ingalls Wilder.

Dialogue

The ability to read and understand dialogue is crucial for successful reading. Most children's books include some dialogue. To support transitional readers, many early chapter books clarify each quotation by specifying which character is talking, often using the word *said*. More complex texts may specify who is talking, but with a greater variety of descriptive words or phrases. In *Pinky and Rex and the New Neighbors* by James Howe, we find the following dialogue:

> *"But he's a boy! And he's seven!" Amanda protested.*
> *Pinky shrugged. "I'm just trying to be fair," he said.*
> *"Right," said Amanda. "You already told me you and Rex don't want to play with him. So why should I?"*
> *Pinky shrugged again as he pushed open the door. "That's life," he called back over his shoulder. (17)*

The least amount of dialogue support occurs when characters converse without any text to identify which one is talking. Here it is up to the reader to follow the conversation and be aware of who the speaker is throughout the conversation. In *Cam Jansen and the Mystery of the Babe Ruth Baseball* by David A. Adler, the conversation is unclear unless the reader is sophisticated enough to deduce who is talking.

> *"He got off on the fifth floor," Cam told Eric. "Now we know where he lives. I'll stay here and watch to make sure he doesn't leave. You go get the police."*

"No!"

"No?"

"You still haven't told me why we followed him. What will I tell the police?" (37)

As teachers we look carefully at the dialogue in the books transitional readers choose and monitor the match between how it is presented and each reader's level of sophistication.

Book and Chapter Leads

The books in our classrooms offer varied support in the way the story begins. Some authors begin their stories with a description of the characters and the setting before moving into the story. *Meet M & M* by Pat Ross begins by presenting the title characters:

Mandy and Mimi were friends. They were such good friends that sometimes they pretended to be twins. But Mandy was two inches taller. So she bent her legs to look shorter. And Mimi was one size bigger. She held in her stomach to look smaller. (1)

The text continues with a description of several similarities the two girls share before moving into the story line. In the other books in the series, this descriptive support is abandoned; it is assumed that the reader is familiar with the characters.

Other writers begin by taking readers right into the story. Here it is up to the reader to determine what is happening, who the characters are, and where the story is taking place. These books require readers to fill in the gaps as the story unfolds. For example, *Anastasia Again*, by Lois Lowry, begins this way:

"The suburbs!" said Anastasia. "We're moving to the suburbs? I can't believe that you would actually do such a thing to me." (1)

Transitional readers need to have strategies for understanding how to make sense of the story no matter how it begins. Some leads set the stage and give readers a great deal of support for understanding the story. Comprehension is less of a challenge when the lead provides important information about the characters and the setting. Less supportive leads are more typical of stories that children will encounter as they become more independent readers.

Continuation or Stand-Alone Chapters

As children move into beginning chapter books, they often have difficulty sustaining comprehension over the time it takes to complete the book. Because these books are longer than those they are accustomed to reading, children often take several days to read them. They therefore need to learn strategies that will help them remember where they are in the story when they pick the book up again.

Many authors of early chapter books are aware of the support these young children need. Some early chapter books have several chapters that are related only by theme. For example, all of the stories may occur on a family vacation to the beach. Aside from the same characters and settings, these chapters can stand alone as individual stories; children need not remember details of previous chapters when they return to the book. In *Gus and Grandpa* by Claudia Mills, the three chapters stand alone. Each can be read without reading the others. In other books, the chapters are sequential and build on one another. The chapters of *Mr. Putter and Tabby Fly the Plane* by Cynthia Rylant tell a continuing story about playing with a toy airplane. In books like this one, children must be able to build on their prior reading in order to understand the entire text.

In some books, the setting changes when a new chapter begins. For example, in most of David Adler's Cam Jansen books, the chapters begin at almost exactly the same time and place as the previous chapter ended. But in books like *A Jigsaw Jones Mystery: The Case of the Christmas Snowman* by James Preller, the time and place change at the beginning of each chapter.

Length of Chapters

Transitional readers are often best able to comprehend texts that can be read in one sitting. Some books, like Cynthia Rylant's *Poppleton and Friends*, have short chapters that can be read in a single sitting. It takes more sophisticated skills to be able to understand a chapter that is longer and might have to be read over several days, such as those in *Poppy* by Avi. Transitional readers often have a hard time keeping track of stories with longer, more complex chapters, or they lose interest before they finish. They need to learn strategies for understanding a more complex story line.

Tables of Contents/Chapter Titles

When they first learn to read, young children are taught to preview the book by looking at the cover as well as the illustrations. This encourages them to predict the story and improves comprehension. Children should continue to preview books as they move from picture books to chapter books, but the features that are most helpful in predicting and comprehending change as they begin to read longer books. Many chapter books have a table of contents listing individual chapter titles that give the reader an idea of what to expect in each chapter. Chapter titles can also support readers when they return to a book by reminding them what has happened in the story. Of course, books vary considerably: some have chapter titles that are very explicit; others have titles that are more vague. For example, in *Pinky and Rex and the Spelling Bee* by James Howe, the chapter titles encourage the reader to predict the events of the story:

> The Big Day
> The Champion Speller of the Whole Second Grade
> Nervous Pinky
> The Worst Thing That Ever Happened
> Laughter
> The Long Walk Home

In other books, such as *Sarah, Plain and Tall* by Patricia MacLachlan, the chapters do not have titles, so readers need to use other clues to make predictions.

Mini-Lesson:	# Building Comprehension
Possible Anchor Text:	*Belle Teal* by Ann M. Martin
Why Teach It?	We want students to know that there are differences between the books they choose to read. Students who have been reading books like those in the Henry and Mudge or Junie B. Jones series are accustomed to having the book set up for them on the first few pages. However, as books get more sophisticated, leads do not give readers all the answers. Students need to know that one way to

decide if a book is right for them is to think about whether or not they are willing and able to invest the time to put the pieces together to figure out what is going on in the book. This lesson also gives students a strategy for making sense of more difficult leads.

How We Teach It:

We teach this lesson as a think-aloud, sharing our own thinking with students on a chart or an overhead transparency. For this lesson, we pay close attention to the way we make sense of the first several pages of a more difficult chapter book. We realize that much of our thinking is asking ourselves questions, suspending our thoughts until the book reveals more evidence. We share our thinking (below) with students.

Thoughts and Questions	**Thinking**
Does Belle live with Gran?	p. 1 I wonder. p. 2 It's the last day of summer vacation.
Inferred that Belle is staying at Gran's for the summer.	p. 2 Changed my thinking when I found out that Mom, Gran, and Belle live together.
How old is Belle?	p. 1 I wonder. p. 5 It wasn't until p. 5 that I found out that Belle is starting the fifth grade.
Gran has become forgetful.	p. 1 I wonder what this will have to do with the story. I may not find out until later in the story.
Gran sees the good in people.	p. 1 Will this be important later in the story?
Does seeing the positive and the good in things have anything to do with a theme in a book?	p. 1 I wonder what the theme of the story will be.
Belle keeps a journal.	p. 2 I wonder what she writes in her journal. I may have to wait to find that out.

Where's Belle's father?	p. 2 I wonder.
	p. 3 Found out that Belle's father died.
Belle's friend is Clarice.	p. 4
They can't wait to have Miss Casey for a teacher.	p. 5

Follow-Up: Students can look more closely at the lead in the book that they are currently reading. Going back to the lead and thinking once they've already read it will give them an idea of how they made sense of it when they began the book. A discussion about things they noticed will show the variety of ways authors start books.

Expanding Our Definition of Just-Right Books

It is important for students to understand that there are many reasons a book is right for them at the time. It's not about levels. Often, there are more complex reasons to consider. If we can help students be in tune with their lives as readers, they will also be able to figure out when a book is not just right for them and why.

Mini-Lesson: When Is a Book a Just-Right Book?

Possible Anchor Text: One from your own reading stack

Why Teach It? Our transitional readers need to know that just-right books depend on several things. A book can be just right for you one day that wasn't just right for you the week before. At this point in their reading lives, they can't merely decide that a book is just right because they know all the words or they understand it or it is interesting. As they become better readers, they have more choices in their reading.

How We Teach It: I brought in a copy of *A Thousand Splendid Suns* by Khaled Hosseini (2007). I explained that I had been looking forward to its coming out. I had read the author's first book and couldn't wait to read this one. I had kept up with summaries and reviews online before the book was published, and I went out to get it the day it was released to bookstores. But, it came out at a busy time for me—the end of the school year. I started the book and had time to read only a few pages at a time. I realized quickly that even though this book was a just-right book for me, it wasn't just right for me at the end of the school year. I wanted to read this book when I could really become immersed in it. So, instead of continuing, I saved it for later. Instead, I chose a book that was lighter and faster to read. When I look for just-right books, I have to make sure that the book fits into my life at the time, that I have the time and energy to become immersed in it. I want to read a book when I know I can read it through completion.

Follow-Up: Follow-up conversations, possibly during whole-class share time or in individual conferences, would bring this idea up again and again. Asking students about books that might be right for them at a different time is a conversation that we want to carry through all year long.

Mini-Lesson:

Just-Right Books—Things to Think About

Why Teach It? We want students to integrate the lessons we are teaching to begin to ask themselves questions about whether a book is right for them. This will help them become more independent in book selection.

How We Teach It: We remind students of past lessons on just-right books and ask them to share ways they find good books. Then we ask them to think about the kinds of things they think about when they are deciding whether a book is just right. We make a chart with the class to hang in the room to remind them of things to think about when choosing books. One class's chart looked like this:

How Do You Choose a Just-Right Book?

How is the length? Will I stick with it?
After I preview, does it sound interesting?
Is it a topic that I like?
Can I understand it after I read the blurb and first chapter?

Are there too many hard words?
Will this book be better for me at another time?
Is this book by an author I like?
Is this book part of a series I like?
What mood am I in?

Follow-Up: For several weeks afterward, we refer to this chart as students choose new books, asking who has used the questions to determine whether a book was right for them.

Our goal as teachers should be for children eventually to be able to read and understand any text they encounter. This can be accomplished by being aware of the supports that books contain to help the transitional reader, by reconsidering our classroom libraries and audience, and by clearly understanding the importance of matching readers with books that will support their growing independence.

chapter five

Taking a Close Look at Series Books

It was amazing how few of my students even knew where to look to find the author's name on a novel. Lack of basic knowledge in using text supports hampers students not only in choosing appropriate books but also in reading them successfully. For struggling readers, these supports are often a mystery and as such require step-by-step shared discovery.

JANET ALLEN, YELLOW BRICK ROADS

When we started teaching intermediate grades, one of our main goals was to get students to read beyond picture books, early series books, and easy chapter books. We got caught up in moving children to more difficult, longer books without realizing that series books, picture books, and beginning chapter books provided supports that could expand and extend our readers without burdening them with longer texts. We tried desperately to move children who seemed "stuck in a series" into what we thought were more appropriate books. We were eager for them to read books we considered more challenging and more interesting.

Over the past several years, we have realized that we were wrong. In his book *What Really Matters for Struggling Readers*, Richard Allington discusses this issue. "There is another often underappreciated genre of reading material that we need to consider when rethinking children's access to books they can read easily, fluently, and with understanding. These are the often maligned series books" (2006, 62). We have come to see the value of picture books, series books, and early chapter books in helping transitional readers move to greater independence.

Just as predictable texts support young readers, Sharon Taberski (2000) reminds us how series books can provide similar support for transitional readers. "Children at the transitional stage read a lot of 'series' books. Through their shared characters, settings, and events, these books support transitional readers' development just as the repetitive language and structure of emergent and early texts supported them when they were starting out" (17).

Students feel comfortable reading books whose characters, style, and likely story progression are familiar. Allowing children to linger in books they can easily read can provide them with the context and support they need to become more effective readers. Just as many adults read every John Grisham book or every book in the Orson Scott Card series, children can benefit from reading a number of books by the same author or in the same series. Often transitional readers struggle with the complexities of text as they progress as readers. They begin to encounter books with more characters, complex plots, and longer text. If we can help them by providing books they can count on, books that have characters they know well, and books with story lines that begin and end in similar ways, we can teach them the more subtle and sophisticated skills they will need to read independently. Even as children move beyond early series books into more sophisticated series books like the Redwall series by Brian Jacques and the Shiloh series by Phyllis Reynolds Naylor, they can still count on consistent characters, settings, and plots.

Early series books that we once viewed as all the same level have a variety of supports for young readers. We have learned to look closely and carefully at each series and each book within a series to see what supports are there for transitional readers. There are many high-quality series books, and some are written by well-known authors of other good children's literature. These authors know and understand readers at this critical stage of development.

Sluggers . . . a Series for Transitional/Reluctant/Emergent Readers from a Dad Who Happens to Live with One

Loren Long

It caught us off guard when my son's first-grade teacher called us in for a parent-teacher meeting at a time when such meetings were not planned or on the calendar. It was just before Christmas, in fact. She informed us that Griff was having serious reading problems. He was not keeping up with her expectations. He would need "extra" help or he might not be able to move on to second grade.

How could this be? After all, I was committed to children's literature, illustrating picture books for a living, and we had read to him nightly his entire life. As troubling as it was to hear this, I'll forever thank this teacher for her conviction that my son, come hell or high water, would not slide by until he developed reading skills up to her standard.

So we went through the proper channels to investigate his reading issues. Did he have a learning disability? Was he dyslexic? Did he have other conditions that we'd never heard of? It turns out, he was a normal little kid. We got the following responses: "Griff is a bit of a dreamer." "Griff likes to draw." "He's pretty much an average little boy who would rather do just about anything under the sun than sit with a book." Hmm, nervous whistle from Dad . . . wonder where he gets that?

So we immediately got Griff some extra help both in and out of school. And we began amping up our at-home reading exercises with him. For the first time, I began to take a close look at the chapter-book world. As Griff advanced into second and third grade, we searched high and low and began to discover wonderful chapter series. My publisher would send me hot-off-the-press books. The biggest thing I noticed about these books was that they were published in series, not just one and done. We would read them aloud with Griff. We would read a page and then he would read a page. We would read two pages and then he would read one page. I noticed he would try to trade me his page when my page was short. I noticed that he would count the pages until the next chapter started. And he would "swim" from picture to picture. I saw firsthand how valuable those pictures were to the psyche of a reluctant little reader. And the series element was key.

Griff still was not an accomplished reader, but when we found a series that he liked . . . BAM! He wanted them all. I'll never forget when we finished reading that first book over many sittings. He had read a novel. Sure, it was a little novel for kids and we had helped him along, but in his mind, it was a real book and he had read it. He had his own sense of pride.

This is how the Sluggers series was born. I wanted to create a chapter series and perhaps I could help spark interest in reading to another little boy or girl who would rather do anything under the sun than sit with a book.

I knew a few of the characteristics that my series would have to have. It had to have short chapters. It had to have lots of pictures. And I wanted to write about what I loved as a kid (and as a grown-up) . . . baseball! I love baseball and I love the history of baseball. I conceived the "seed" idea for the series and needed a writer to help create the books with me. This is where my co-creator Phil Bildner stepped in. Phil has written about baseball and sports for children, and we shared similar interests. Together, we built on my initial premise and we were off.

Sluggers is about three main characters—Griffith, eleven, Ruby, nine, and Graham, seven—who travel around the country with a quirky band of barnstorming baseball players in the summer of 1899. The series is filled with baseball, history, mystery, love of family, love of country, and a little baseball mystique and magic. It has short chapters, lots of art (each chapter starts with a drawing of old-time ballplayers in the shape of a letter), and historical references from each city the team travels to and is peppered with the baseball vernacular of the day. For example, in 1899 they called a ground ball a "daisy cutter." As of March 2008, there were three books out in the series, with plans for as many as nine in all.

And just so you know, my Griff is in sixth grade now, and thanks to a tough first-grade teacher, he's doing fine. In fact, this has been the first year he did not need in-school "extra" help. I truly feel that this very special reading specialist saved my son's life in many ways.

And it's been a family affair as well. Two of the main characters in the Sluggers series are named for my own boys: Griff, of course, and his little brother Graham.

Thanks for reading!

Loren Long is illustrator and creator of the Sluggers series for transitional readers. In addition, Long is the New York Times *best-selling illustrator of the re-creation of* The Little Engine That Could *by Watty Piper,* Toy Boat *by Randal DeSeve,* Angela and the Baby Jesus *by Frank McCourt, and* Smash

Crash by Jon Scieszka. His newest book, Drummer Boy, *is the first picture book he has both written and illustrated. To learn more about his work, visit www.LorenLong.com.*

Mini-Lesson:

Possible Anchor Text:

Why Teach It?

How We Teach It:

Follow-Up:

Introducing a New Series to the Classroom

Game One (The Sluggers series) by Loren Long and Phil Bildner

As we get to know our students as readers, we find new series that seem like good matches for them. These could be series that were recently published, series that students haven't yet discovered in the classroom, or series that we just haven't had in the classroom library. This lesson helps students learn about new books but also teaches them that they can think about the kinds of series they might like.

When Sluggers was new to the classroom, Franki brought in the first in the series, *Game One*, to share with a couple of her students who were hooked on Matt Christopher books. These two boys had been reading Christopher's books for a while, and Franki wanted to introduce them to other sports series that they might enjoy. She asked them to read it and to see if they thought it would be a good series to add to the classroom library. Both boys enjoyed the first book and went on to read the next one. Franki asked them to think about others in the class who might enjoy the series and to generate a list of characteristics of readers who might enjoy Sluggers. The students did this and then introduced the series to the class, using this list to highlight the kinds of readers who might enjoy it.

Asking students to think about other readers who would like a series is an important piece of building community in the reading workshop. After a lesson like this, we ask students to think about series that other readers in the class might enjoy. Encouraging them to share new series they find with others and to seek out others' recommendations then becomes a natural part of the reading workshop talk.

Series books can provide various supports and challenges to young readers. Once we have become familiar with the books, we can better determine which one may be the perfect fit for a young reader. Although individual titles in a series may have different supports, it is likely that many books in a given series will offer similar supports. When children read five or six books in a series, their comprehension improves. Table 5.1 (see pages 98–121) summarizes the supports in some common series. When reviewing series books that may be added to the classroom library, we ask ourselves the following questions:

- Do the cover illustration and title help predict the story?
- Is there a blurb on the back or inside flap to set the scene?
- How well do the size of the print and the line spacing support readers?
- Do the line breaks support the reader, or is the book written in paragraph form?
- How long is each chapter? Can a chapter be read in a single sitting?
- Are there chapter titles that can help readers predict what will happen next?
- Is each chapter a continuation of the story, or does each stand alone?
- Are there time lapses between chapters that readers need to infer?
- How do the pictures support the reader? Is there a picture on each page? Do the pictures match up with the text?
- Is the dialogue easy to follow? Is the speaker always identified?
- Does the lead of the book or chapter provide a quick introduction to character and setting?
- What other supports are there for the reader?

Mini-Lesson:

Possible Anchor Text:

Why Teach It?

How Do You Read Series Books?

A few books from series that have been read in the classroom.

Readers read series books differently. Some read the series in order and can't read book number four before they have completed book three in the series. Some readers stay stuck in a series for a very long time, whereas others read a few books in a series, take a break, and come back to that series later. This lesson is intended to help students think about those choices, and to remind them that they are in charge of this process and that we all go through many choices as we decide on next-reads.

How We Teach It: Franki shares different series books that she has read throughout her life: those she read as a child, such as Betsy by Carolyn Haywood, Nancy Drew by Carolyn Keene, and The Secret Seven by Enid Blyton, and those she has read as an adult, such as the Boleyn series by Philippa Gregory. Franki tells students that books in a series have always been an important part of her reading life. She shares the story about how she would go to her grandmother's attic every single week to choose a new Nancy Drew book from the bookshelves there. She read Nancy Drew exclusively for months until she nearly finished the series. The Betsy books were a bit different for Franki. She would read one or two, read some other things for a while, and then go back to Betsy books. After she discovered the Boleyn series as an adult, she was excited to read another book with the same characters right away. But then she realized that she wanted a break from the same characters and might come back to them later. She then asked students to think about the series books they have read: Did they read them in order? Did they read them all at once or take breaks in between? Did they sometimes need or want a break from a series they loved? Did they enjoy going back to series books that they hadn't read in a while?

Follow-Up: This lesson is intended to be the beginning of a conversation that extends throughout the year as students think about books. It places value on series books but more value on the readers' decisions to stick with or abandon a series. This conversation comes up in conferences and share times as students notice their own behaviors when reading series books.

Series books and early chapter books are a great bridge for children at the transitional stage of reading. As they mature as readers, they will encounter texts with more complex plots, a variety of characters, and changes in time and setting. When children read series books, they can begin to notice some of these features and discover ways of understanding them in text. Series books introduce new complexities to young readers, but they do it in a way that is supportive and comfortable.

Making Predictions in Series Books

Franny K. Stein, Mad Scientist: Lunch Walks Among Us by Jim Benton

This lesson is similar to the lesson in Chapter 2 using *Llama, Llama Red Pajama*. When students read about familiar characters and books by the same author, they build knowledge that helps them understand new books in the series differently. This lesson allows students to recognize that when you read books about the same characters in a series, you can more easily understand the books because you know the characters better. The Franny K. Stein series is a good choice for several reasons. It is an easy book that we can place value on by reading it aloud. It also sets the stage for students, who need a bit of support for the first book in a series, to read subsequent books in the series.

We use read-aloud time to read the first book in a series, such as *Franny K. Stein, Mad Scientist: Lunch Walks Among Us*. After the reading, we hold up the other books in the series. We let students know that the book we just read was the first in a series. We tell them that after we have read a book or two in a series, we can better predict what might happen in the next book because we know the character and the author's writing much better after each book we read. We read the blurb from the back cover of the second book aloud and talk about all the things we know about the book. We then use what we know to predict what might happen in the next book. What can we expect from the second book? What predictions do we have, now that we have read the first book in the series?

Sometimes we read the second book aloud, go back to our predictions, and make new, more precise predictions about the third book. (When students have read two books in a series, it is easy to pick out things that might become common to all books, such as plot turns.) If reading aloud the second book would take too long, we use this conversation for small-group and individual work. We carry this conversation over to support those students who may not comprehend all that they can. We talk to them about what they know about the characters they are reading about and ask them to make predictions based on what they know from the other books.

Sometimes our most challenged students need access to series books because so many of their peers are reading them. Following is a list of easier series that even our third graders would not be embarrassed to read:

Fly Guy by Tedd Arnold
Elephant and Piggie by Mo Willems
Mercy Watson by Kate DiCamillo
Keeker by Hadley Higgenson
Flat Stanley by Jeff Brown

More sophisticated readers still enjoy series books and benefit from the supports they have to offer. Following is a list of series for more sophisticated readers in grades three to five:

Molly Moon by Georgian Byng
Peter and the Starcatchers by Dave Barry and Ridley Pearson
Among the Hidden by Margaret Peterson Haddix
A Series of Unfortunate Events by Lemony Snicket
Sisters Grimm by Michael Buckley
Septimus Heap by Angie Sage
Tales from Dimwood Forest by Avi
The Underland Chronicles by Suzanne Collins
Charlie Bone by Jenny Nimmo
Warriors by Erin Hunter
Books of Ember by Jeanne DuPrau

We have learned a great deal from our transitional readers since we began teaching intermediate students many years ago. We have spent time alongside students understanding the ways that these books support their reading development. Series books have become a valued part of our classrooms. They are the most popular books read during independent reading time. We have realized the importance of series books for these readers and continue to learn more about them.

Table 5.1 Beyond Leveled Books—Series Books

Series and Author	Text Setup	Chapter Titles	Hooks	Dialogue
A to Z Mysteries by Ron Roy	Paragraph form Sentences often continue on the next page	No chapter titles	Page 1 offers a scene from the book just before the mystery is solved Map of Green Lawn Home of A to Z Mysteries is included before the title page Back cover sets up the mystery	A great deal of dialogue with several characters involved in one conversation Breaks in conversation may make dialogue difficult to follow
Babymouse by Jennifer Holm and Matthew Holm	Graphic novel	Series is not broken into chapters	Covers are inviting Combination of pink and silver and lovable main character make readers want to pick them up Inside flap has a blurb about the book (in graphic form, of course!)	Great introduction of talking bubbles as a way to write dialogue
Sluggers by Loren Long and Phil Bildner	Paragraph form Sentences often continue on the next page	Titles offer great clues for the chapter to come Great for prediction	Inside cover offers a map of the United States Trip from the game played before the book opens is mapped out on front inside flap, and route to the next game is mapped out on back inside flap Color team photo of the main characters on the first page Table of contents Graphics with short pieces of text pull in readers	Speakers are easily identified with moderate to maximum use of dialogue

continued on page 100

Table 5.1 Beyond Leveled Books—Series Books

Pictures	Book and Chapter Leads	Continuation of Chapters	Length of Chapters	Teaching Thoughts
Black and white every 2–5 pages Offer some support	Story begins in setting Main characters often involved in action as mystery presents itself	Chapters are sequential All based on one main event Must sustain minimal comprehension between chapters	9 chapters, 10–15 pages each Can be read in one sitting	This is not a first chapter book series It has a more difficult style as far as use of dialogue, spacing, text size, sentence structure, and sentence fluency.
A great deal of picture support Graphic novel setup means the pictures are just as important as the text All illustrations are done in black, white, and pink Pink lets the reader know when Babymouse is dreaming or thinking	Story starts in the middle of the action Scene is set and moving when you enter the story	N/A	N/A	This series is a great first graphic-novel series. The engaging story, lovable characters, and simple text setup make it perfect for readers new to chapter books and/or graphic novels. The humor allows more sophisticated readers to fall in love with the books, too.
The illustrations alone could almost tell this story Beautiful and full of detail Readers can use them as a major source of support Baseball theme is carried throughout, with first letter of each chapter drawn with baseball players in action Full-page and sometimes 2-page spreads of illustrations	Books start in action but have been set up before with background information Chapters continue in the action	Chapters continue in chronological order with some time lapse Somewhat sophisticated in nature, so readers must sustain some information as the books progress	20 chapters 6–15 pages each Can be read in one sitting	This series offers some real perks! It appeals to a wide variety of readers. The pictures and chapter titles offer support. Difficult or historically dated phrases are identified on the side of each page. It is somewhat sophisticated, but students will have the baseball background information to help them, and with its short chapters, all readers will be sucked in. This series fills in gaps for those who are reluctant to read but need some adventure in their text.

continued on page 101

Table 5.1 Beyond Leveled Books—Series Books (continued)

Series and Author	Text Setup	Chapter Titles	Hooks	Dialogue
Beezy by Megan McDonald	Large print Space between lines One phrase or short sentence per line Most line breaks at natural pauses	Titles do not give a great deal of information about the chapter	Table of contents	Great deal of dialogue Speaker usually identified No paragraph breaks for dialogue Several characters involved in same conversation
Cam Jansen by David A. Adler	Paragraph form Sentences often continue on the next page	No chapter titles	Title helps give mystery topic Brief description on back of book Inside page has a scene from the book	Great deal of dialogue Speaker not always identified Words like *announced, said, told*
Clementine by Sara Pennypacker	Paragraph form Sentences often continue on the next page	No chapter titles	Cover illustration—Clementine just looks like someone to be friends with Inside jacket includes a bullet summary Back jacket provides scene from the book	Often—Clementine with herself or with one other person

continued on page 102

Table 5.1 Beyond Leveled Books—Series Books (continued)

Pictures	Book and Chapter Leads	Continuation of Chapters	Length of Chapters	Teaching Thoughts
Colorful Illustration on every page or spread Provide some support for comprehension	Story begins in setting; reader must infer what is going on No introduction of characters Chapter leads begin without introduction of chapters or setting	Chapters are sequential All based on common theme Must sustain minimal comprehension between chapters	3–5 chapters 5–15 pages each Can easily be read in one sitting	This series provides a great deal of text and comprehension support. The text is large and set up to support fluency. However, it expects the reader to be able to infer setting and dialogue at a more complex level. Support for fluency is greater than support for comprehension.
Black and white Every few pages Provide minimal support	Story begins in setting; reader must infer what is going on Chapter leads merely a continuation of story	Chapter begins where last chapter ended Very sequential; no change in setting between chapters	7–10 chapters 4–6 pages each Can usually be read in one sitting	This is a good introductory mystery series. The chapters build on one another and do not require the reader to change scenes between chapters. It is important that the reader sustain comprehension because the chapters are dependent on one another.
Full of support for comprehension and evolution of character personality Black-and-white illustrations offer support for comprehension	Story starts with action and explanation of events to follow Introduces narrator and her friend	Chapters are sequential and all based on common themes Must sustain minimal comprehension between chapters	10 chapters 10–13 pages each Can be read in one sitting	Clementine seems like a favorite for those who loved Junie B. Jones. Her voice is strong and could be used to teach about writer's craft. The illustrations are supportive, and there is a good mix of support for both fluency and comprehension. Strong lessons in friendship, empathy, cultural differences—lots to talk about! The illustrations are full of personality and charm.

continued on page 103

Table 5.1 Beyond Leveled Books—Series Books (continued)

Series and Author	Text Setup	Chapter Titles	Hooks	Dialogue
Commander Toad by Jane Yolen	One phrase or short sentence per line Most line breaks at natural pauses	No chapter titles	Brief description on back of book	Some dialogue Speaker usually identified No paragraph breaks for dialogue Words like *says, asks*
Dragon Slayers' Academy by Kate McMullan	Paragraph form Few sentences continue on the next page	No chapter titles	Back of book includes DSA Yearbook with pictures and descriptions of the characters as well as a map of the school campus and philosophy Back cover asks readers a question and gives reviews	Quite a bit of dialogue with a number of people involved Transitions are smooth, allowing for comprehension support Breaks in conversation
Elephant and Piggie by Mo Willems	Conversation bubbles of few words	N/A	Familiar characters Character descriptions on back cover	In bubbles with no quotation marks Speaker is identified through illustrations

continued on page 104

Table 5.1 Beyond Leveled Books—Series Books (continued)

Pictures	Book and Chapter Leads	Continuation of Chapters	Length of Chapters	Teaching Thoughts
Black and white alternate with color On each page Provide some support	Story begins with introduction of main character and setting First few pages introduce other characters	No chapters—one continuous story	N/A	This series is full of puns and sophisticated humor. The text setup helps readers who require a great deal of support, but the story and humor appeal to those who are interested in more age-appropriate humor and topics. This series is often successful with older transitional readers.
One every other chapter with the exception of the yearbook	Books begin in setting with reintroduction of characters within the first few pages Often a recap of a former situation to catch readers up to current days and the conflict to come	Chapters are chronological, taking place within a few days All actions focus around one main story line	9–14 chapters 7–10 pages each Can be read in one sitting	Good series for those new to fantasies Yearbook can help readers keep track of the various characters
Cartoonlike on every page	Books start in the action	No chapter divisions	N/A (all one chapter)	Elephant and Piggie is a great first series. The illustrations are simple yet let the reader know everything necessary about the characters or the situation at hand. Dialogue is simple but full of voice. The author captures complex characters in language and illustrations that help readers feel satisfied that they've really connected with Elephant, Piggie, and the adventure.

continued on page 105

Table 5.1 Beyond Leveled Books—Series Books (continued)

Series and Author	Text Setup	Chapter Titles	Hooks	Dialogue
The Fairy Chronicles by J. H. Sweet	Large print Space between lines Paragraph form Pages sometimes end in middle of sentence	Chapter titles are direct and can be used for support and prediction	Cover and illustrations are full color Illustrations of the "Fairy Team" within the first few pages Fun fairy facts at the end of the story with a constant reminder that "inside you is the power to do anything"	Although dialogue is used throughout the story, the attribution is usually set before the quote Direct with little figurative language The story is told. Dialogue is used in much the same way. E.g., "She broke down and sobbed, 'I am not ready to be a fairy.'"
Fly Guy by Tedd Arnold	Large print with space between lines Each page has 1–2 sentences	No chapter titles	Bright illustrations Shiny covers Covers of other books in the series highlighted on the back	Dialogue, identified in most cases by word *said*
Franny K. Stein, Mad Scientist by Jim Benton	Paragraph form Sentences are not broken between pages Text is medium size, with spaces between lines	Titles are often a play on words Can be used for prediction, but readers need background knowledge for a full understanding of the intended humor	Cover has comic-book look to it Table of contents Back cover gives a brief description of the story	Little dialogue All is easily identified, with the speaker's name directly after the quote
Hank Zipzer by Henry Winkler and Lin Oliver	Paragraph form with little space between lines Main character writes lists here and there as well	No chapter titles	Cover offers great illustrations of older characters facing some sort of challenge Inside back cover lists other books in the series, and back cover provides a page from the text to bring readers in	Much use of dialogue, with the speaker easily identified

continued on page 106

Table 5.1 Beyond Leveled Books—Series Books (continued)

Pictures	Book and Chapter Leads	Continuation of Chapters	Length of Chapters	Teaching Thoughts
Full color Within every 2–5 pages is a picture or graphic to support the text for comprehension	Books begin with introduction of characters and setting First few pages give some basic fairy information, setting the scene for the remainder of the story Chapter leads are a continuation of the story	Chapters are sequential; Chapters begin where last chapter ended Some settings change between chapters, requiring minimal comprehension between	Average of 8 chapters 6–19 pages each Can be read in one sitting	This is a basic fantasy/fairy series. It is substantial in length yet basic in storytelling approach. There is little use of figurative expression, but some use of strong vocabulary that may require strategies outside of what's required for rest of text.
Large, bright illustrations on each page Illustrations offer support to the action	Books and chapters begin in a simple action	Chapters are chronological, with little comprehension necessary to sustain understanding	3 chapters per book 7–13 pages each Entire book could be read in one sitting	This is a chapter book for students new to the concept. The character is amusing and students will find early success with easy-to-follow format.
Comic-book-style illustrations on every page	Books start with a description of Franny's mad scientist lab Chapters continue in the action	Chapters are chronological Minimal comprehension must be sustained between chapters	4–11 pages Chapters can easily be read in one sitting Books average close to 17 chapters	Franny K. Stein is a mad scientist. The front cover compares the character to Captain Underpants. Although Franny is a female character who loves science, both female and male students will enjoy this quick-paced series.
The only illustrations are with the chapter number Can be used for minimal support or for making minimal predictions	Books start in the action with quick identification of the main characters and a reference to Hank's learning challenges	Chapters in chronological order with some time lapse between events Readers must sustain minimal comprehension between chapters	1–14 pages Can be read in one sitting Books run about 25 chapters	This is a more sophisticated series, offering adventure and some great life lessons. The main character has learning difficulties, and readers will enjoy getting to know him and his friends as they face the challenges of growing up.

continued on page 107

Table 5.1 Beyond Leveled Books—Series Books (continued)

Series and Author	Text Setup	Chapter Titles	Hooks	Dialogue
Henry and Mudge by Cynthia Rylant	One sentence or phrase per line Most line breaks at natural pauses, with few exceptions	Titles can be used to predict One chapter usually the book title	Brief description on back of book Table of contents	Alternating dialogue Speaker identified for each line No paragraph breaks for dialogue
Horrible Harry by Suzy Kline	Paragraph form Sentences sometimes continue on next page	Titles can be used to predict	Table of contents Brief description on back of book Chapters often end with interesting surprise that invites prediction	Alternating dialogue Speaker sometimes identified for each line Paragraph breaks for dialogue Words like *howled, said, whispered*
Ivy & Bean by Annie Barrows	Large print Space between lines Few sentences broken between pages	Titles can be used to predict	Table of contents Inside page includes scene from book Last page hooks reader to next book in series with "sneak preview"	Great deal of dialogue Speaker easily identified with paragraph breaks Clarifiers such as *asked, said, repeated, added, explained*

continued on page 108

Table 5.1 Beyond Leveled Books—Series Books (continued)

Pictures	Book and Chapter Leads	Continuation of Chapters	Length of Chapters	Teaching Thoughts
Colorful One per page Provide some support	Beginning sets stage Introduces two main characters and setting	Chapters are sequential All based on one main event Must sustain minimal comprehension between chapters	5 chapters (average in series) 5–15 pages each Can be read in one sitting	This is a good series to begin to sustain comprehension over time. Each chapter is a separate story, but connects by theme and sequence to previous chapters. Chapter titles can be used for prediction or to remember previous chapters.
Black and white Usually one on each spread Provide some support	Chapter leads provide good introduction Chapter is often a new time and place	Chapters are sequential Time and setting often change Good introduction to each chapter	5 chapters (average in series) 10–15 pages each Can be read in one sitting	In this series, the chapters are very dependent on one another. The characters are often the same in all of the books so readers come to know them easily. The chapters provide solid introductions so that the reader can determine the characters and setting. This is a good series to introduce change of time and place between chapters.
Black and white almost every page Provide some support for comprehension	Story starts in the action with introduction or clarification of the main character Chapters also begin in the action	Chapters are sequential and based on a common theme Time and setting remain the same between chapters Must sustain minimal comprehension between chapters	10–12 chapters 7–14 pages each Can be read in one sitting	This series provides support for the transitional reader. The events all happen within a few hours, allowing for comprehension support. With few scene changes and continual action, readers remain engaged.

continued on page 109

Table 5.1 Beyond Leveled Books—Series Books (continued)

Series and Author	Text Setup	Chapter Titles	Hooks	Dialogue
The Jackson Friends Series by Michelle Edwards	Large print with space between lines Pages rarely end in the middle of a sentence	Titles are vague and can be used to make general predictions about chapter content	Table of contents Author note at the end Section with illustrations and information about the four friends from Jackson Magnet School	Clear and easy to follow, although not always immediately followed with the speaker's name Main character's thoughts are also written in italics to help new readers follow what is actually being said and what is going on in the character's head
Jake Drake by Andrew Clements	Midsized text in paragraph form Sentences often break at end of page	Titles work well for predicting the content	Table of contents Back cover gives a great description as well as illustrations of other books in the series	Some dialogue Speaker not always clearly identified
Judy Moody by Megan McDonald	Paragraph form with space between lines Sentences sometimes break between pages	Chapter titles are vague but can be used for prediction Often titles are a play on words or situations	Jackets are all brown paper so they are easy to recognize First few pages provide an illustrated who's who of the characters for a reference as well as an interest builder	Dialogue used throughout the text Speaker is clearly identified and easy to follow Often the conversation is with herself or with one other person

continued on page 110

Table 5.1 Beyond Leveled Books—Series Books (continued)

Pictures	Book and Chapter Leads	Continuation of Chapters	Length of Chapters	Teaching Thoughts
Illustrations on each page Some pages have multiple thumbprint-sized illustrations to help guide the reader	Books start in the action Chapters start in the action as well, with few starting with a description of setting	Chapters follow in chronological order with minimal comprehension required to sustain understanding	6 pages, with the first chapter a few pages longer Can easily be read in one sitting	This is a basic story for new readers of chapter books. The stories start with an introduction and move to a school-related conflict, resolution, and conclusion. The characters are fairly flat, with the multicultural aspect included mostly in the illustrations and the author's note. This is a great series for a reader who requires little distraction.
One black-and-white full-page illustration in each chapter	Jake, the narrator, begins with the background of his elementary school career Chapters continue in the action	Chapters are a continuation of the former Readers must sustain minimal comprehension between chapters	5–11 pages Can be read in one sitting	This series has such a strong voice, struggling readers are motivated and more accomplished readers find it refreshing. To this point we've had a number of female characters like Jake, but this series is great for both boys and girls.
Pictures every 3–5 pages and can be used for support	Story begins in setting; introduces the Moody family and the adventure to come Sets the stage	Chapters are sequential, beginning where the last left off, with minimal comprehension between chapters required	10 chapters (average in series) 7–11 pages each Can be read in one sitting	Judy Moody is such a well-written series for young readers that it lends itself to support comprehension as well as fluency. Students who have read books from the Stink series about Judy Moody's brother will be able to use that schema when reading this series. Judy Moody is a well-developed character readers can depend on to support their reading strategies. This series is full of puns, allusions, and sophisticated humor, but it works on all levels.

continued on page 111

Table 5.1 Beyond Leveled Books—Series Books (continued)

Series and Author	Text Setup	Chapter Titles	Hooks	Dialogue
Just Grace by Charise Mericle Harper	Large with spaces between lines Many breaks in the text where plot illustrations have been inserted In some spaces there are comic strips; in others there are conversation balloons Extras are helpful in supporting comprehension for those readers with a little more experience Text often breaks between pages	Chapters are titled with single word or phrase descriptions Somewhat supportive for making predictions	Cover is bright with a cutout to Grace on the hard cover Back cover has pictures of the four Graces from the class Reader can predict why the main character is called "Just Grace"	Not a lot of dialogue Most of the text is internal conversation or descriptions from Grace
Keeker by Hadley Higginson	Medium-sized text with space in between lines Paragraph form with few sentences broken between pages	Numbered with no titles	Illustrations are especially inviting to those who love horses Back cover has a short description of the book and a sneak peak of other stories in the Sneaky Pony Series	Dialogue is limited and easily identified
Little Bill by Bill Cosby	Paragraph form Large print Space between lines Page always ends with the end of a sentence	Numbered chapters	Very brief description on back of book	Alternating dialogue Speaker identified for most lines Paragraph breaks for dialogue Words like *said, explained*

continued on page 112

Table 5.1 Beyond Leveled Books—Series Books (continued)

Pictures	Book and Chapter Leads	Continuation of Chapters	Length of Chapters	Teaching Thoughts
Author was first an illustrator, so there are plenty of illustrations In many cases story is retold through pictures Illustrations are set up throughout text. For early readers they could be a distraction, but for others, the visuals can add to the story.	Starts with description Chapters often start with a list, map, or comic. Chapters continue into the action	Chapters are chronological with few time-lapse situations	Most are 1–2 pages Reader in most cases can see the next chapter Some longer chapters (8 pages), but those are filled with natural breaks because of lists or illustrations Can be read in one sitting	Just Grace has a familiar voice. The text itself will hold the reader's attention, but the added supports could go either way. Students with a little more reading experience may have the best luck. We found new readers to have fun with it as well.
Illustrations are adorable and on every page Easily used for making predictions	Books begin with introduction of the main characters Chapter leads are set in the action	Chapters are in chronological order and in some cases a continuation of the former Readers must sustain minimal comprehension between chapters	5–8 pages with plenty of pictures Readers could get through a couple of chapters in one sitting	Keeker is a perfect series for those early readers looking for a "chapter book." The text and illustrations offer support. The story is set with a beginning, a middle, and an end to help readers with story structure. The illustrations are an asset as well in terms of comprehension support.
Colorful One per page or spread Provide some support	Told in first person by Little Bill Beginning sets stage for story Chapter leads often a continuation of story Change of setting described when setting changes between chapters	Chapter begins where last chapter ended Time and setting often remain the same between chapters Must sustain comprehension over chapters	3–5 chapters 5–15 pages each Can usually be read in one sitting	The large text in these books makes them perfect for children just ready for chapter books. Often the stories take place over a short period of time. Because most chapters begin where the last chapter ended, children do not have to determine change in setting.

continued on page 113

Table 5.1 Beyond Leveled Books—Series Books (continued)

Series and Author	Text Setup	Chapter Titles	Hooks	Dialogue
Magic Tree House by Mary Pope Osborne	Paragraph form Space between lines Page often ends with the end of a sentence; sometimes ends in the middle of a sentence	Titles can be used to predict	Brief description on back of book Title usually tells time period of book Inside cover has an excerpt from the book that can help support comprehension	Great deal of alternating dialogue Speaker not always identified Paragraph breaks for dialogue Chapters often begin with dialogue
Mallory by Laurie Friedman	Paragraph form with little space between lines	Can be used for prediction	Mallory writes a note at the beginning of the book to set the scene. She also closes the book with a note. Mallory has her own website for students to visit Table of contents Paragraph description on the back cover Front cover illustrations are inviting because illustrator gives Mallory so much personality	Used often Speaker is not always directly identified
Martin Bridge by Jessica Scott Kerrin	Set in paragraph form with little space between lines	Each book contains three short stories. They are titled and can be used along with the illustrations to make predictions.	Title character is drawn in action on cover Table of contents for short stories One story highlighted on back cover	Used often Speaker clearly identified

continued on page 114

Table 5.1 Beyond Leveled Books—Series Books (continued)

Pictures	Book and Chapter Leads	Continuation of Chapters	Length of Chapters	Teaching Thoughts
Black and white Many throughout, but several spreads without Can assist in visualizing time period/setting	No introduction of characters Story often begins with dialogue; reader must infer setting, characters, etc. Connections sometimes made to other books First chapter similar events in all stories	Chapter often begins where last chapter ended Time and setting often remain the same between chapters Must sustain comprehension over chapters Chapters dependent on one another Chapters often begin with dialogue	10 chapters 6–10 pages each Can usually be read in one sitting	The text and comprehension supports in this series allow the reader to understand time periods with which they are unfamiliar. Because the chapters continue without setting changes, the reader can concentrate on the interesting information. This series also has a companion nonfiction book for some titles, so it is an easy way to bring nonfiction text into instruction.
Every few pages, offering support to the action	After initial note by Mallory, the chapters begin in the action	Chapters are chronological, with some time lapse Reader must sustain minimal comprehension to follow the events	About 15 chapters 9–14 pages each	Mallory has a strong voice, and young readers seem to really relate to her adventures. The website is engaging, and students can't wait to get their hands on the next Mallory book. The text offers support, and the conversational tone works well to encourage fluency, leading to stronger comprehension.
On each 2-page spread Can be used as support to the action	Each chapter is the start of a new story Setting is clarified within first few paragraphs	Chapters are not continued, but new stories start with each chapter title	30–42 pages May be difficult to finish an entire story in one sitting	Students like Martin Bridge as a character; his adventures offer subtle life lessons. The short-story idea works well for readers who haven't built up the stamina to complete an entire chapter book.

continued on page 115

Table 5.1 Beyond Leveled Books—Series Books (continued)

Series and Author	Text Setup	Chapter Titles	Hooks	Dialogue
Mercy Watson by Kate DiCamillo	Text is large with space between the lines Set up to look like a "storybook" from the 1950s	No chapter titles; only numbers	Illustrations Sneak peek of the next book in the series at the back	Plenty of dialogue within the action of the story Easy to follow, and quotes are directly identified. E.g., "'Mercy?'" said Baby."
Mr. and Mrs. Green by Keith Baker	A few lines per page Sentences not broken between pages	Each short story has a title that can be used for prediction	Color illustrations Table of contents Back cover gives a "favorites" list for both characters	Plenty of easily identifiable, simple dialogue
Nate the Great by Marjorie Weinman Sharmat	One sentence or phrase per line Most line breaks at natural pauses Page sometimes ends in the middle of a sentence	No chapters	One continuous story	Alternating dialogue Speaker usually identified No paragraph breaks for dialogue

continued on page 116

Table 5.1 Beyond Leveled Books—Series Books (continued)

Pictures	Book and Chapter Leads	Continuation of Chapters	Length of Chapters	Teaching Thoughts
Illustrations are bright and cartoonlike Illustrations on each spread; some full page, others bleed together across bottom Illustrations are major part of book, for storytelling as well as support	Books start with description of the setting Chapter leads continue in the action of the story	Chapters are a continuation of the former Readers must sustain minimal comprehension between chapters	3–5 pages each Readers could get through a few chapters in one sitting	Mercy Watson is a humor-filled series. The main character is a pig, and the other characters are cartoonlike adults. The action is silly, but it moves quickly and the text offers plenty of support for all readers.
Bright green alligators decorate every spread	Books start in conversation, setting up the action	Each chapter is a new story; three in each	20–25 pages but could be read in one sitting Readers need not sustain comprehension between chapters	Mr. and Mrs. Green are wonderful characters. They love each other and it makes for an enjoyable read. The individual stories are short enough that early readers can read them in one sitting, then come back to read the next without having to remember the first. This is a good series to start with because the characters remain true, allowing for support and for making predictions.
Black and white One per page or spread Minimal support	Introduces main character and setting	No chapters; one continuous story	N/A	These books can often be read in a few sittings. Although there are no separate chapters, the reader must sustain comprehension over the longer text. The text setup and illustrations support those readers who are just beginning to read longer text.

continued on page 117

Table 5.1 Beyond Leveled Books—Series Books (continued)

Series and Author	Text Setup	Chapter Titles	Hooks	Dialogue
Pinky and Rex by James Howe	Paragraph form Large print Space between lines Page always ends with the end of a sentence	Titles can be used to predict	Brief description on back of book Table of contents	Great deal of dialogue Speaker usually identified Words like *repeated, muttered*
Shredderman by Wendelin Van Draanen	Paragraph form with space between lines Sentences break between pages	Can be used for prediction/ support	Colorful front cover with character ID Summary inside front jacket Scene from book on back jacket	Plenty of conversation, mostly between two people and identified with words like *said* or *asked*
The Sisters Grimm by Michael Buckley	Paragraph form	Chapters are numbered with a silhouette illustration that can be used for prediction	First pages set the scene Stories start in the action Fairy-tale guide in the back with questions List of websites for the Brothers Grimm to really get readers involved in this series Back cover has an explanation of the situation and the mystery at hand	Plenty of dialogue In most cases the speaker is immediately identified

continued on page 118

Table 5.1 Beyond Leveled Books—Series Books (continued)

Pictures	Book and Chapter Leads	Continuation of Chapters	Length of Chapters	Teaching Thoughts
Colorful One per page Minimal support	No introduction of characters Story often begins with dialogue Chapters sometimes begin with dialogue	Chapters in sequence, but one does not necessarily begin where the last one left off	6 chapters (average in series) 5–10 pages each Can be read in one sitting	Pinky and Rex books are a bit longer and are a good series to help children jump into a story without having the characters and theme set up for them. The connection between chapters is important, and the reader must sustain comprehension.
Every few pages and can be used for support	Book begins with character descriptions and insight into the main character	Chapters are chronological, with entire story unfolding in just a few days Reader must sustain comprehension, as chapters build on common theme	16 chapters 7–15 pages each Can be read in one sitting	This book is perfect for those learning to follow a plot over time. There are many opportunities for predicting things that might happen next. The characters are likable, and the length of the book is perfect for those moving to chapter books.
Few and far between: one per chapter	Book leads with the setup of the mystery at hand Chapter leads bring reader immediately into the situation with clear descriptions	Chapters are continuations of the former Often set in the action Readers must sustain minimal comprehension between chapters	Up to 20+ pages Readers may not finish a chapter in one sitting	This is a sophisticated series that involves many reading skills. Readers will need background knowledge to fully understand the plot but will be pulled in immediately because of the fast pace and additional information provided at the end of the book.

continued on page 119

Table 5.1 Beyond Leveled Books—Series Books (continued)

Series and Author	Text Setup	Chapter Titles	Hooks	Dialogue
The Spiderwick Chronicles by Holly Black and Tony DiTerlizzi	Written in paragraphs with sentence breaks between pages Text is small with little space between lines	Each starts with the words *In which* . . . and can be used for prediction	Chapter titles Cover picture Short poem on back cover from the story Review from Amazon on back cover Notes to the reader Maps and full-page illustrations	Use of dialogue is clear Usually one character at a time followed by *said*
Stink by Megan McDonald	Large print Space between lines Sentences continue from page to page	Can be used to predict Are *huge* on left page in a variety of fonts	Use of color on cover Character is Judy Moody's brother Chapter titles are funny Inside flap provides brief summary Fun Stinky Fact page in each chapter	Easy to follow with words like *said* and *asked* Speaker clearly identified Paragraph breaks for dialogue
Willimena Rules! by Valerie Wilson Wesley	Paragraph form Little space between lines	Titles are perfect for making predictions	First page is a journal entry setting up the story, followed by title page and then table of contents titled "My Rules Step by Step" Book ends with a journal entry as well as pictures of the other books in the series	Dialogue used throughout Immediate identification of the speaker
Zack Files by Dan Greenburg	Paragraph form Medium-sized print with space between lines Sentences often broken between pages	Chapters do not have titles	Fun illustrations on the cover as well as catchy subtitles Readers can join a fan club Page in the back from another story to hook readers into yet another Zack story	Plenty of dialogue Speakers easily identified

continued on page 120

Table 5.1 Beyond Leveled Books—Series Books (continued)

Pictures	Book and Chapter Leads	Continuation of Chapters	Length of Chapters	Teaching Thoughts
Illustrations are outlined in table of contents Black-and-white full-page illustrations with a caption from the chapter Usually one from the current chapter and one from the chapter to come Great for supporting young readers	Book starts with introduction of characters, then moves to the setting, then goes on to the story line for the rest of the series	Chapters are chronological, taking place within a few days All actions focus around one main story line Must sustain minimal comprehension between chapters	7 chapters 11–21 pages each	What a great series! It offers a lot for readers to dive into. There is a field guide, the situation is intriguing, and there is room for plenty of discussion between readers.
Black and white Every few pages Provide some support	Story begins in setting Reader then introduced to main character and others	Chapters begin where last chapter ended Time and setting remain the same between chapters Must sustain minimal comprehension	10 chapters 9–20 pages each Can be read in one sitting	This series is high interest with lots of stinky, smelly talk! There is much support for fluency as well as comprehension. The reader can follow the events without confusion. The chapters build on one another so the reader is responsible for sustaining comprehension.
Every few pages	Books start in the setting Chapters continue in the action	Chapters are in chronological order Readers must sustain minimal comprehension between chapters	10–15 pages each Can be read in one sitting	This is a great series for all readers. The messages are great, and the support is evident within the text as well as with chapter titles and illustrations.
One per chapter	Books start in the action followed by a brief introduction of Zack Chapters continue in the action	Chapters are chronological, with little comprehension necessary to sustain understanding	Close to 6 chapters each 4–12 pages per chapter	Zack has a strong voice in this series. Readers seem to really get to know him as a character and find the situations worthy of making it to a "file" a lot of fun. Each story is as wacky as the one before it.

continued on page 121

Table 5.1 Beyond Leveled Books—Series Books (continued)

Series and Author	Text Setup	Chapter Titles	Hooks	Dialogue
Ziggy and the Black Dinosaurs by Sharon M. Draper	Paragraph form with little space between lines	No chapter titles	Cover is inviting with color picture End offers a note from the author with websites to visit Illustrations of the other books in the series at the end encourage readers to keep reading Last page offers an introduction of what's next for the Black Dinosaurs	Dialogue is used often and the speaker is easily identified

Table 5.1 Beyond Leveled Books—Series Books (continued)

Pictures	Book and Chapter Leads	Continuation of Chapters	Length of Chapters	Teaching Thoughts
One per chapter, can be used for text support	Book begins in the action, closely followed by introduction of club members, the Black Dinosaurs	Chapters are chronological with some time lapse between Reader must sustain minimal comprehension for understanding	About 10 pages each About 9 chapters per book Chapters could be read in one sitting	Ziggy and the Black Dinosaurs is the name of a club. The series offers readers a chance to get to know the characters. There is strong family involvement with the characters as they face each adventure. The books offer insight to educational situations.

chapter six

Using Picture Books, Nonfiction, and Graphic Novels with Transitional Readers

So we surround kids with text that includes a variety of perspectives, opinions, ideas, issues, and concepts to read about, write about, and talk about. When students read and respond to text that provokes thinking, they are much more likely to become active, engaged readers. We flood our classrooms with text of all different types and on tons of topics, so we have a better shot at reaching all of our kids. How we choose text and how kids choose their own makes a difference in their literate lives.

STEPHANIE HARVEY AND ANNE GOUDVIS, STRATEGIES THAT WORK

Often when transitional readers move to chapter books and series books, they abandon picture books and nonfiction. We need to continue to invite students to read a variety of texts that include picture books and nonfiction. More recently, we are also encouraging our students to consider graphic novels. A broad range of texts can help them move toward independence and a lifetime of reading.

Picture Books

We use picture books daily with our transitional readers. We read picture books aloud to the whole class, use them in mini-lessons, and share them during small-group instruction. We value these books during independent reading time and often use them when conferring with students. Because children are so familiar with picture books, they can easily identify their unique features and elements. Some people might not think about using picture books in their teaching because they think the text is easier than what students can read on their own. But we have learned that there are many ways for a book to be complex, and it is important that we value these picture books in all parts of our reading instruction. Using picture books in whole-group and small-group instruction places value on them so that students are more likely to choose picture books later for independent reading.

Literary components common to all good literature can be easily introduced using picture books. These books can be enjoyed daily to foster discussions about leads, setting, use of italics, and other literary techniques. Years ago, we used difficult novels to teach students new skills. This was a mistake. We used a difficult book to teach a difficult skill. We have learned that students learn the skill much more quickly when we use a less challenging book. Later that skill transfers to more difficult text. For example, we use picture books to show students that words can have more than one meaning. This sophisticated concept is easily taught with picture books that have the right instructional supports.

Mini-Lesson: Understanding New Vocabulary/Words with Double Meanings

Possible Anchor Texts: *Agatha's Feather Bed* by Carmen Agra Deedy or *Tough Cookie* by David Wisniewski

Why Teach It? Students will continue to encounter new vocabulary in their reading. They will also begin to encounter humor in text. Often the language provides the humor, and students can see how writers use words to convey it. In this lesson, students come to realize that the literal meaning of words is not always intended.

How We Teach It: Each student should have a copy of the text for this lesson. Read one of the books to the group. After the reading, reread the text, searching for words with double meanings. Create a three-column (word, first meaning, second meaning) chart for the students to fill in. Chart the words and phrases the children find that could have two meanings.

Follow-Up: Share books from a series, such as Amelia Bedelia by Peggy Parish or Commander Toad by Jane Yolen. These series books use words and phrases in similar ways and have picture supports for the reader.

The use of picture books allows all students to participate in discussions, regardless of individual reading levels. Discussions around picture books can become springboards for similar discussions around longer, more difficult texts.

Mini-Lesson: Supporting Predictions by Finding Proof in the Book

Possible Anchor Text: *Goldilocks Returns* by Lisa Campbell Ernst

Why Teach It? Often transitional readers make predictions and conclusions about text without using what they have read to support their thinking. They infer the author's meaning without regard to clues that are in the text and consequently miss important meaning in the story. *Goldilocks Returns*, a sequel to the original story, tells the story of how Goldi tries years later to make up for her mistakes as a child by doing something nice for the bears. Most transitional readers have a great deal of background knowledge to bring to this lesson. Using a simple book with an engaging story line, this lesson invites students to go back into the book looking for evidence to support their predictions. It will be easier for them to support their thinking with excerpts from text after they have had experience trying the strategy with a simple picture book.

How We Teach It: In a small group, we give each child a copy of *Goldilocks Returns* and ask them to preview the book by looking at the pictures. We ask them to make predictions about what is going to happen in the book. After we list their predictions, we ask, "What in the book makes you think that?" We then list the evidence that they find in the book on the chart alongside the prediction. A chart created by second graders is shown below:

Prediction	Evidence in the Book
Goldilocks will be old.	Looks old on the cover—her earrings and shoes look old. It looks like she has a job because she has tools.
Goldilocks will bring food.	She has grocery bags.
Goldilocks can get in the house.	She has a key shop and tools.
Goldilocks will fix things.	In the pictures she is using her tools and putting away food.
The Bears won't like what Goldilocks did.	Their expressions look unhappy and surprised.

We follow the charting with a shared reading of the book and then discuss how we did in our predictions (see prediction chart).

Follow-Up: This lesson provides an introduction to students on supporting their thinking based on the text. Throughout the rest of the school year, we refer to this lesson. Children are consistently asked, "What in the book makes you think that?" when making predictions, inferring from the text, and so on.

The picture books in our classroom libraries offer a great deal of support for the transitional reader. When we combine what we know about the supports these books have and what we know about individual readers, we can make better matches between individual students and the books they read. As children begin to explore various genres, such as science fiction and historical fiction, they will encounter many new and unfamiliar settings. Picture books provide a bridge to understanding stories set in different times and places.

Mini-Lesson:

Reading Descriptive Language to Visualize Settings

Possible Anchor Text: *All the Places to Love* by Patricia MacLachlan

Why Teach It? Students will encounter texts with unfamiliar settings. It is important that they be able to use the details of the setting when it is important to the story.

How We Teach It: Read aloud the book *All the Places to Love*. Each page describes a place on a family farm. The language helps readers visualize the scenes the author is describing and learn about life on the farm. As the book is read aloud, ask students to list phrases on a piece of paper that help them visualize the farm. After the reading, talk with them about the things they learned about the farm. Ask them to use the phrases they wrote down to support their comments. Students can then illustrate a favorite phrase from the book.

Follow-Up: Read *Twilight Comes Twice* by Ralph Fletcher to provide students with another opportunity to visualize the text. To help students transfer this skill to their independent reading there are many novels that contain descriptions of the setting without illustrations. Descriptive language invites readers to visualize the setting. When reading aloud a book such as *Where the Red Fern Grows* by Wilson Rawls, find paragraphs that describe the region. Ask students to illustrate different paragraphs, using the words to support their illustrations.

Students will continue to meet more challenging texts as they move beyond the transitional stage of reading. Each text may have a feature that is new to the reader. For example, in Ralph Fletcher's book *Flying Solo*, readers will need to understand that each of the chapters looks closely at a different character in the book. They need to put the information together to understand the story. Or they may read *Mick Harte Was Here* by Barbara Park, in which the main character is grieving the loss of her brother. She moves back and forth from her present grief to her happy memories throughout the book. Students also need to learn how to read and understand texts written in first person and texts in which the setting changes or is in an unfamiliar time period. We can use

Table 6.1 Using Picture Books to Introduce Literary Elements

Literary Elements	Picture Books	Complex Chapter Books
Journals and letters tell story	*The Gardener* by Sarah Stewart *Yours Truly, Goldilocks* by Alma Flor Ada	*Dear Mr. Henshaw* by Beverly Cleary *Trial by Journal* by Kate Klise
Historical information embedded in fiction text	*The Little Ships* by Louise Borden *You Forgot Your Skirt, Amelia Bloomer* by Shana Corey	*Johnny Tremain* by Esther Forbes
First-person narrative	*Fireflies!* by Julie Brinckloe *Good Luck, Mrs. K.!* by Louise Borden	*Fig Pudding* by Ralph Fletcher
Descriptive language Visualizing an unfamiliar setting	*All the Places to Love* by Patricia MacLachlan	*The Lion, the Witch, and the Wardrobe* by C. S. Lewis
Going back and forth in time	*The Sunsets of Miss Olivia Wiggins* by Lester Laminack *The Summer My Father Was Ten* by Pat Brisson	*Mick Harte Was Here* by Barbara Park
Told from different points of view	*The Pain and the Great One* by Judy Blume	*A View from Saturday* by E. L. Konigsburg

picture books to teach transitional readers how to make sense of specific challenges they will encounter in future reading (including, for example, multiple narrators, use of flashback, sophisticated changes in setting, and unfamiliar vocabulary). Table 6.1 provides information on using picture books to introduce literary elements that readers will encounter in complex chapter books. When we are aware of the skills transitional readers need, we can more easily choose books that will help them move toward independence.

Nonfiction

Understanding nonfiction requires a different set of strategies for young readers. A reader's purpose in reading nonfiction is often to learn new information. There are many picture books in bookstores and libraries that can support the teaching of nonfiction reading. For example, several years ago Franki was working with a small group of fourth graders who were reading pages from the nonfiction text *Children Just Like Me* by Barnabas and Anabel Kindersley. The book is laid out like many current nonfiction books for children, with photographs on each page and related text placed accordingly. On page 14 was a short piece of text that read, "Every day Celina collects water from the village well (right)." To the right of the text was a photograph of the well. As they discussed the text, Franki asked the students if they knew what "(right)" meant in the text. Justin answered excitedly that "(right)" was intended to serve as an exclamation point: "The author wanted us to know that it was really important. It meant 'Yeah! Right!' to tell us he thought this was really important." The three other students in the group agreed with Justin.

This story reminds us of how critical explicit teaching is for transitional readers. Franki assumed that her students understood this text feature, which is so obvious to an experienced reader. But many of these "obvious" features require explicit instruction. A quick mini-lesson on directional words in nonfiction text was sufficient to teach Franki's four students. However, because young readers often have little experience with nonfiction text, we find that much of our explicit teaching is concerned with ways to make sense of it. We now use *Children Just Like Me* to teach our students about directional words.

Mini-Lesson: Recognizing and Using Directional Words

Possible Anchor Texts: A variety of nonfiction books that use directional words, such as *Children Just Like Me* by Barnabas and Anabel Kindersley

Why Teach It? Many nonfiction texts contain graphics, photos, and illustrations that support information contained in the text. Sometimes directional words are used to point out to the reader the appropriate illustration. Common words and phrases used are *right, left, above, below, center,* and *clockwise from left.* Children do not always know how to use these words (and the accompanying graphics) to help them make sense of the text.

How to Teach It: Use a page from *Children Just Like Me* to point out the directional words. After introducing the words, begin a chart with the directional words that were found. Then ask children to go on a directional-word search using the other nonfiction books in the classroom. As students find words, list them on the chart and keep track of the number of times each is found. After the search, discuss the words on the chart and how often each was discovered.

Use current newspapers and magazines and invite students to search for directional words.

Many transitional readers read nonfiction in the same ways they read fiction. For many nonfiction texts, especially biographies such as *26 Fairmount Avenue* by Tomie dePaola and *The Story of Ruby Bridges* by Robert Coles, this works adequately. But narrative reading strategies will not work for nonfiction texts that contain more graphics and photographs. Students often read nonfiction texts from beginning to end, without paying attention to the photographs, diagrams, time lines, and subheadings that are interspersed within the text. In the book *Nonfiction Matters* (1998), Stephanie Harvey identifies the following features of nonfiction books (77):

- fonts and special effects
- textual cues, such as *for example*, *for instance*, and *in fact*
- illustrations and photographs
- graphics
- text organization

Although nonfiction texts vary greatly in supports and challenges, teaching students how to use the common features that Harvey identifies will assist children in understanding many nonfiction books.

It has become the norm in many schools to teach students the features of nonfiction text. We agree that this is valuable for the students. But understanding the way text features work is not the goal of a unit on nonfiction. Knowing a feature does not mean that students can integrate all the features of a nonfiction text to gather information. It is important that we go beyond a unit on nonfiction text features if we want our students to understand and use all pieces of nonfiction text appropriately.

Mini-Lesson:

Beyond Browsing Nonfiction Text

Possible Anchor Text:

Time for Kids Almanac

Why Teach It?

We have found that in the last several years, our students know the features of nonfiction text. They can point to a caption, name a graph, and so on. However, with so much information on a page, it is often difficult for them to pull information from these sources. We often find them browsing pages of nonfiction, picking up a fact or looking at a photo. But they don't dig into the visual pieces as deeply as they could. At the transitional stage of reading, we want to make sure our students are doing more than merely browsing visual information.

How We Teach It:

Our kids love trivia books, especially the yearly *Time for Kids Almanac*s and other books filled with information. We like to use the *Time for Kids Almanac* because each page is packed with information in a variety of forms. To teach this lesson, we try to find a page with several different forms of information—a chart, a graph, a photo and caption. (The more information on a page, the more likely children are to browse if they do not know how to actually make sense of the visuals.) We enlarge the page on the overhead and give each student a copy to look at. We then do a think-aloud, breaking the page apart. "I see that on the left side is an interview with a doctor in question-answer form. I also see an illustration of the food pyramid with labels. In the bottom left corner is a 'Did you know?' box that may give me information about the article. On the right side, there is a chart with the top five fruits. Now that I know what is on the page, I am going to take some time to really read one of these things. It is important that I browse the page and then focus on one piece at a time. I am going to focus on the chart of top five fruits." We then go on to tell the things that we learn from looking at the chart and point to the places that tell us that particular information on the chart.

Follow-Up:

We may go back to this same page on the next day and move to another piece of the page. We may also do this with other pages and let students share their own process for browsing and then focusing in.

Nonfiction Books for Independent Reading: Moving Beyond Content Connections

Franki Sibberson

What we too often forget when considering the importance of non-fiction reading is the pleasure, the art, the wonder of it. We do not want to develop students who read nonfiction just for function, or for school success, but students who read nonfiction for enjoyment, to be fascinated, to discover.
    Nell Duke, Foreword to *Reality Checks*

I realized years ago that my fourth- and fifth-grade students were not choosing nonfiction for their independent reading time. When we discussed this as a class, the kids were honest. They had found many great novels to enjoy, and they were hooked. They didn't want to give up reading the fiction that they had come to love in order to read nonfiction. This made a lot of sense to me. When I think about my own reading, I make time for nonfiction reading, but it never gets in the way of my fiction reading. I set aside separate times for each.

I reflected on our conversation and realized that although we did do a lot of nonfiction reading in the class, almost all of it was in some way connected to content we were studying. Every so often I'd read aloud a book or an article just because it was an interesting topic, or something would be in our weekly news magazine that was unrelated to our curriculum in science or social studies. But, most often, I chose books that were connected in some way to our social studies or science content.

I looked through the large nonfiction library I had in the classroom. As I suspected, most of the books I had purchased over the years were somehow linked to science or social studies content. It was no wonder that my students saw nonfiction reading as "school reading." I knew I had to do something to hook this class on nonfiction.

Nonfiction-Reading Time

I decided to start a nonfiction-reading time in the classroom. Each morning when the students arrived, I began the day with nonfiction-reading time instead of a more traditional morning assignment. For about fifteen to twenty minutes each morning (except for Friday, which was Poetry Friday!) time was set aside for students to read nonfiction of their choice. Because we didn't often share our nonfiction reading with others as a class, I made time (two to three minutes each day) for informal sharing of great nonfiction facts and books that students wanted to share.

This routine was one of the simplest things I've implemented in my twenty years of teaching. The effect it had on students' reading lives was huge. Students became readers of nonfiction because I provided time and great nonfiction books. They quickly fell in love with nonfiction, and many began choosing nonfiction books for their reading workshop time. Their nonfiction reading skills improved because they were reading about topics of their choice. Nonfiction-reading time has allowed my students to become independent readers of both fiction and nonfiction.

Because the routine was so successful, I've continued it over the past few years. Instead of a daily routine, two mornings a week are devoted to nonfiction-reading time. To keep the reading time interesting, I am always on the lookout for new nonfiction titles to add to our nonfiction library.

I look for books that are visually appealing as well as books on topics that interest my students; I also look for books that can be read from cover to cover in a few sittings. I realized after observing my students that many of them were comfortable browsing nonfiction that was scattered across the page. Yet having books they could read cover to cover was important, too. Below are some of our favorite nonfiction choices.

Nonfiction Books You Can Easily Read Cover to Cover

It is important to provide students in the upper elementary grades with nonfiction books that are written in a more narrative form. Many of these books are in a nonfiction narrative form that is comfortable for students to read. When students experience reading a book from cover to cover, they learn many new things and build new questions about a topic. I have been looking for good nonfiction narrative books that have great illustrations and/or photographs to support the reader.

The Journey That Saved Curious George by Louise Borden
The true story of Margret and H. A. Rey's escape to the United States with a draft of the first Curious George manuscript in their bag.

Hey Batta Batta Swing! The Wild Old Days of Baseball by Sally Cook and James Charlton
A fun look at the history of baseball, this book shares many facts in a kid-friendly way. The illustrations are perfect for the subject.

You Forgot Your Skirt, Amelia Bloomer by Shana Corey
It is always surprising to our students that there was a time when girls were not allowed to wear pants. They love to read this simple picture book about Amelia Bloomer, who made bloomers popular. A great author's note provides additional information.

Hero Dogs: Courageous Canines in Action by Donna M. Jackson
The stories of several "hero dogs" are shared in this book. In narrative form, the author tells the stories of working dogs that have had a huge effect on the world. The photos help make the information accessible to students.

Sneeze! by Alexandra Siy
This book shares a great deal of information about sneezes, with a focus on the reasons people sneeze. The magnified photographs add interesting information and make this book visually appealing.

Nonfiction Books with Interesting Topics for Intermediate Students

Here are some of the books my students find most engaging; and they have few if any connections to the content-area topics we explore each year.

Albino Animals by Kelly Milner Halls
This book presents information on many albino animals around the world. The photographs are intriguing and draw the reader in.

Dogs and Cats by Steve Jenkins
Chock-full of information, this is a great book for animal lovers. The format and illustrations make it one of the best dog and cat books I've seen.

What Stinks? by Marilyn Singer
This book obviously focuses on things that stink. It is written with humor and packed with facts. The photos and illustrations are colorful and spread out across the pages.

Transformed: How Everyday Things Are Made by Bill Slavin
Kids love to know how things are made. In this book, each two-page spread shares the steps necessary in making an item such as a football. The funny cartoonlike illustrations make this a delightful read.

You Wouldn't Want to Explore With Sir Francis Drake: A Pirate You'd Rather Not Know by David Stewart

This book is part of a favorite nonfiction series in our classroom. Each book is filled with information about a certain period in history. The illustrations are colorful and humorous.

Girls Think of Everything: Stories of Ingenious Inventions by Women by Catherine Thimmesh
A great collection of short pieces that share stories of things invented by women.

Often we can use a single, stand-alone page in a nonfiction text to teach a mini-lesson or to instruct a small group about nonfiction text features and reading strategies (see Table 6.2). We also look through our daily newspapers and favorite magazines to find short pieces of nonfiction to share with our students. We have found that the weekly

Table 6.2 Teaching Points for Books with Stand-Alone Pages

Title and Author	Possible Teaching Points
A Seed Is Sleepy by Diana Hutts Aston*	This book invites reader to read it cover to cover or as stand-alone pages. Each page focuses on a unique characteristic of seeds. More information detailing that characteristic is included on the rest of the page in text and illustrations.
All by Herself by Ann Whitford Paul	This book of nonfiction about famous women contains poems. Each page includes a poem and illustration about a woman in history.
Buzz by Caroline Bingham	*Buzz* is filled with amazing photos and interesting information about all sorts of bugs. This book is a smaller size than most large nonfiction DK books, and the size makes it easier for readers to navigate the various information on each page.
Home Run by Robert Burleigh	This poetic story of Babe Ruth uses great language. Each page contains a "baseball card" with information about Babe Ruth. The cards can be used individually to teach students about nonfiction text.
Hooray for Inventors! by Marcia Williams	This book is set up in a comic/graphic form. Frames tell stories and trivia about various inventors. Bordering each page are related facts. A good table of contents and glossary are included.
Living Color by Steve Jenkins	This book is organized by color. Each two-page spread focuses on one color and the ways it is important to various animals. Each page has good subheadings.
The Living House by Nigel Hester*	This book uses photographs, directional words, symbols, and labels to describe things in our homes.
Welcome to Kirsten's World, 1854 by Susan Sinnott*	Books in this series successfully combine many elements of nonfiction text such as photos, artifacts, maps, keys, labels, and subheadings. To read and understand this book, it is necessary to use the graphics that support the text.
Where in the Wild by David Schwartz	This book contains great poems about various animals in the wild. The poem gives some clues about where the reader can find the creature in the accompanying photo. Lift the photo and several paragraphs of nonfiction text give more information. A unique combination of writing.
Yo! I Know! by the editors of World Almanac	This book contains charts, graphs, photos, and more. Each visual is different in its setup and can be used to teach students how to make sense of visuals in their nonfiction reading.

*one of several titles in a series

publication *Time for Kids* provides great nonfiction text that can be used in this way.

We use books like *Kidbits* by Jenny E. Tesar and Bruce Glassman to teach our students how to read graphs and charts. This book is a collection of a variety of charts and graphs that can be used to help students interpret information. We have found, however, that we also need to teach them how to use charts and graphs in conjunction with text in nonfiction books. Transitional readers do not always use the supports that are provided in nonfiction texts, such as boldface type, chapter subheadings, photographs, and time lines. Although students can usually read and understand these things independently, they often must be taught how to use these supports in combination with the text to help them construct meaning.

To support nonfiction reading, we use a variety of nonfiction and historical fiction picture books that have a narrative style to them. Students need to be able to recognize the important information within a narrative text. In the book *The* Mary Celeste, for example, readers can speculate what happened to the people aboard the ship and go back into the text to find evidence to support their theory.

Mini-Lesson: Supporting Thoughts with Lines from the Text

Possible Anchor Text:

The Mary Celeste: *An Unsolved Mystery from History* by Jane Yolen and Heidi Elizabet Yolen Stemple

Why Teach It?

Transitional readers need to know how to find proof in the texts they read to support their thinking. Often, as text becomes more complex, more inferring is required for complete understanding. When children are able to do this, they become more thoughtful readers.

How We Teach It:

Read the book aloud with your students. It would be helpful to have a copy for each student in the group. While reading, discuss the various features: the story, the field notes, the boxed definitions, and the illustrations. On the final page of the book, six theories are described that could explain the disappearance of the ship's passengers. Have students read the theories and find supporting evidence in the text to support the one they believe is the most likely expla-

Follow-Up: nation. Create a chart for each theory and record the words from the text that support each one.

Share the book *One Boy from Kosovo* by Trish Marx, and have students discuss how the boy's life is similar to and different from their own, using the text to support their thinking.

Some nonfiction picture books have an epilogue with factual details that relate to the book. In *Sleds on Boston Common: A Story from the American Revolution*, for example, Louise Borden tells the story of nine-year-old Henry Price, who approaches General Thomas Gage to ask if Henry and his friends can sled on the Boston Common, where British troops have camped. In the back of this book, the author includes a page of information on Boston Common and a biographical page on General Thomas Gage. This not only helps readers understand the kind of research that is involved in writing nonfiction and historical fiction, but also clarifies factual information included in the narrative. Following is a list of books of historical fiction and narrative nonfiction that we have used to nudge readers into reading nonfiction:

The Little Ships by Louise Borden
The Story of Ruby Bridges by Robert Coles
Eleanor by Barbara Cooney
Hey Batta Batta Swing! The Wild Old Days of Baseball by Sally Cook
    and James Charlton
You Forgot Your Skirt, Amelia Bloomer by Shana Corey
The Amazing Life of Benjamin Franklin by James Cross Giblin
Owen and Mzee: The True Story of a Remarkable Friendship by Isabella
    Hatkoff, Craig Hatkoff, and Dr. Paula Kahumbu
Dirt on Their Skirts by Doreen Rappaport and Lyndall Callan

Graphic Novels

The Invention of Hugo Cabret by Brian Selznick took the world by storm when it was published in January 2007. In 2008, it became the longest book to ever win the Caldecott Award. This book broke new ground—combining text, illustrations, and photos in new ways to create an amazing reading experience.

Our students are growing up in a visual world. Understanding the ways that visual information and text can work together is a skill that is and will be important to them. As teachers who did not grow up in as visual a world, it is sometimes difficult for us to see the importance of including this type of text in our teaching.

Graphic novels have become a popular genre for all age levels. When we visit libraries and bookstores, we are amazed at the variety of graphic novels available. We know this genre could be a key component for many of our transitional readers. Catching up on all the graphic novels that are available is a challenge. Terry Thompson (2008) tells us, "As students learn to think about their thinking, they need texts that intrigue them and make them anxious to read. Here's where graphica can play an important role. . . . Motivation and engagement are powerful forces. Because of its novelty—and its engaging text and pictures—graphica often motivates readers even when other texts fail to do so" (51).

Mini-Lesson: Understanding Graphic Novels

Possible Anchor Text:

Babymouse: Our Hero and other Babymouse books by Jennifer Holm and Matthew Holm

Why Teach It?

Graphic novels are becoming more and more popular with all ages. Graphic novels often provide transitional readers with the picture support they need to understand the text. Reading graphic novels requires paying attention to both the text and the visuals. We use lessons like this to both introduce new graphic novels and give students strategies for understanding them.

How We Teach It:

We give each student a copy of a Babymouse book or enlarge some of the pages so that all children can see the page. We let children know that graphic novels take some different kinds of thinking—putting the words and pictures together in ways that they may never have done before. Since most students at this stage are good at looking at and using pictures, we focus this lesson on the words. We may say, "In graphic novels, the author uses words in different ways. Take some time to look at the way the author writes words in this book to see what you notice."

Chart the things they notice. The chart may look something like this:

Some words are in talking bubbles.
Some words are in the top of the box.
Some words are in the bottom of the box.
Some words are bigger than others.
Some words are smaller than others.
Some words are in pink boxes.
Some words are in white boxes or talking bubbles.
Some words are in shapes above the characters.
Some words are sound effects.
Some words label things.
Some words are in bubbles that are unique shapes.
Most words are written in all capital letters.

We then read the page and make predictions about how the author uses these different ways to tell us things. We might list those in the next column on the chart. For example, "The words in the top of each box give us a clue about what is happening in the box."

Follow-Up: We ask students to be on the lookout for different ways that graphic-novel authors share words with their readers. We continue the discussion about this and how to use this information to better understand the text.

Comprehending Graphic Novels: A Primer for Teachers

Mary Lee Hahn

Just recently, I discovered a whole new "room" in the library, one I'd never visited before. Likewise, I have found shelves in the bookstore that I've only ever walked by. I have discovered graphic novels.

I'm not talking about comic books. I grew up reading those flimsy magazines featuring Richie Rich, Archie and his pals Veronica and Jughead, Uncle Scrooge, and many others.

Graphic novels are book-length works of sequential art. Calling them graphic *novels* would seem to indicate that their story lines are always fiction.

This could not be further from the truth, as I've come to realize. In recent months, I've read graphic fiction, graphic memoir, graphic documentary, graphic nonfiction, graphic fairy tales, and graphic mythology. I've also dipped my toe into Manga, or Japanese-style comics/graphic novels.

The children's book publishing world has recently responded to the rising popularity of graphic novels. At least five popular series are being re-released as graphic novels: Time Warp Trio, Baby Sitters Club, Nancy Drew, Hardy Boys, and Goosebumps. Scholastic now has an imprint (Graphix) expressly for its line of graphic novels. A young-adult librarian who buys graphic novels for her library explained the popularity of graphic novels by estimating that some of the most popular volumes circulate forty times per year. Traditional print novels might circulate five times per year.

What is it about graphic novels that is so attractive to kids? Yes, of course it's the pictures, but it's bigger than that. Marc Prensky (2001) defines the current generation of children as Digital Natives. They have never lived in a world that didn't have the Internet, cell phones, video games, iPods, and all the other digital media that exist now. He believes that these children's brains are wired differently because of this upbringing:

> Digital Natives are used to receiving information really fast. They like to parallel process and multi-task. They prefer their graphics before their text rather than the opposite. They prefer random access (like hypertext). They function best when networked. They thrive on instant gratification and frequent rewards. They prefer games to "serious" work. (2)

Graphic novels, then, give Digital Natives a reading experience that matches the way their brains are wired.

Unfortunately, most teachers are not Digital Natives. We are Digital Immigrants. We struggle to understand and teach a classroom of children who live in a different world and speak a different cultural language than we do. Fortunately, I can also explain the importance of graphic novels in terms that a Digital Immigrant will understand. Graphic novels are an important tool for engaging reluctant and less able readers (often, but not always boys). The pictures provide a powerful support for readers who struggle with text. Struggling students are able to read books that are popular, interesting, and motivating, which is often not true when those struggling readers are working with text-only books. Graphic novels are primarily produced in series, which allows a struggling reader to stay with familiar characters and plot lines. Finally, readers who struggle with text can still use all of the comprehension strategies with which we are familiar.

Let's use *Babymouse: Heartbreaker* by Jennifer L. Holm and Matthew Holm as an example of the ways a reader can use comprehension strategies (Keene and Zimmerman 2007) to maneuver through a graphic novel:

Prior Knowledge: This isn't just a book about a mouse that wants a date to the Valentine's Day dance. The book is rich with invitations to the reader to use what he or she knows about *Romeo and Juliet, Cinderella*, the first Babymouse book, *Snow White and the Seven Dwarves, Sleeping Beauty, The Frog Prince, Grease,* and *Gone with the Wind.*

Determining Importance: If you've never read a Babymouse book, go read one now. I'll wait here while you read. I want you to see for yourself if you can determine the importance of the use of the color pink in *Babymouse.* . . . Well, how long did it take you to figure out that the parts of the book in pink are Babymouse's dreams or imagination, and that the black and white is reality?

Asking Questions: We're pretty sure Babymouse is going to make it to the dance, but will her handsome prince appear to take her? Will not calling him work? How about a makeover? Will she have luck asking someone? Will she be brave enough to go to the dance alone?

Drawing Inferences: It is a natural function of the brain to "read," or fill in, what happens *between* the pictures in a graphic novel. But the pictures can also provide clues that help the reader predict what will happen through the use of foreshadowing. You did notice all the bits and pieces of Georgie the giraffe that showed up on pages 14, 21, 24, 25, 31, 32 . . . well, you get the picture. Literally. The observant reader knows *way* before Babymouse how the Valentine's Day dance will turn out.

Retelling: With the pictures as a support, retelling is a cinch.

Using a Variety of Fix-Up Strategies: In the same way that there is no penalty for a video gamer to "die" and start the game over again, there is no penalty for the reader of a graphic novel to misread the sequence of the panels or images on a page and then go back as far as necessary to reread and make sense of the story. The best way to experience this firsthand (if you are unfamiliar with Manga) is to pick up a book of Manga written in the "Native Manga" style: written in English, but formatted in the Japanese way of reading left to right. Not only will you feel like you are starting at the back of the book, but you will have to remember to read the panels left to right. And you'll forget. And you'll realize you made a mistake and you'll go back and reread.

Should we be using graphic novels in our classrooms? Absolutely. Aren't we supposed to do whatever it takes to reach every reader?

Will graphic novels replace traditional texts in our classrooms? Absolutely not. Think back to the literary references a reader needs to get the fullest meaning of *Babymouse: Heartbreaker: Romeo and Juliet*, *Cinderella*, the first Babymouse book, *Snow White and the Seven Dwarves*, *Sleeping Beauty*, and *The Frog Prince*.

Should we buy every graphic novel we can find for our classroom libraries? No. As in every publishing format, there's a lot of junk mixed in with the jewels. You'll have to stretch yourself as a reader and come join me in that new and unexplored room of the library—graphic novels.

Here's a short list of books to get started:

Easy for Digital Immigrants (most like American comics):

Babymouse series by Jennifer L. Holm and Matthew Holm
The Baby-Sitters Club graphic novel series by Raina Telgemeier

Medium for Digital Immigrants (blend of American comics and Japanese Manga styles):

Time Warp Trio graphic novel series by Jon Sciezka
Amelia Rules! series by Jimmy Gownley

Hardest for Digital Immigrants (beginner Manga):

Kat & Mouse series by Alex de Campi
Mail Order Ninja series by Joshua Elder

Mary Lee Hahn teaches at Daniel Wright Elementary in Dublin, Ohio. She is the author of Reconsidering Read-Aloud *published by Stenhouse.*

References

Prensky, Marc. 2001. "Digital Natives, Digital Immigrants." *On the Horizon* 9 (5). Available online at http://www.marcprensky.com/writing.

We don't know what other genres will surface in the reading lives of our students. With new advances in technology our students will need to be open to new genres and to figuring out the best strategies for making sense of these new forms of text. What we can give them now are the strategies to understand any text they encounter.

chapter seven

Organizing for Thoughtful Instruction

Teachers who encourage a wide range of reading, who give their students plenty of opportunity for sustained, silent reading, who read aloud to their students on a regular basis, who provide ongoing opportunities for students to discuss—in small- and large-group settings—their understanding of a text, who encourage extensive rather than intensive reading, who encourage self-selection of some texts, and who recognize that students become better readers by reading, not merely practicing reading skills, increase students' opportunity for developing a positive attitude toward reading, for improving fluency, for improving vocabulary, and for improving comprehension.

KYLENE BEERS, WHEN KIDS CAN'T READ

When we work with teachers of transitional readers, we find that their biggest question is what to teach and how to teach it. There is no one right answer to this question for all teachers in all classrooms. But when teachers begin each year by looking closely at their individual students, they can design instruction that meets their students' unique needs.

When we begin the school year, we think hard about how we are going to set up our instructional program to assist transitional readers. We ask ourselves the following questions:

- How will the books and reading materials be organized? Will I use baskets? How will I create space to display books face out?
- Will the entire classroom library be in one area of the room, or will it be in different parts of the room?
- What type of reading materials will students have access to during reading time?
- Where will students be able to read? Can I arrange the room to create spaces for quiet and buddy reading?
- Should reading time be silent, or will I allow reading aloud?
- Will children be allowed to read with friends?
- How will students keep a record of their own reading throughout the year?
- How long will children read each day? How will I begin the year to support them so that they can build to this amount of sustained reading time?
- When and where will I meet with individuals and small groups for literature circles, guided reading groups, mini-lessons, and conferences?
- How will I provide opportunities for conversations?
- Will students have the opportunity to share their reading with others?
- How will I keep records of students' reading and our conversations about reading?
- Which type of yearlong assessments will I use?
- How will I share information with parents?
- What opportunities will children have for daily self-reflection?

On Kidney Tables: Small Changes for Big Effects

Karen Szymusiak

Our staff is opening a new elementary school this fall, and we have been buried beneath the many decisions required to establish a new place for learning. When you start with nothing, it is easy to fall back on the experiences you have had. It's tempting to do things the way we have always done them. But a new school offers us many chances to shed our previous teaching and learning experiences, rethink what we do, and make the most thoughtful decisions for our children. What are the messages our children will come to understand from the decisions we make? How can we keep the perspective of children at the surface as we plan the way we live and learn together in our new school?

When we met for one of our earliest staff meetings last spring, we began talking about the furniture we were purchasing for the school. Some teachers asked about ordering kidney-shaped tables. It seemed like a reasonable request, and we began to consider how many we would need.

But small moments in our lives can bring clarity to our thinking if we slow down enough to recognize them. Near the end of the school year, I participated in a parent conference. As we entered the classroom, the parents and I sat on the outside of the kidney-shaped table and the teacher sat in the cutout section on the other side. The teacher was delightful and professional. We had a productive conversation about supporting a child who was struggling, but it felt uncomfortable to me. Nothing the teacher did or said made me feel that way. It was the message represented by the position of the teacher at the head of the table. It signified a sense of authority and power that was not conducive to shared problem solving or collaboration. It didn't encourage a conversation among four people who cared deeply about the student's success.

When I drove home from school that evening, I began thinking about the kidney table and imagining what it feels like to sit there as a child. I wondered if children feel less responsible for their own learning as they wait to be directed by the teacher sitting on the other side of the table.

What Kidney Tables Represent

Does the kidney table represent a hierarchy that we don't want to promote in our lovely new school? I hope we treat children as equals in the learning process. The teacher and the child both learn. I hope we portray that we are learners, too—that when we sit at a table with children, we are all teaching and learning. If we talk to children as peer learners, they will respond in positive ways in their own learning.

It is not our job to make children feel small and insignificant. Children have wisdom beyond our imaginations, and sometimes they have even more wisdom than the adults in their world. I will never permit a staff member to make a child feel small, embarrassed, or "bossed around." I want to discourage children from making each other feel small. I will not promote the teacher as the all-knowing expert or the person who always gets to make the decisions. There won't be big people and small people at Glacier Ridge Elementary. There will be learners—all of us together on a level field where we can learn from each other every day.

Our school will be a place for the children. The school belongs to every child and not to the adults who work there. It should be a place that promotes collaborative and interactive learning with many thoughtful conversations about learning. Can that happen at a kidney table? We think not, because the design sets the teacher up as the all-knowing authority who is taller, bigger, and smarter than those sitting on the other side.

Can we consider other ways to talk with children? Can we gather at round tables or in a circle of stools or pillows, or gather casually on the rug where the teacher sits at the same level as the children? We want to raise the question and to think about other possibilities. We want our children to get clear messages that they have the power to become learners for a lifetime. We want our school to be a place where learners are equal and the conversations we have move us toward excellence.

We did order round tables to replace the kidney tables in our new school. As we open the school this fall, we are hoping for many thoughtful and collaborative conversations that help us discover who we are as learners. We will look for ways to help children take charge of their learning and become part of a learning community.

Organizing Classroom Libraries to Support Transitional Readers

If children become readers by reading, then we must have texts that will entice them to pick up a book day after day. This has as much to do with having texts that are accessible in terms of students' reading fluency as with having literature that interests them because of the topic.

JOANNE HINDLEY, IN THE COMPANY OF CHILDREN

Because learning to choose appropriate books is necessary for independent reading, we try to set up our classroom libraries to support transitional readers who are trying out new ways of selecting books independently. Our classroom libraries are organized in ways that invite students to begin to think about favorite authors and purposes for reading. Since people who work in bookstores understand how to display and market books to customers, we pay attention to the way we browse in bookstores when we think about how to design our classroom library, mimicking some of their inviting display strategies. Just as we do with our early readers, we want our libraries for transitional readers to support our students in making their own good choices about what to read. We want to highlight books with characters we love and books by favorite authors just as we do in kindergarten and first-grade classrooms. We want books to be accessible and inviting to our transitional readers. And we want to use the library design to support readers in finding new challenges. The big difference between the organization of classroom libraries in kindergarten and first grade and those in grades two–five is the types of books that are highlighted. Early series chapter books are more visible, whereas books for very beginning readers may be less visible.

Transitional readers benefit from having books placed face out so that they can see the covers and preview them easily. Series books and books by favorite authors can be separated into baskets that are easy to find and browse. Sequels to read-alouds and new books that have been highlighted in class can be placed in a basket near the read-aloud area so students can choose a book that they know something about. Baskets allow books to be placed face out and in helpful categories. By organizing the classroom library like this, we encourage transitional readers to begin to choose books in ways that independent readers do. They may, for example, go to the Magic Tree House basket because they have read

Books organized in baskets according to author.

Books displayed face out and organized in baskets by series.

one book in that series and would like to try another. They may browse the Beverly Cleary basket, because she is becoming a favorite author. They may find a book in the basket near the read-aloud area because the teacher recommended it.

Second-grade teacher Molly Foglietti places different series books with similar features in the same basket or in baskets next to each other, thus encouraging readers to expand their choices. For example, if a child is reading a Cam Jansen book and is searching for another one in the Cam Jansen basket, she may find an Invisible Inc. book that she wants to try. Table 7.1 can be used to find series that contain similar features.

With the pressure to read longer and harder chapter books as early as second grade, it is important that we make sure to value all kinds of reading in our classrooms. We have to make sure our students recognize that reading bigger, fatter books is not the only way to demonstrate that they are good readers.

Heidi Wolfer, a teacher with whom we work, has a Quick Read basket in her second-grade classroom. The basket is filled with short books that can be read in one sitting. The label on the basket gives students the message that sometimes you are in the mood to read something quick, and it values the choice that a reader has over his or her own reading. Heidi started off with one quick-read basket at the beginning of the year and then moved to two baskets—Quick Read Fiction and Quick

Table 7.1 Series Books with Similar Features

Series Books in a Basket	Reason for Grouping
Frog and Toad by Arnold Lobel Little Bear by Maurice Sendak Poppleton by Cynthia Rylant Minnie and Moo by Denys Cazet	Animal characters have human experiences
Mr. Putter and Tabby by Cynthia Rylant Henry and Mudge by Cynthia Rylant	Human characters with animal companion
Cam Jansen by David A. Adler Invisible Inc. by Elizabeth Levy Magic Tree House by Mary Pope Osborne A to Z Mysteries by Ron Roy Something Queer Mysteries by Elizabeth Levy Jigsaw Jones by James Preller	Mystery adventure themes
Horrible Harry by Suzy Kline Spider Storch by Gina Willner-Pardo Pee Wee Scouts by Judy Delton Triplet Trouble by Debbie Dadey Bean by Susan Wojciechowski Annie Bananie by Leah Kamaiko	Adventure with friends
Aliens by Jonathan Etra Funny Firsts by Mike Thaler Amelia Bedelia by Peggy Parish The Stupids by Harry Allard Mrs. Piggle-Wiggle by Betty MacDonald Pippi Longstocking by Astrid Lindgren	Humorous stories
Ida Early by Robert Burch Little House by Laura Ingalls Wilder Time Warp Trio by Jon Scieszka American Girls by Pleasant Company	Stories that take the reader back in time

Read Nonfiction. The children helped decide what books would be good for a quick-read basket.

One year in fourth grade, Maty discovered *Heartbeat* by Sharon Creech. She fell in love with it for several reasons. I thought that she would then start reading other books by Sharon Creech. But instead, she fell in love with novels in verse. After she finished *Heartbeat* and told everyone she could about it, she made a list of the things she loved about the book—so you can see how important the verse was to Maty. One book can show readers new possibilities for their reading. When they know that the choice is theirs, they often discover things about themselves as readers that change the way they choose books forever. Following is a list of books placed in a Novels in Verse basket in an intermediate classroom:

Where I Live by Eileen Spinelli
Heartbeat by Sharon Creech
The Trial by Jen Bryant
Home of the Brave by Katherine Applegate
Amber Was Brave, Essie Was Smart by Vera B. Williams
Almost Forever by Maria Testa
Becoming Joe DiMaggio by Maria Testa
Locomotion by Jacqueline Woodson
Spinning Through the Universe by Helen Frost
Love That Dog by Sharon Creech

Mini-Lesson:

One Book Can Change You as a Reader

Possible Anchor Text:

Book from your own stack (For Franki: *Girl with a Pearl Earring* by Tracy Chevalier)

Why Teach It?

We like for students to know that their tastes as readers will constantly change. So we share our own reading to show them that we are always thinking about how our own tastes change. It is often one book that helps us realize that we might be interested in genres and authors that we hadn't been interested in before.

How We Teach It:

Franki shows her students the cover of *Girl with a Pearl Earring* by Tracy Chevalier. She tells them that she read this book several years ago. It was recommended to her, but it was not a book she normally would have chosen. She *loved* the book and told all of her friends about it. Previously, Franki thought that she did not like historical fiction. She had never enjoyed it in the past. But she loved this character. This book made Franki reflect on her reading choices. She decided to try some additional historical fiction books and read more by Chevalier, and also found another author of the same genre, Philippa Gregory. For Franki, this book opened up a whole new set of possibilities—books she had never paid attention to, but now was adding to her next-read stack. One book can do that for you.

After telling her story, Franki asks students to go back into their reading logs and think about those books that seemed to change the way they chose books. (See list below.)

Follow-Up: We sometimes follow this lesson with more mini-lessons on the subject. We might ask one child to share the ways that one book opened up new possibilities for him or her. We might chart ways that a book can extend your choices. A chart asking a class to think about how one book can do that may include the following:

How can one book expand the way you choose books?

You may try more books by the author.
You may try more books in that genre.
You might like the new format.
You may read other books about characters like this.
You might read other books with similar themes.

Books in the nonfiction library are displayed face out in baskets organized by topic.

In our classroom libraries we have a separate area for nonfiction, and the various nonfiction books are separated into baskets by topic. This supports readers in finding the information they are interested in. Many teachers invite their students to sort, categorize, and label their nonfiction books for placement in the library.

Poetry texts, too, are separated out into baskets in inviting ways. This encourages children to easily find their favorite books and poems.

When the library is set up to support good choices, transitional readers will not only spend more time engaged in reading, but also begin to develop book selection skills that will last a lifetime.

Reading Workshop

Our goal in reading workshop is to get to know each student as a reader and to provide each one with opportunities for growth. For detailed information about how to set up a reading workshop and launch the routines that are characteristic in the intermediate and upper elementary grades, teachers may want to refer to *Day-to-Day Assessment in the Reading Workshop* by Franki Sibberson and Karen Szymusiak (2008), *In the Middle* by Nancie Atwell (1998), and *In the Company of Children* by Joanne Hindley (1996). Below, we briefly discuss common elements of a reading workshop that we have found to be successful.

These common elements are supported by rich conversations that provide a foundation for literacy learning. It is critical that students be engaged in conversations about their reading lives. These interactions with classmates and the teacher support the development of a reader identity. Students engaged in conversations learn about reading strategies that others have found helpful and are able to communicate their own strengths and challenges. A classroom rich in literary conversations opens up a world of books and reading to our students.

Read-Aloud Time

> *Read-aloud may look like an ordinary event in a typical classroom, but it feels*
> *extraordinary when the teacher who is reading is aware of the power of the*
> *book and importance of her role in not only reading to her students, but*
> *leading them through the book—using read-aloud as a teaching time.*
>
> MARY LEE HAHN, RECONSIDERING READ-ALOUD

Although reading aloud is often overlooked in the upper elementary grades, research has shown that it remains the most important activity for helping children of all ages to build the knowledge necessary for success in their own reading. As Regie Routman reminds us in her book *Invitations* (1994), "Read aloud is seen as the single most influential factor in young children's success in learning to read" (32). We use read-alouds as springboards into discussions about skills and strategies transitional readers need. No longer is it an activity we do after recess to quiet students down. Instead, reading aloud has become a powerful instructional experience. Read-aloud time is enriched by the conversations that surround the text and the "think-aloud" remarks the teacher makes to model what effective readers do. The conversations bring all readers into a community that values response to the books we read and offers a strong model for the behaviors that characterize successful readers.

Mini-Lessons

Mini-lessons provide the structure for short but explicit instruction in every aspect of reading. As we gather information about our students in conferences and observations, we can design mini-lessons that meet the needs of our transitional readers in a whole-class setting. Some mini-lessons provide opportunities for readers to respond to the books they are reading, discuss literary elements, and examine supportive features of books. Others focus on specific comprehension strategies, such as those suggested in *Strategies That Work* by Stephanie Harvey and Anne Goudvis (2007). Whole-group mini-lessons provide students with a common language for the skills and strategies they are learning. As Nancie Atwell points out in her book *In the Middle*, "mini-lessons create a communal frame of reference" (1998, 78).

Reflection

If readers are going to move toward independence, they need opportunities to think about their reading experiences and reflect on their strengths and challenges. Reading workshop provides many opportunities for students to talk with others about the reading process and think about the books they are reading. As they interact with other readers in the classroom, they can think about their own reading lives.

When students reflect on their own reading lives, they set goals for themselves. After reflecting on their recent reading choices, they might think about moving to a new genre. If they discover that they are always losing track of the characters as they read, they might plan a strategy and set a goal to improve. They plan ways to become more competent readers.

Independent and Partner Reading

Students spend most of their time in reading workshop reading alone and with others. They develop strategies for choosing books and sustaining independent reading. Sometimes they may engage in partner reading as a support for developing independence.

Reader Response

In the reading workshop, students respond to the texts they read. They may do so individually in a reading log or share responses in a small group. Through these activities, readers learn to appreciate the range of responses to a given text.

Reading Conferences

During the first month of school, we spend at least one hour a day meeting with students in individual conferences to discuss their reading. Our goal is to assess each child's instructional level, including the skills and strategies each needs to work on, and to match readers with appropriate books for independent reading. By October or November, the time used for these conferences is reduced to two or three days a week, with more time given over to small-group instruction.

Literature Circles

Student- or teacher-led literature groups promote thoughtful discussion of books and reading. Literature circles are small, temporary discussion

Informal small-group reader response.

groups composed of students who choose to read and respond to the same book (Daniels 1994). We help our students prepare for literature circles and recognize the responses to the text that can generate the most useful discussions.

Share Time

Share time is when we come back together as a reading community at the end of reading workshop. This important component allows time for reflecting on our own reading, connecting with other readers, and thinking more deeply about how we are growing and changing. In *Don't Forget to Share* Leah Mermelstein tells us, "As I've begun to conduct share sessions as discussions, I've been dazzled by the ways in which these meetings have the capacity to lift energy, build morale, encourage participation, and most of all instruct" (2007, 8).

In short, reading workshop provides a structure that allows students to read appropriate books independently while they learn from a community of readers. Each component of the workshop provides support and instruction for transitional readers.

Getting to Know Our Students

It is important to know the supports various books have to offer as we plan instruction for transitional readers, but unless we know our students well, the match between book and reader will never be one that moves them toward independence. The match needs to propel the reader to new understanding and to more sophisticated strategies for constructing meaning. We make very calculated instructional decisions based on both knowing the supports that books have to offer transitional readers and understanding the needs of individual students.

We approach the beginning of a new school year armed with everything we know about the stages readers go through, our state-mandated curriculum, and the books and materials that will support reading growth. Like architects, we have planned and organized a classroom that supports transitional readers. Now we begin the complex but fascinating work of getting to know the individuals in our classroom. Instead of focusing on the required curriculum, or what students need for the yearly mandated test, we concentrate at the beginning of the year on learning about our students as individual readers.

We gather information about our students from many sources—running records, individual interviews, observations of how they select and discard books, analysis of early reading log entries, and whole-class discussions of reading. Our goal is to see how our students define reading and what their perspectives of themselves are as readers.

Starting conversations about readers and reading is often an easy way to begin to get some of this information. Children's stories of their own histories as readers and preferences in books are particularly useful. In addition, there are some wonderful children's books written about characters and their reading experiences that are appropriate for whole-class or small-group discussion. Students respond easily to a book that is shared with the whole class. Teachers can read these books aloud and engage the class in conversations that provide invaluable insights.

The Library by Sarah Stewart is a particular favorite, about a character who loves reading so much that she surrounds herself with books. Before too long she has so many books she doesn't know what to do with them. The books are everywhere, and she is running out of places to put them. This book encourages students to talk about the books they have at home, people they know who are like the character, and their own interest in reading.

The book *Jeremiah Learns to Read* by Jo Ellen Bogart is another thought-provoking selection about an older man who starts going to school with the children because he wants to learn how to read. At the end of the story, he surprises his wife by reading a poem to her. What better way for students to begin conversations about what it must be like not being able to read, and about how dedicated Jeremiah is and how hard he works to become a reader. The character serves as a wonderful model for the transitional reader and, once again, helps teachers gather insights about their students as the class discusses responses to the book.

The following list describes other books about readers and reading that are appropriate for this type of discussion.

Wolf by Becky Bloom
A hungry wolf intending to eat the farm animals is surprised when they tell him to stop disturbing their reading. The wolf decides to learn how to read to impress the farm animals and eventually becomes their friend.

More Than Anything Else by Marie Bradby
This story portrays the early years of Booker T. Washington, who works with his father in the saltworks of West Virginia. All he wants is to learn to read.

The Wednesday Surprise by Eve Bunting
This story is about a young girl who teaches her grandmother to read and surprises her father for his birthday.

Book by George Ella Lyon
This free-verse poem accompanied by watercolor illustrations presents a collection of rich metaphors that celebrate the connection between author and reader.

Tomas and the Library Lady by Pat Mora
This is the true story of Tomas Rivera, a migrant worker who became the chancellor of the University of California, Riverside, and the librarian who helped him learn to love books.

The Girl Who Hated Books by Manjusha Pawagi
Although she lives with parents who love to read, Meena hates books. When a pile of books topples and all the characters fall

out, Meena must read the books to get all the characters back into the right books. In the process, she learns to love reading.

Aunt Chip and the Great Triple Creek Dam Affair by Patricia Polacco
The residents of Triple Creek watch so much television, they forget how to read. Aunt Chip steps in, teaches the children to read, and turns the town around in this funny tale.

Thank You, Mr. Falker by Patricia Polacco
Trisha, excited about starting school and learning to read, is frustrated when she struggles with the letters and words on the page. Her classmates make fun of her until Mr. Falker, the new teacher, helps her overcome her reading difficulties. This story is an autobiographical tribute to Patricia Polacco's fifth-grade teacher, who recognized her learning disability and helped her learn to read.

How Reading Changed My Life by Anna Quindlen
Noted author and journalist Anna Quindlen tells about the influence books and reading have had on her life. Excerpts from this book will stimulate conversations about reading.

Reading Grows by Ellen B. Senisi
This book contains wonderful photographs of children from various cultures and of various ages as they read books.

Library Lil by Suzanne Williams
Lil is a librarian in a town where people watch too much television. When the electricity goes out in a storm, she turns the townspeople into readers again.

Maybe a Bear Ate It! by Robie Harris
When the child in this story loses his favorite book, he goes on an adventurous and imaginative search.

Souperchicken by Mary Jane and Herm Auch
Because Henrietta the hen can read, she realizes that her aunts, the pigs, and the cows are headed for danger. She saves them all and encourages them to learn to read.

The Day Eddie Met the Author by Louise Borden
Eddie is prepared to ask the visiting author an important question about writing, but time runs out. By chance, he runs into the author and gets his question answered.

But Excuse Me That Is My Book by Lauren Child
When Charlie's younger sister, Lola, sees someone else carrying her favorite book, he tries to get her interested in other books.

The Incredible Book-Eating Boy by Oliver Jeffers
Henry loves eating books, and the more he eats, the smarter he gets until he has eaten so many books that the information gets all mixed up. Henry eventually learns to enjoy reading his books instead.

The Library Lion by Michelle Knudsen
Lion is permitted to stay in the library as long as he doesn't break the rules. An occasional roar gets him in trouble, but he saves the day when the librarian falls and breaks her arm.

Jake's 100th Day of School by Lester Laminack
Jake puts together an album of 100 family pictures, but on the 100th day of school he forgets his bookbag. The principal helps him put together another collection, but to everyone's surprise, Jake's grandma Maggie arrives with her 100-year-old aunt Lulu, and the day is saved.

The Librarian of Basra by Jeannette Winter
Under the threat of war in Iraq, the librarian moves all the books to a nearby restaurant just nine days before the library burns down.

We also observe and listen carefully to the conversations among students, especially when they are given time to choose books and read independently. Informal conversations can provide teachers with a wealth of information about individual readers. In addition, it helps to observe students' reading habits, to notice those students who have difficulty choosing a book to read and those who cannot sustain reading for an extended amount of time. These observations add to our data on individual students. Our observations and the things we learn from listening to students add clarity to our perspective of each child as a reader.

We also take notes on interesting behavior and stories about our students' reading lives. We often ask the students' parents to write to us about their children before school begins. Often these letters contain important information about the children as readers. We listen when parents tell us stories. We were, for example, especially interested when Sandra's mother told us that one evening during the fourth week of school one of Sandra's friends called her to come outside to play. But Sandra wanted to stay in so she could finish her book. Sandra's mother was eager to share the story with us, since Sandra had not previously enjoyed reading. Now she was enjoying it so much that she chose to read instead of playing with friends.

We also use surveys to learn about our students. We've used and adapted surveys from many sources. We ask questions such as these:

- Who is your favorite author?
- Where do you like to read?
- What kind of books do you like to read?
- What was a book that you read this summer?
- Do you read with anyone at home?
- Is there a type of book that you don't enjoy?
- When do you read?
- What are your strengths as a reader?
- What is difficult for you as a reader?
- How do you choose books to read?

We do more formal assessments of individuals as issues come up in reading conferences. Many teachers use running records to assess how students are integrating reading strategies to decode the text. But transitional readers are often fairly adept at decoding. They often read fluently and have developed some sophisticated strategies for figuring out unfamiliar words. Running records can be used to validate the high level of decoding skills most transitional readers possess and may help us find which students are not using a range of strategies for decoding.

Reading conferences also give teachers opportunities to ask a student to retell a story or respond to a text so they can begin to put together an understanding of the student's ability to comprehend what is being read. Transitional readers often appear to be able to decode and read fluently. But when asked to discuss what they read, their responses may reveal that they are less able to monitor the meaning of the words. For this reason, we use the first conferences to find out whether students can understand the texts they read. Often we do this by asking them to retell the part of the story they have just finished. When we ask children to retell, we are quickly able to determine if they understand the main ideas and issues in the story. We notice whether they are sequential in their retelling or whether they move randomly from one event to another. We pay attention to the ways in which children connect specific events to the whole story. We listen for gaps in their understanding.

By listening carefully when children retell the story and paying attention to what they choose to share in reading conferences, we can determine whether they are choosing appropriate books for independent reading. When we ask them to read us a part of the story, ask for a retelling, and chat informally about the characters and details, we gather critical information about our students as readers.

These early conferences also give us the opportunity to get to know our students' reading habits and behaviors, as well as how they define reading. The conferences often feel like informal conversations. We ask some of the following questions:

- Why did you choose to read this book?
- How do you choose books to read?
- Do you like to read?
- Do you read with anyone at home?
- Why do you read?
- When do you like to read?
- Where is your favorite place to read?
- Tell me about one of your favorite books. Why is it a favorite?
- Is there a type of book that you do not like to read?
- Do you have a favorite author?
- Do you read any magazines?
- What do you like best about reading?
- What is something that is hard for you when you are reading?

As we begin to create profiles of our students as readers and recognize each one's unique qualities, we watch for behaviors that will help us plan instruction. We try to gain insights about the children's reading process that help us identify transitional readers who will need a variety of instructional supports. For example, they may

- choose books that are too difficult or too easy;
- hesitate to choose new genres or new authors or even a more complex text;

- focus on decoding rather than meaning;
- perceive reading to be a chore or something to do at school and not part of their lives outside of school;
- appear to be fluent readers but without comprehending what they read;
- have difficulty comprehending longer, more complex texts;
- be unable to stick with a book for any length of time.

All the data, formal and informal, that we gather help us determine what we will need to do in individual, small-group, and large-group instruction.

chapter eight

Grouping for Instruction

There must be a match between what we teach and the child's needs, interests, engagement, and readiness to learn. It takes a knowledgeable teacher, not a program from a publisher, to determine and assess what needs to be directly taught and how and when to teach it.

REGIE ROUTMAN, CONVERSATIONS

Flexible, small-group instruction helps us use our time wisely with transitional readers. Because these students have such a wide variety of needs and interests, it is essential to individualize instruction. Small-group instruction can save time spent in individual conferences by grouping students with similar needs. In addition, groups build students' sense of themselves as readers by giving them a chance to talk with small numbers of classmates regularly.

We group in several ways throughout the year. We think about the students' needs, the students' own goals, our state's standards, and the time we have. Some groups are designed to stay together for only one session. Other groups stay together for a few days based on the purpose of the group. To group effectively, it is important that we know our students well and constantly look for patterns in the class.

Every few weeks, we reflect on the students' needs for reading instruction and use it to form flexible small groups and plan whole-class lessons and individual instruction. When we plan for small-group instruction, we take into account what we know about our students, what we know about reading, and what we know about the books that are available to us. We are constantly observing our students and paying attention to the ways in which they respond to various books. We keep track of features that we notice in books that may help us with a lesson later when a certain need arises. Sometimes the needs of our students make us think that a guided reading group would help them learn how to use reading strategies independently; at other times, we know that putting together a group of children for a literature circle will best meet their needs. Often, children just need quick conversations with us to get through new challenges in a text. Grouping students by skill need frees us to choose books that support the skill rather than limiting us to a list of books based on level. We group children for a variety of reasons; here are some of the most common ones:

- Help students choose just-right books
- Introduce students to a new genre or author
- Talk to others about a book to gain deeper understanding
- Share good or recommended books
- Enhance comprehension strategies (questioning, visualizing, inferring, synthesizing, predicting, connecting)
- Teach a word study or vocabulary skill
- Discuss a book or piece of text
- Teach a specific skill or text element (dialogue, nonfiction captions, etc.)
- Conduct an author study
- Have self-reflective discussions about literacy
- Create or add to portfolios
- Be part of a reader's theater (possibly fluency work)
- Share strategies
- Help sustain comprehension over time
- Help students stick with a book through the end
- Practice word work that supports fluency
- Expand written responses to reading
- Explore several books of a specific genre

Throughout the year, we take our cues from observations of students during whole-class discussions, assessments from individual conferences, and answers to surveys (discussed in Chapter 4). We tend to work primarily from the anecdotal notes we jot down about each child. We make a list of our students and write down what we believe they need to become more independent readers. We are aware of the strategies they already have that are making them successful with some texts, and we pay attention to the things that are creating confusion or roadblocks in their reading.

When we think about flexible grouping of transitional readers, it is important that we not limit our thinking about how they should be grouped. We group children for a variety of reasons, not necessarily for guided reading instruction. Rather than guiding students through the book, our role is to help them become more thoughtful readers who are able to comprehend more complex text. As teachers, we need to look carefully at our students' needs and find books that provide the right supports for them.

An Example of Flexible Grouping

When we talk with teachers about planning instruction for transitional readers, observational assessments and flexible grouping are what they find most challenging. By examining an actual list of students, needs, and instructional plans, we hope to demystify this process. Here is a list that Franki created for a class of students (a blank form is in the appendix). On the list, she jotted down next to a student's name the one thing that she felt could benefit that student most.

Name	**Most Critical Need**
Michael	Reading for meaning
Anthony	Sustaining comprehension with longer text
Austin	Stretching to more challenging books
Zachary	
Jeffrey	Sustaining comprehension
Matthew	
Robert	Finding a new genre
Ryan	
Donald	
Neil	
Trevor	Comprehending with fewer picture cues
Scott	Vowel sounds along with meaning to decode

P. J.	Fantasy at his level
Brad	
Danielle	Maintaining reading/comprehension
Lori	Sustaining longer books
Mollie	
Gabriella	Sustaining comprehension over longer books
Lynnie	
Paula	Sustaining interest over longer books
Katie	Partner reading with Kelly
Kristin	
Kelly	Partner reading with Katie
Anna	Read another biography
Libby	
Amanda	Using all decoding skills together

When Franki studied her completed list, she noticed several patterns. She could easily see which children had similar needs at that moment. These children she grouped together for teaching purposes (see Table 8.1).

Franki decided to group Michael, Danielle, and Trevor because of comprehension issues. Although their needs were not identical, she knew she could teach them ways to sustain comprehension for books that take longer than one day to read. Danielle and Trevor were hesitant to try books that were longer than one-day reads. Michael read fluently, but rarely read for meaning. His goal was to "get it finished." Franki was confident that the strategies she would teach Danielle and Trevor for getting through longer text would also help Michael redefine reading and pay more attention to his comprehension. These students were at various reading levels, but this was not a problem. Franki looked for a book for the three to read whose chapters connected in some way, so that she could teach the children ways to start reading the next day after thinking back or reading back to remember where they were in the story.

Henry and Mudge and the Long Weekend by Cynthia Rylant was a book that was easy for all three group members. The three students could breeze through decoding the text and as a result could focus on learning the strategies they would need to remember the story over time. The chapters were connected, they were sequential, and the action in all of them took place on the same weekend. Readers needed to recall only minimal information before starting a new chapter. Franki chose this book because throughout the guided reading group the members were able to look back at past chapter titles and pictures to remember what

Table 8.1 Possible Groups for Instruction

Group Members	Reason	Text/Book
Michael, Danielle, Trevor	Sustaining comprehension, predicting and reading for meaning	*Henry and Mudge and the Long Weekend* by Cynthia Rylant
Anthony, Jeffrey	Sustaining comprehension	
Robert, Anna, Libby, Donald	Biography/new genre	*The Story of Squanto: First Friend to the Pilgrims* by Cathy East Dubowski
Gabriella, Paula, Lori	Sustaining reading, comprehending longer books	A book from the Pinky and Rex series by James Howe
Scott, Lori, Amanda	Using vowels and meaning	*To Market, to Market* by Anne Miranda
Austin, P. J.	Fantasy at good level	*Indian in the Cupboard* by Lynne Reid Banks or *Mrs. Frisby and the Rats of NIMH* by Robert O'Brien

Kids to keep an eye on—invite into book talks, conference with, etc.

Matthew   Ryan   Mollie   Kristin   Neil   Zachary   Libby   Lynnie   Donald   Brad

happened before they resumed reading. Sometimes they also read the last page of the previous chapter to help them remember what they had read the day before.

Anthony and Jeffrey also were having difficulty sustaining comprehension over time. Both had very good comprehension of what they were reading that day and knew strategies that would help them resume reading the next day. However, neither boy used those strategies independently. Because they both understood the strategies to help them begin reading but were not using them independently, they could not be included in the Michael-Danielle-Trevor group. The goal for Anthony and Jeffrey was to become more aware of which strategies would help them understand the text they were reading and monitor which ones they were using on their own. Franki hoped that if they began to pay closer attention to what was working, they would begin to use the strategies independently. The boys were in the middle of different books, so Franki chose to have quick daily meetings with the two of them to remind them of strategies to use and discuss those that seemed to be working. After reviewing with them how to begin the day's reading, she would send them off to read independently.

Robert and Anna were placed together, although their needs were different on the class assessment sheet. Robert was stuck in his reading and unable to find a new book. He had just read several books from a series he liked but had had his fill of it. He had gone several days without finding a book that interested him. Franki thought this might be the perfect time to introduce him to a new genre. Anna had recently finished a biography and was eager to find another one she would enjoy. Both Anna and Robert were very capable readers who would require minimal support once they began reading. This was a group that Franki thought Libby and Donald might join. Neither had an immediate need on her list, but Franki knew that neither of them was choosing much nonfiction. She thought this might be a good way to broaden their reading tastes. Although they were progressing well in their reading, Franki decided to invite Libby and Donald to join Robert and Anna in reading *The Story of Squanto: First Friend to the Pilgrims* by Cathy East Dubowski. After an initial meeting at which Franki introduced the book and the genre, she planned to meet with the group once or twice during their reading to discuss the features of nonfiction, which were fairly new to them. Because these students were capable of reading the book with minimal support, Franki's meeting with them to introduce nonfiction and touching base with them periodically while they read were sufficient.

Gabriella, Paula, and Lori were all having trouble finding books that held their interest. They were able to read and comprehend over time, but all too often they wanted to quit reading a book after a few days. They seemed to lose interest in the story about halfway through. The Pinky and Rex series by James Howe included chapter books that were a bit shorter than the books they had been abandoning, but had stories interesting enough to possibly keep them engaged to the end. Franki wanted to meet with this group daily to talk about the book they were reading, encouraging them to make predictions and listening to them talk about it to find out where they were losing interest. This series has chapter titles that can be used to predict what will follow, a text support that often helps students sustain interest. The chapters also offer more complex leads, making readers infer quite a bit when starting a new chapter. Franki suspected that the three girls would be able to make these inferences and that the more challenging text might help keep them engaged. She wanted to offer them a genre that could help them over this hump and at the same time find out more about their reading needs.

When Franki listened to Scott read over several weeks and analyzed his running records, it became obvious that decoding unknown words with complex vowel sounds was affecting his fluency and thus his comprehension. Scott definitely read for meaning, and he had many strategies for making sure the text made sense, but too often he confused vowels, making decoding take longer than it needed to. Franki hoped that spending a few days with Scott discussing vowels using a rhyming picture book would help. Amanda was able to use all decoding strategies independently but had trouble using them together. She often relied too heavily on phonics first. Franki knew that combining Scott's strength of reading for meaning with Amanda's "phonics first" method would allow both children to see how important it was to use the two together. Franki added Lori to the group because Lori could benefit from a vowel brush-up lesson. For their book Franki chose *To Market, to Market* by Anne Miranda, a picture book that highlights words with certain vowels. The students were able to look at rhyming words with common vowel patterns such as *goose* and *loose*. This book helped remind the students of vowel patterns they had been exposed to in the past.

Austin was a very good reader, but he did not enjoy reading. He was hesitant to choose books that were engaging enough for him because often they were too long for him to finish. Austin tended to stick to very short chapter books; he read only because he had to. P. J. had recently started *Mossflower* by Brian Jacques. He realized it was much too difficult for him, but he really liked the fantasy. He had asked Franki to help him find something that he could handle on his own. Franki thought that P. J. might provide the support Austin needed to read a more challenging book, so she put them together.

Interestingly, the Austin–P. J. group never met. By the next week, when Franki planned on bringing them together, P. J. had discovered *Mrs. Frisby and the Rats of NIMH* by Robert O'Brien. His cousin had recommended it to him, and he was hooked. Austin had asked to partner read with his good friend, and they were reading *My Side of the Mountain* by Jean Craighead George. Although *My Side of the Mountain* is not a fantasy, it is a complex book that Franki knew might hold Austin's attention and might, she hoped, change his ideas about reading. She knew that a friend's support could spur him on to read more complex books independently.

Several students in Franki's class were not put into any of these groups. Not every child needs to be in a group all the time. We meet with children during reading conferences, converse with them during read-aloud time, and otherwise interact with them throughout the day. If the children are at a point in their reading where they seem to be rapidly gaining new skills and independence, meeting in a group may not be more valuable for them than reading independently. That is why it is important to go through the class list every few weeks to ensure that we are meeting the children's current needs and remaining flexible in how we think about their evolving needs.

For example, Trevor's need was very individual. He had spent a great deal of time reading the Arthur books by Marc Brown. He also read many Garfield comic books. He was hesitant to read books without pictures. When Franki met with him, she realized that pictures provided a great deal of comprehension support for Trevor. He did not have strategies in place for getting much information from the text. Franki met with him in a series of individual conferences to help him find books that provided some support from the illustrations, but not as much as the Arthur picture books. She introduced him to the Mr. Putter and Tabby series and the Poppleton series, both by Cynthia Rylant. Although many of these books were at an easier reading level than the Arthur books, not as much of the story was told through the pictures. They were easy enough for Trevor to read to allow him to focus on strategies for understanding the text without the support of detailed illustrations.

When Students Initiate Their Own Groups

There are also several times throughout the year when students have input into the groups that are formed. Much of our time is spent building reader identity, helping students see their strengths and needs as readers, and setting goals. Student-chosen groups become a very natural part of this.

When Franki began a nonfiction unit of study with her third and fourth graders, they talked about the need to integrate all that was on a page of nonfiction text. She had noticed that many of them browsed nonfiction but did not necessarily understand how to add information from a graph to the text on the page. To begin their thinking, the class charted all of the things that readers need to understand when reading nonfiction. Franki then wanted to tie this much-needed skill in with the standards that she was required to teach.

Early in the unit, she shared with the class the five big things that would be part of their learning, taken from the state standards and her district's target standards. After sharing the list with the students, she asked them to think about the one that each child would want to learn more about first.

I can understand different nonfiction text structures.

I can understand what is important in nonfiction texts.

I can retell what I have read.

I can decide if something is a fact or an opinion.

I can find answers to my questions.

I can figure out new words in my nonfiction reading.

I can add information to what I know by reading the graphs, charts, and captions.

It was clear during the conversation that students felt confident about some parts of their nonfiction reading and uncomfortable with others. Students each chose one area that they thought they needed to work on. They signed up on the chart of statements, and Franki began to form groups based on their feedback.

Students use sticky notes to indicate their goals in nonfiction reading.

These early groups gave students ownership of their own nonfiction reading and gave Franki huge insights into the things that they could and could not do comfortably while reading nonfiction.

Literature Circles as Small-Group Instruction

We are flexible in the ways and the reasons for which we group students for instruction. We think talk about books and reading is important in all components of the reading workshop. Some of our small-group work occurs as students are talking together about a common book. This allows the group to pull their thinking together and to understand the book more deeply than if they had read it on their own.

Our good friend Shari Frost shares some amazing insights on some mistakes we can make with our highest readers when putting them in literature circles based on levels.

Just Because They Can Doesn't Mean They Should

Shari Frost

"Whatever you are doing tomorrow, cancel it! You have got to come and see Jan's literature circles." That was the message that Patty, a literacy coach, left on my voicemail. She had been working with Jan, a third-grade teacher, for about six weeks on getting literature circles started in her class. Intrigued, I rearranged my morning appointments so I could be in Jan's classroom the next day.

When I arrived, Patty steered me toward a group of five children sitting on the rug with their literature response journals and a black paperback book. As I got closer, I saw the title of the book, *The Giver* (Lowry 1993). I was completely dismayed, because it takes a sophisticated reader to understand this book. Why would Jan select this book? Why didn't Patty make another suggestion? I decided to block out my internal questions and concentrated on the children's discussion.

The children were discussing Chapter 5. The character, Jonas, was telling his parents about a strange dream that he had had the previous night. In the dream, he was in a bathtub and was trying to persuade a female classmate to join him. His parents told him he was having "stirrings" and would have to take a pill to get rid of them. Three of the children had written *stirrings* in the vocabulary section of their journals. One child said, "What do you think that means? I don't think it has anything to do with mixing things up." Another child said, "I looked it up. *Stirrings* means 'the beginning of motion or action.'" One of the other children wondered why Jonas's society didn't want people to take action. Then the children began to share their own strange dreams. They tried to figure out why this society would want to ban strange dreams so much that they would invent a pill to prevent someone from having them. Finally, the children turned to another page in their journals. They added *strange dreams* to a list of things that were not permitted in Jonas's village.

I met Patty in her office after the observation. She was practically jumping for joy. I certainly understood her excitement. She and Jan had done a great job getting the literature circles started. Many good things were in place. Jan's students had all actually read the chapter. They came to the literature circle prepared to discuss it. The children were focused, stayed on topic, and did a good job taking turns and listening to each other. I was really impressed that the children were able to do all of this without the teacher's overt supervision. I finally asked Patty why these eight-year-olds were reading *The Giver*. She replied, "Because they can. They are all very strong readers. I think they can handle sophisticated books."

Those children *were* strong readers. They were capable of reading a book that is usually read in middle school, with accuracy and prosody. However, they didn't have the life experiences to support the reading of that book. It was not an age-appropriate selection. Every middle school student completely understands what is happening to Jonas when he has "stirrings." Talk about text-to-self connection! The themes in *The Giver* are well beyond the comprehension of most eight-year-olds. These are children who believed in Santa Claus and the tooth fairy just last year. Are they really ready to grapple with the concept of utopian societies? Can they comprehend and discuss the idea of giving up individuality, choice, and independence for safety and security? Is it even fair to ask them to think about such ideas?

Think of the books that these third graders are missing! When they are thirteen, they are probably not going to go back and read novels featuring eight- and nine-year-old characters like those in *Love, Ruby Lavender* (Wiles 2001). I strongly suspect that they won't pick up the picture books that they missed, like *Chicken Sunday* (Polacco 1998). It is also very unlikely that they will willingly go back and reread *The Giver* when they have the life experience, cognitive development, and emotional maturity to truly comprehend the book.

Jan and Patty are not the only teachers who are guilty of giving children books "just because they can read them." I routinely see books that are traditionally read in high school being read in sixth-grade classrooms. Many first-grade teachers think they haven't done their job if they don't have a group of children in their class reading chapter books by the end of the school year. These book choices are encouraged and applauded by school administrators and parents. Once I went to a school to conduct a professional-development workshop. The principal eagerly led me to a fifth-grade classroom so I could see the students reading Shakespeare.

I understand the importance of giving children books to read that support their growth and development as readers. They won't make progress as readers if they read only easy books. However, there are better options for young advanced readers than young-adult books. Teachers need to look at more than the readability level of the book when making book selections. A book's theme, the students' interests, and the possible teaching opportunities should also be considered.

A good source of books for advanced young readers is probably right at any teacher's fingertips: the books that a teacher would select for a class read-aloud. No third-grade teacher would consider reading *The Giver* aloud to a class. Class read-alouds are generally above the instructional reading level of most of the children in the class, which probably makes them just right for those advanced readers. These books have rich and challenging vocabulary, yet the ideas and themes are comprehensible for younger children. Most of all, teachers always select age-appropriate books for read-alouds.

The following books are written at a fifth- through eighth-grade readability level and are good choices for advanced young readers:

Poppy by Avi
This exciting, fast-paced book features Poppy, a timid mouse. She and the other mice of Dimwood Forest are terrorized by Mr. Ocax, the owl. Poppy tries to find the courage to stand up to him. This book lays the foundation for the themes and ideas expanded upon and further developed in *The Giver*. There are five sequels to this book suitable for independent reading choices for children who can't get enough of these characters.

The Tale of Despereaux: Being the Story of a Mouse, a Princess, Some Soup, and a Spool of Thread by Kate DiCamillo
Despereaux is a mouse that is different from all the other mice. He's smaller and has very big ears. He likes to read, and most alarming, he is in love with a human girl. In DiCamillo's Newbery Award–winning

book, children will meet colorful characters, encounter interesting language, and become totally engrossed in this charming fairy-tale-like story.

The Cricket in Times Square by George Selden
Mario is delighted to find a cricket while picnicking with his family. He decides to keep it as a pet. Chester, the cricket, charms Mario with his music and befriends Harry, the cat, and Tucker, the mouse. However, Chester finds living in New York City a big adjustment.

The Borrowers by Mary Norton
I have yet to meet a child who doesn't love this book! The Borrowers are little people who live under the floorboards of a house. They borrow things (stamps, matchbooks, keys) from the big people who live in the house. Their "borrowing" could have gone on indefinitely, but a little boy and his ferret see one of them. This book also has several sequels for ongoing independent reading fun.

Shari Frost has been a teacher for grades K–5 and reading specialist in the Chicago Public Schools. Currently, she is supporting literacy coaches in the Coaching Collaborative at National-Louis University.

Implications for Whole-Group Instruction

Although individual needs are a critical factor to consider when determining groupings, it is also important to analyze those needs to determine which teaching strategy would be effective in whole-group instruction. Because students read at different levels, having the entire class read the same book would not be effective. Instead, we use read-aloud sessions as a vehicle for teaching many skills that children will need as they move forward in their reading. Inspired by a visit to Judy Davis's fifth-grade class at the Manhattan New School in New York City, we began to share strategies during read-aloud time, allowing the whole class to see how we use them in our own reading. Students can then transfer skills they learned in mini-lessons with picture books, short series books, and novels to the challenge of reading longer chapter books independently.

Because many of Franki's students were having difficulty sustaining comprehension and/or interest over the course of an entire novel, she decided this would be an important focus for her read-aloud sessions. She had observed that many of her students did not preview a book before reading and that, as a result, they had trouble following the story line once they got started. She also noticed that many students seemed to resume reading where they had left off the previous day, neglecting to look back in the book to help them recall where they were in the story. These observations and notes suggested that her students needed to find and use strategies to help them comprehend longer text in order to sustain interest.

Franki chose *Shiloh* by Phyllis Reynolds Naylor as a read-aloud book, knowing she would use it to demonstrate previewing strategies for her students. She also planned to demonstrate how reading the last few paragraphs from the previous day can help readers. Franki knew that guiding the whole class through a preview of the book would be important. She began by asking her students to look carefully at the cover and to listen as she read the blurb on the back of the book, the reviews, and the first page of the text.

After spending time on each of these, Franki and her students listed everything they had already learned about the book. By the end of this forty-five-minute previewing session, the class had created a chart with an incredible amount of information:

Before You Read—*Shiloh*

Read the back cover summary
    the boy will do anything for the dog
    the dog's name is Shiloh
    what the title means
    Shiloh runs away
    boy's name is Marty
    boy thinks dog is being abused
    dog's master is cruel
    a place called Shiloh School House
    happens in West Virginia
Read the reviews on the back
    tells us why they think it is good
    compares to other books
Read the first page
    boy is telling the story
    dad shot rabbit

      dad is probably a hunter

      there are two sisters—Dara Lyn and Becky

      Mom wants respect for her cooking

Read "about the author" blurb

      she did see a dog in Shiloh

      in West Virginia

      based on something true that happened

      likes to write about things she sees

Look at the cover

      about a boy and a dog

      title

      won Newbery Medal (1992)

      dog is a beagle

      boy and dog like each other

      might be fall/autumn

Other things we could do to find out about a book:

      ask someone who has read it

      check to see if there are any pictures

      look at pages

      look at the number of pages (144) and number of chapters

      look at the dedication, copyright, etc.

      look at the table of contents

The students were surprised by how much information they could discover about a text before they had even started to read it. Franki talked with them about how authors and publishers put many supports in books for readers so that they can better understand them once they start reading. Throughout the reading of the book, Franki went back to the chart, reminding the children of how much more difficult it would have been to understand the book without the preview.

Franki did this same previewing activity with each read-aloud throughout the year. Before reading *Stone Fox* by John Reynolds Gardiner, she asked students to preview it independently and jot down things they knew about it before reading. Figure 8.1 shows one student's notes. (A blank form is in the appendix.)

Students began to notice that different books had different supports. For example, *Poppy* by Avi has a map of the setting on a page before the story begins. Many novels have chapter titles or poems or epigraphs that can be used when previewing. Franki encouraged her students to find and use these supports in their own reading. To reinforce their use of

Figure 8.1
Casey's
prereading notes
about *Stone Fox*.

BEFORE YOU READ

What do you know/predict from looking at the cover?

There is a big dog race. The kid only has one dog. The kid could win the race.

What do you know after reading the blurb about the book?

The grand father ran out of many. The dogs name is searchlight. The grand father could loos the farm.

What do you know after looking at the table of contents?

There is 10 chapters. There is 77 pages. willy macks it to the finish line. The race is on chapter 9 the pag is 68.

What do you know after reading the first page?

Thay gr00 potatos. Thay Live in Wyoming. The grand father wouid int get out of bed.

previewing when reading independently, she asked the class to brainstorm a list of things that readers could do when starting a new book. This is the list they came up with:

Things to Do When You Start a New Book

Read the back blurb.
Read "About the Author."

Read the first page.

Look at the table of contents.

Read the reviews on the back.

Look at the cover.

Talk to someone who has read the book.

Look at the dedication and copyright.

Flip through and look at pictures.

Look at the number of pages and number of chapters.

Franki posted the list in the classroom for students to refer to when they needed it. Transitional readers benefit from reminders that will help them transfer strategies learned during read-aloud to their own reading.

Throughout the school year, Franki chose books to read aloud that would support strategies her students needed to learn to become independent readers. She chose the books carefully, based on her observations, conferences, and assessments.

Conversations are at the heart of our reading workshop. Whether we are working with the entire class, a small group, or an individual, we have created routines that support talk about books in the classroom. Besides encouraging student-directed talk, we choose books, ask questions, and lead discussions, keeping in mind the teaching we need to do.

chapter nine

Building a Reading Community

We'd like to think that we are working in such wise ways that our students will care about their own literacy long after they graduate. In fact, there is only one reason we work so hard to create such a beautiful and inviting literary setting filled with extensive collections, schoolwide literacy rituals, and ways to keep up with children's literature. We want our students to make a lifelong commitment to reading and writing. And so we begin by painstakingly caring about the literary landscape, and then we proceed to do the best literacy teaching imaginable.

SHELLEY HARWAYNE, LIFETIME GUARANTEES

Much of what we know about ourselves as readers can help us understand what transitional readers need to become more independent. The starting point for helping all transitional readers is to think about what we ourselves do as confident, independent adult readers, and then carefully translate these insights into classroom instruction. We know ourselves as readers and our friends and family members as readers. For example, Franki and her grandmother have been sharing books for as long as she can remember. As a child, Franki would go up to the attic each Sunday to pick a new Nancy Drew book from her grandmother's shelf. Now, as adults, they share books that they know the other will enjoy. Each time a new Mary Higgins Clark book is published, Franki buys it for her grandmother, knowing that her grandmother will give it back to her with a grin on her face, saying, "You'll never be able to figure out how this one ends!" Conversations about books have always been part of their relationship. Readers swap books with neighbors and friends, discuss favorite authors in their conversations, and suggest books to each other over email.

When we are immersed in a great book, we eagerly anticipate the end of the workday so we can get back to our reading. Karen recalls the days when her mother would be reading such a book. On those days the family would know that things around the house might not get done and that dinner might be a few minutes late. Karen's mother would get so involved in her book that she would notice little else until she reached a place where she could put it down.

Our reading reflects our favorite authors, our favorite genres, and our moods. When we choose a book, we think about whether we want it to be long or short, sad or funny. We spend hours talking about books, browsing in the bookstore, and sharing books. The sharing comes from many thoughtful conversations and a relationship built on what we know about each other as readers.

Teachers of reading know what successful readers do. Teachers reflect on their own reading practices, talk with other readers about the reading process, and identify the strategies they want to teach in the classroom. Teachers search for ways to make reading real to their students, to engage them in reading they will value, and to help them build lifelong reading habits. Independent readers can understand complex story lines, gather pertinent information, and become engaged in choosing their own books, talking to friends, and pondering the meaning that the author intended. Our students need to learn how to do these things.

The conversations about the reading process in classrooms make the difference. Drawing children into conversations about their own reading helps them clarify the way they construct meaning. The conversations they have with other readers, both adults and peers, propel them toward independence. We need to become architects of classroom cultures that support focused conversations about reading and provide children with a variety of experiences that draw them back into the world of reading with new skills and a better understanding of how texts work.

We need to facilitate discussions that help our young readers move toward independence.

Several years ago in Franki's intermediate multiage classroom, the children brought in a morning snack from home. Snack time was scheduled for 10:15, but Franki rarely remembered this. Every day, David would remind her that it was snack time. Months after the school year ended, a student from the class mentioned David and his reminders. Franki learned that David had a watch with a timer, and that he would set it each day to remind him and his classmates that it was snack time. (He had learned that his teacher would not remember on her own.) It was a job David created for himself. The entire class knew about the snack timer and knew that David would make sure snack time happened at 10:15 each day. Although they had not deliberately kept this information from Franki, she had never realized it.

This story reminds us that students can have purposeful conversations with and without us. As teachers of transitional readers, our goal is to have our children talk about books and their own reading in the same independent way Franki's students talked about snack time. We celebrate when we overhear children like Christopher, who takes a new student under his wing and shows him which books he and his classmates have enjoyed. Just as Christopher asked Joey which sports teams he liked and where he used to live, he asked what kinds of books he liked to read. Christopher had been part of many classroom conversations about books and reading and was beginning to think and talk about reading on his own. He invited Joey into the world of reading that he had just discovered for himself. Christopher was able to initiate this peer conversation because he had been involved in talk about books and reading throughout the school year.

We are sometimes lucky enough to catch a glimpse of the kinds of conversations that occur without us. Having returned from buying books at the school book fair, Corey, a third grader, told Franki he had bought a new sports book and was going to begin reading it. He said, "It's by that guy—" and Ethan piped in, "The guy that wrote *Soccer Halfback*." Obviously, the two had talked at the book fair about their favorite authors, and the dialogue became part of their process for choosing books. Talk about books and authors was part of their peer chat.

We have not always valued or understood the power of talk about books for the transitional reader. Often we are afraid to use much time with students to have conversations about literacy. We had the experience in our early years of teaching of having colleagues and principals drop in while we were doing mini-lessons on sampling books from a new genre or organizing the series books in the classroom library. We feared that the visitor considered the task merely "housekeeping" and would inquire when she might return to see some "real teaching." We sometimes felt a little guilty that we were not really instructing students with these conversations, and we worried that they were mostly fluff—something to do only if we had some extra time. We now realize that how we structure brief lessons, how we select texts for small-group and whole-classroom instruction, and how we orchestrate seemingly impromptu conversations are at the heart of reading instruction for transitional readers. Without this work on the part of teachers, these students will not develop new skills.

Fostering Extended Conversations

Early in the school year, Franki sent this invitation home for her students' parents:

> *You're Invited!*
> *We are learning about ourselves as readers. As we learn about ourselves, we would like to learn about other people as readers. When we learn about others, it helps us reflect on what we do as readers. If you are a reader and would like to come visit our classroom for 15–20 minutes to share your reading with us, we would love it! You could show us some of your favorite books, talk about your favorite places to read, how you choose books, etc. A great time to do this would be from 1:00 to 1:15 P.M. each day. If you would like to come share with us, please fill out the form below and return it ASAP. Thank you!*
>
> *Name:*
> *I would like to come in and share my reading with the class. I am available on the following dates at 1:00 P.M. (If 1:00 P.M. is not convenient, please write down an alternate time for you.)*
>
> *Convenient dates/times:*

The invitation allowed us to set up a long-term schedule of visitors.

Nick's father was one of our first guests. He began by saying that the first reading he does each day is to find jokes on the Internet. He shared the following joke that he'd found in his email that morning:

Mrs. Stewart talks about her reading.

Q: Why do gorillas have big nostrils?

A: Because they have big fingers.

As he continued, we learned that his grandfather had read to him every Sunday before they watched *The Wonderful World of Disney* on TV. Every Sunday he and his grandfather would read a story while they ate a bowl of ice cream. His favorite book from those evenings was *Rikki Tikki Tavi* by Rudyard Kipling. We also learned that he liked reading so much as a child that his friends called him "Robbie Reader." He read every day on the playground, and the teachers often got angry with him because he didn't want to play.

Because our goal with transitional readers is to move them toward independent and lifelong reading, we should provide opportunities for them to explore their lives as readers both in and out of the classroom setting. By inviting adult readers into the classroom, Franki got her students to begin to think about readers—their tastes, habits, similarities, and differences. Transitional readers can begin to see themselves as part of the larger reading community. We can help them understand ways that adult readers make decisions, monitor reading, and choose books. Adults are important role models for transitional readers.

Nick's father was followed by other family members, teachers, school staff, and community members who shared their reading lives with us. Over the course of a month, the adult readers carried in bags of books and talked to students about ways they choose books, their likes and dislikes, their memories of childhood reading, and so on.

Franki's students quickly began to see how these adult readers made choices about their reading. They were fascinated by the fact that Meggie's mother loved to read any book she could find on how to raise children. They were even more fascinated when Beth's mother shared her bag of books and said that she liked every kind of book except books about parenting. She had read one parenting book when her first child was born and hated it. Although both of these mothers were avid readers, the children began to realize that every reader defined him- or herself differently. Eventually, the students began to recommend books to the visitors and asked questions based on previous conversations.

Students spent time listening closely to real readers talk about themselves. Slowly, they started asking their classmates questions about their reading similar to those they had asked the parents and other adult guests. Eventually, the children began thinking about their own lives as readers. Having visitors talk about their reading turned out to be a powerful way to encourage the children to begin to think about how they fit into the world of readers.

Once children begin to think about their own reading, it is easy to get them to talk about their growth as readers. To begin such conversations, Karen asked her class to bring in books from their younger days that their families had saved over the years. The next day the classroom was filled with the cloth books, board books, classic tales, and favorite books of the students' childhoods. For more than an hour, the children pored over each other's books, shared stories of sitting on their parents' laps, and talked about how they had learned to read. Connections were made when individual students realized that they were not alone in reading and saving books like *Where the Wild Things Are* by Maurice Sendak. Wonderful, rich conversations filled the classroom and lasted for days, weeks, and well into the school year. The experience of exploring their reading histories allowed these children to create a community that valued where they came from as readers and affirmed their membership in a community of learners.

Using Our Own Literacy in Our Teaching

Early in our teaching, we felt the need to read silently during independent reading time. We would bring a novel to school and spend thirty minutes each day reading alongside our students. We wanted them to see us as adult readers. Although we still believe our role as adult models is critical, we have realized that by telling students what we are reading, encouraging meaningful conversations about books, and talking about our own struggles in reading, we can send a more powerful message. Instead of just reading silently when our children are reading, we now realize how important it is to use that precious time to meet with them individually or in small groups and instruct them. We find other avenues for showing our students that we are readers, and we provide other models of adult readers, who explain their reading histories, quirks, and preferences.

For very young readers, just seeing the teacher read can communicate a powerful message about the value of reading. But transitional readers need far more. We need to give them windows into our thinking as readers, such as how we deal with difficult text and how we plan for the next reading we will do. And if our hope is that students will develop these same independent reading behaviors, we need to structure class activities, lessons, and experiences that encourage similar thinking and self-reflection.

Early in the school year, Franki realized that many of her students were having a hard time choosing appropriate books. She noticed that they often were not engaged in their reading, quit a book midway through, or consistently chose books that were too difficult. When many of them did finish a book, they approached the bookshelves without any idea of what to read next. As a result, much of these students' reading time was spent looking for a book.

Franki thought about her own reading and asked herself how she decided what to read next. She realized that many adult readers think ahead—about what they might read next. We listen to friends, remember names of favorite authors, and reread books we loved years ago. Most of us have a bookshelf or nightstand that houses the books we expect to read as soon as we have time.

Franki realized that her students were not thinking ahead in their reading. She decided to talk about her own strategies for thinking ahead and choosing books. She brought in a stack of eight books from her nightstand pile that she hoped to read in the near future. She encouraged her students to begin to think ahead in their own reading by having each fill a bookbag with "next read" books. Franki demonstrated a variety of ways that adult readers choose books. She pointed out how she chooses books that friends have recommended, books by favorite authors, magazines about topics of interest to her, books that she loves so much that she wants to reread them, and sequels to books she has already read. She hadn't just pulled the top books on her nightstand pile and brought them to class. She had chosen each one for a specific teaching purpose. She wanted the children to see a variety of ways to choose books.

Selecting from his bag of "next read" books.

Here are the books Franki showed her students, with her reasons for wanting to read them.

Title and Author	Why Read It?
A Lesson Before Dying by Ernest Gaines	My book club decided to read this book for its next meeting.
In the Company of Children by Joanne Hindley	I have already read this nonfiction book about teaching reading. I like to reread it each school year.
Lifetime Guarantees by Shelley Harwayne	I have been waiting for this book. I had heard about it long before it was published, and I knew it was a book I wanted to read. It is about the teaching of reading.
Staying Fat for Sarah Byrnes by Chris Crutcher	I heard the author, Chris Crutcher, speak at a conference. I wanted to read a book that he wrote.
The Honk and Holler Opening Soon by Billie Letts	I had read and enjoyed the book *Where the Heart Is* by the same author. I was eager to read her next book.
Have a Great One! A Homeless Man's Story by Laurie Anthony	A teacher who works with us wrote this book. I am eager to read it because I know the author.
Working Mother	I subscribe to this magazine and enjoy reading it each month when it arrives. I like to read the articles in it that are on topics of interest to me.
The Poisonwood Bible by Barbara Kingsolver	This book was recommended to me by a friend. She loved it and thought I would, too.

We are always thinking of ways we can bring our own experiences with books into the classroom. Our students come to expect that we will share thoughts about new favorite authors, struggles in our reading, and things we've learned about ourselves as readers.

Self-Reflection for Independence

As children begin to know themselves as readers, it becomes easier to continue the talks about reading that began earlier in the school year. Children come to enjoy sharing their discoveries and struggles with

Figure 9.1
Sean's reflections
on his reading.

I know I am reading more chapter books. I am reading a lot of books that tell about something. I like true and fact books. I try to read about 20 pages a day. When I come to a word I don't understand I read the sentence over and figure out a word to go with it.

classmates. Self-reflection becomes a part of their reading. Along with great picture books, quotes, and poems about reading, individual student reading logs can be great conversation starters. Throughout the year, we ask our students to write to us about their reading (see Figure 9.1). In addition, we often ask them to review their reading logs and see what they notice about themselves as readers. We purposefully designed the reading logs to get students to notice such things as the genres and authors they read, how often they complete a book, and so on.

When we want students to examine something specific about their reading, we create focused questions. On a recent survey, we asked them to look at their reading logs and answer these questions about the ways they choose books (see the appendix for a copy):

What types of books have you read?
Have you tried any books that were too hard? Which ones?
Were most of the books on your reading list too hard, too easy, or
    just right?
How do you know when a book is just right for you?
How do you decide which books to read?
How have you changed in the way you choose books?
Is there a book that you know of that you'd like to read soon?
What is one of your favorite books on your reading log? Why?

figure 9.2
A student's tally
from the reading
log.

Reading Log Tally

How many books have you read that are:

	TALLY	TOTAL
realistic fiction?	|||| |||	8
fantasy?	||	2
science fiction?		0
mystery?			1
biography?	/	1
nonfiction?	||||	4
adventure?		0
historical fiction?	||	2
poetry?	||	2

Looking over your reading log, what do you notice
about the genres you have read so far this year? I have read
alot of realistic fiction and nonfiction but not as many mystery
books or biography books.
What else do you notice about your reading? (length
of books, authors, completing a book, etc.) I think I
have been reading longer books in the nonfiction
Section.
Using your log and this survey, what is a goal you
have for your reading? My goal is to read more
biography books

These questions encourage children to think about different aspects
of their growth as readers, rather than just doing daily, piecemeal log
entries of what they've read. When we want children to reflect on a certain aspect of their reading, we may ask them to tally information from
their log. Figure 9.2 is an example of such a tally (a blank form is in the
appendix). It was designed to get children to think about the variety of

genres they had been reading. Often they are surprised at how little or how much variety there is in their reading. Using this type of record, we often ask them to set goals to expand their reading experiences.

When we make self-reflection a part of our reading workshops, children learn how to recognize their own strengths and limitations as readers. Being reflective helps them make better choices about their reading and notice when they are having difficulties. Jennifer came up to Franki one day during reading workshop to tell her that she was having trouble concentrating on her book. She was thinking about her grandmother, who was ill, and she couldn't keep her mind on the story. She asked if she could read a familiar picture book that day because she was not comprehending the book she was reading. Jennifer would not have known to ask this question had she not been part of a reflective community of readers.

Partner Reading

Reading with a friend has always been an option for students in our classrooms during independent reading time. They can choose to read a book with a classmate as long as they both have a copy of the book. Students often choose to find a quiet corner and read together.

We have found that partner reading is often an important aid for transitional readers who are not confident enough to take risks on their own. When children are given the opportunity to partner read, they are often more willing to try a new genre, sustain interest over time, or read a more complex book. When we give children the opportunity to partner read, they

- are more comfortable taking a risk with book choice;
- have natural, informal conversations about the book and their own reading;
- monitor their own reading more carefully;
- sustain interest and comprehension over time;
- expand the variety of authors and genres they read;
- have a peer model for reading;
- get to know themselves as readers by making comparisons to their partner.

Appropriate instructional supports must be in place to help make partner reading useful and enjoyable for transitional readers. We allow

Looking at Our Reading

I read with/interviewed _Trey + Evan_ **about his/her
reading. We found out that we are the same in some ways
and different in some ways. Here is what we learned.**

We are the same because: | **We are different because:**

We read as fast as each other.

We agree on Different things.

We both agreed to read the Same book

We both picture it in our heads

We pernownce the words different

we picture it in our heads differen

I never remember what happend last but trey does

I always want to read back and he does not.

I read louder than trey

I always forget to take turns

---

our students to partner read during reading workshop. Those who plan
to read together may each get a copy of the book and read it aloud. They
often take turns reading aloud. Or they might choose to read the book
separately and then meet to discuss it. Although we do not believe students should partner read every book, we know that many of them need
this support to take risks they would not take on their own.

As students continue to think about themselves as readers, partner
reading allows them to get to know another reader well and to learn more
about their own reading. After students have read a book with a friend,
we ask them to think about ways in which they are the same as and different from their partner. Evan discovered quite a bit of information after
reading with Trey, as shown in Figure 9.3 (a blank form is in the appendix). This added dimension encourages children to pay attention to a

variety of strategies, conversations, and reading habits. By adding this self-reflective piece to a routine that we have always had in place, students gain important insights about themselves as readers.

Sharing Reflections with Parents

As students become reflective about their reading and become able to monitor and set goals, we make sure that we communicate their growth to parents. Family members can offer additional support to their children at home.

For example, after several individual conferences with Niko, it became obvious that he had good comprehension of the text that he was reading. He was able to retell with detail, infer important points, and respond to the text. However, as he began to read longer books, Niko was unable to sustain comprehension over several days. When he went back to a book on the second or third day, he had trouble recalling what had already happened and where the new chapter began. As Niko and Franki discussed this problem, Niko told Franki that he read a chapter from one novel each evening at home and a chapter from another novel at school. Niko was reading two books at a time. He said he was worried that if he took the book he was reading at school home each day, he would not remember to bring it back.

Franki knew that for the comprehension strategies she was teaching him to work, it was important that he read only one book at a time. She suggested that he begin reading the same book at home and at school, carrying the book home and back each day. Because this was so important to Niko's development as a reader and because he was worried about getting the book to and from school, Niko and Franki composed a letter to his mother, explaining their discovery of Niko's needs and what each person needed to do to make their plan work:

> *Dear Mrs. Smith,*
>
> *Niko and I have been reading together during reading workshop today. I have noticed some good improvements in his reading. Today, he started the book* Dinosaurs Before Dark. *When he comes to a word he does not know, I am reminding him to read to the end of the sentence and try to find a word that makes sense. (It seems like he is using phonics cues by themselves, and I would like him to use both phonics and meaning cues.)*

When I meet with Niko, he has a good understanding of what hap-pened in the part of the book he is reading on that given day. I think it would be helpful for Niko to read the same book at home that he is read-ing at school. This will help him comprehend the book better. I am encouraging him to remember what happened last before beginning to read again each day. Niko will be bringing his book from reading work-shop home each evening. Please help him remember to bring it back to school the next day.

Thanks!

Franki Sibberson

By sharing discoveries and plans with parents, transitional readers can find the supports they need at home and at school. The reading lives of these students are also enriched by inviting adults into the classroom to talk about their reading. In the following chapter, we show more ways to build extended communities of readers. Once children start seeing adults around them as lifelong readers, the possibilities are endless for expanding the conversations about reading beyond the classroom walls.

chapter ten

Taking the Conversation Home

> *"What is the use of a book," thought Alice, "without pictures and conversations."*
>
> LEWIS CARROLL, ALICE'S ADVENTURES IN WONDERLAND

One morning several years ago, one of Franki's students, Josie, came into class with a book for her—*Plain and Simple* by Sue Bender. It was a gift from Josie's mother. A note from Josie's mother attached to the book told Franki that this was one of her favorite books and that she had shared it with many of her friends. Josie's mother was a frequent visitor to the classroom, and this gift was an extension of the many conversations she had had with Franki about books and reading.

Parents often send us favorite books, jot suggested titles on their child's homework, or let us know when a new book by a favorite author is available. Students like Josie carry the books and notes to and from school. They begin to see their parents and teachers as readers, and they enjoy being part of this ongoing dialogue. They become involved in these conversations between readers and are interested in becoming part of this larger community.

Figure 10.1
Beth and Katie's
note.

Dear Mrs. Foglietti & Mrs. Sibberson
Why didn't you invite
us to your Book Talk.
Have you read the book
HOLES? We could have a
book talk on that book.
Mrs. Sibberson are we going
to finish talking about our
Poetry? Hope to see you
soon. We miss you

At a recent parent-and-teacher book talk, Beth asked her mother to take a note to Franki and Molly, two of her former teachers who were part of the group (see Figure 10.1). Beth and Katie clearly wished to join a larger community of readers.

Home is a natural place for our students to continue this type of conversation. The bridge between school and home is crucial for transitional readers. As teachers, we can provide the starting point for the kind of support that would be most beneficial.

Many parents of emergent readers feel very comfortable supporting their children at home. They read aloud to their children, talk about favorite stories, and celebrate the accomplishments their children make along the way. Their children's early reading experiences are a natural extension of the preschool literacy experiences with which they became familiar before their children's first year of school. By the intermediate grades, when children are beginning to read independently, parents may spend less time reading with their children. But transitional readers continue to need support as they are exposed to more difficult and often longer texts. Parents may be frustrated because they do not know how to support their children as they become more fluent readers. Like teachers, they may even make dangerous assumptions about their children as readers. Because these often fluent readers appear to be decoding the texts, parents may assume that their children are well on their way to becoming independent readers. They may simply focus on oral reading skills, or they may think that reading with their children is no longer helpful, or they may assume that talking to their children about the books they are reading is no longer necessary.

When we consider ways to support our students' reading at home, we know that if we are not careful, we run the risk of being contrived—sending home activities or homework assignments that do not resemble the rich learning experiences they know from the classroom or, worse yet, that do not reflect the rituals of real readers and real-life experiences. Parents are often eager to be involved with their children's learning. But without a strong link to classroom experiences, their efforts may convey confusing messages.

Fostering Talk About Books with Family Members

Consider the notion of independence in reading. As adults, we can and do read independently. But we also talk to each other about our reading—the newspaper articles we read, Oprah's magazine, the novel we just finished, and the books we want to read next. We talk about the information we found on the Internet, and we discuss job-related texts that we are reading. We should invite transitional readers to have these same conversational experiences.

It is an easy step to bridge the conversation from school to home. If we begin early in the school year, these conversations can be ongoing and can develop over time. To help start these conversations, Franki asks her students to interview the members of their family about reading and to share their discoveries with the class. Here is an assignment that Franki gives to her students early in the year, knowing that it will begin to build connections between readers at home and in the classroom (a blank form is in the appendix):

Interview the people in your family about their reading. After your interview, write about each reader in your family. These questions may get your interview started:

- *What kinds of books do you like?*
- *What kinds of books are your least favorite?*
- *When do you read?*
- *Why do you read?*
- *Where do you like to read?*
- *How do you choose books?*
- *What is the title of the best book you have ever read?*

Use these questions to begin, but let each person tell you as much as he or she can about him- or herself as a reader.

Meggie learned the following about her family:

Katie
Favorite series—Amelia Bedelia, Berenstain Bears
Favorite book—*Welcome to Dead House*
Series she would like to read—Magic Tree House
Where she likes to read—in the rocking chair
Likes to be read to by Meggie
Facts
Sort of likes pictures
Likes fictional books

Mom
Favorite series—Gessell Institute of child development
Favorite book—*The Long Journey*
Where she likes to read—her bed

Dad
Favorite series—Chronicles of Amber
Favorite book—*Software*
Where he likes to read—computer

When students bring this kind of information back to school, they talk with their classmates about their discoveries. They continue to learn about what other readers do and make connections to their own reading.

Having discussions about learning to read is another way to invite family members into the conversations. Sharing books like *Thank You, Mr. Falker* by Patricia Polacco and *Wolf* by Becky Bloom, which both describe a reader's halting first attempts to decode text, can help them recall their first attempts to read.

Karen remembers the first book she learned to read. A friend or relative could not enter Karen's home without having to sit beside her and watch Karen demonstrate her newfound talents. She can remember pointing to the page and carefully saying the words. She can picture the book in her mind and recall the feel of it in her hands. She can remember with remarkable clarity the praise she received. And she can remember feeling part of this very special group of people who knew how to read.

Children of all ages love to talk about how they first learned to read. They remember the board books they read as toddlers and the stories they memorized because their parents read the books to them so many times. They remember with passion their favorite books and characters. All of those experiences bring shape and form to their lives as readers. When someone starts talking about these experiences, others can't help but recall stories from their own past. Children are fascinated with their own reading history and become very curious about the histories of others. Children have these stories, adults have similar stories, and the conversations connect us in powerful ways.

Years ago, Franki came across a book called *Books I Read When I Was Young*, edited by M. Jerry Weiss and Bernice E. Cullinan. In it, famous adults discussed the three books they remembered most from childhood. Although the book was old and Franki's students did not recognize many of the adults featured, they were interested in the fact that adults remembered books from their childhood.

Franki decided to give her students a home assignment that would extend their conversation about early reading to home. She purposefully gave this assignment over Thanksgiving vacation, knowing that many students would be with their extended families and would start conversations with relatives outside of their immediate family (a blank form is in the appendix):

Interview any adults in your family. You should interview as many as you can. Have them answer the following questions.

What are three books that you remember from your childhood that have lived with you—those books that are your all-time favorite childhood books? Why do they stand out for you?

Figure 10.2
Three favorite
books.

Figure 10.2 is an example of one boy's completed form.

Jackie, a third grader, shared a special story about her grandmother's favorite book. Jackie reported that reading *Heidi* by Johanna Spyri was one of her grandmother's favorite childhood memories. It had such an effect on her that she chose to name her first daughter, Jackie's aunt Heidi, after the character she had come to know and love. Jackie was thrilled to discover the history of her aunt's name.

Once family members are engaged in conversations about books, it is easy to help them move into good discussions about books their children are reading independently. Parents learn how important it is for children to talk about the books they are reading. Franki helps parents begin these conversations by providing them with a list of open-ended questions they can use (see the appendix):

Talking about books and reading is an important part of your child's learning. Below are some questions to help you get started in conversations about books and reading. It is important that your child read daily at home. The questions below will support the things we are doing in school.

- *Why did you choose this book?*
- *What do you think will happen next? Which part of the text makes you think that?*

- *Does this book remind you of anything that has ever happened to you?*
- *What have you been wondering as you read this?*
- *Does this book make you think of anything else you have read?*
- *Were there any words or phrases in your reading that you really liked? Which ones?*
- *What has been your favorite part of the book so far? Why?*
- *Was there a part of the book that surprised you? Why?*
- *Would you like to read another book by the same author? Why or why not?*
- *Can you think of someone else you know who would like this book? Why?*
- *Is this book too hard, too easy, or just right for you? How do you know?*
- *Were there any places in the book that had you confused? Did you reread to help you understand?*

Many of these questions are similar to the ones Franki uses to start discussions during read-aloud sessions, small-group instruction, and individual reading conferences. This list helps parents understand the nature of the conversations that take place in the classroom and have similar conversations with their children at home.

Helping with Book Selection

One of the more challenging aspects of reading at home for parents is choosing books that appropriately support their children as they move toward independence. Parents appreciate the insights we provide and welcome strategies for choosing books. The take-home page that follows represents some of the helpful information that we have sent to parents (a blank form is in the appendix).

Helping Your Child Choose Appropriate Books
Reading at home should be a positive experience for both you and your child. Providing time to read and having books available are keys to your child's reading success. Your child can learn a great deal about reading from hearing you read aloud as well as from reading to you. You can support your child by providing opportunities to read alone and with others.

To help your child choose a book that is just right, encourage him or her to

- *read the back of the book and ask, "Does it sound interesting?"*
- *look at the table of contents and ask, "Can I predict what may happen in the book?"*
- *talk to someone who has read the book and ask, "Would you recommend it?"*
- *flip through the book, looking at the print, pictures, and organization, and ask, "Does it look like a book that will keep my interest?"*
- *read the blurb about the author and ask, "Does it tell anything new about the book?"*
- *read the first page and ask, "Is it written in a way that is interesting to me?" and "Are there too many words that I don't understand?"*

Many readers choose books because

- *someone has recommended it;*
- *they have enjoyed other books by this author;*
- *it is about a topic of interest.*

Many teachers send home monthly book order forms (from book clubs such as Scholastic) to give parents the opportunity to build home libraries for their children inexpensively. Parents are eager to link the reading their children do at home with the reading they do at school. Franki sends parents her recommendations with each book order (a blank form is in the appendix). For example:

Title	Reason for Recommendation
Junie B. Jones . . . Pocket	Good series book
Weslandia	Picture book by Newbery author
Henry and Ribsy	Good author, Beverly Cleary
Candy Corn	Holiday poetry/favorite author
Time Warp Trio Pack	Great introduction to fantasy genre
Weather	Good nonfiction author
Baseball Big Shots II	Short nonfiction pieces about baseball

She mentions books that she knows are appropriate, recommends authors that the class has been reading, and calls attention to the series books she knows can provide the type of support her students need.

Families appreciate having help in making good book choices for their home libraries.

Providing Opportunities for Shared Reading at Home

Parents are comforted when their child returns home at the end of a school day and shares a snippet of classroom life. We try to design homework that both encourages children to talk about something they did at school and has them bring the discussions from home to school the next day. The note below came from an idea we got from Judy Davis, a teacher at the Manhattan New School. We often attach it to a poem, story, or news article that we have read and discussed at school. Students enjoy sharing the reactions of family members to something they have read in class (see the appendix).

> ### Homework Assignment: Sharing Reading at Home
> *We read this piece in school this week. For homework, share it with one or more members of your family. Discuss the piece. Share the things we talked about in our classroom. After your discussion, write down things about the discussion that you want to share with the class tomorrow.*

Hannah's response to "Papa's Parrot" from Cynthia Rylant's *Every Living Thing* reads as follows:

> *The part on page 23 that is highlighted is my favorite part of Papa's Parrot. My Dad's favorite part of Papa's Parrot was when Harry understood what the parrot was saying. (Highlighted on pages 24–25.) Dad: I like the descriptions of the types of candy. Me: A word that stood out in my head the first time I read it was* stroll. *Dad: I would like to have a better description of the store so I can picture it in my mind's eye. Dad: I like the story. Me: I like the story. Dad: I highly recommend the story.*

We have hosted "Grand Discussions" with our intermediate students. This idea came from an article in *Teaching K–8* titled "'Bookends': A Program for Pairs" by Diana Titus. Grand Discussions are opportunities for families to read together and then gather at school to talk to other families that have read the same book.

We choose a book and invite families to participate in the Grand Discussion. We send the following note home:

You and your child are invited to participate in another Grand Discussion! To prepare for the Grand Discussion, you and your child should read Sun and Spoon *by Kevin Henkes before January 13. On January 13, we will meet in our classroom to celebrate and discuss the book with other families who have read it.*

I would encourage you to read this book aloud with your child (possibly a chapter a night before bedtime). Please send back the form below if you are interested in participating on January 13. I will then send a copy of the book home for your family to use. All family members are welcome!

Student Name:
Our family would like to participate in the Grand Discussion group on January 13 at 7:00 P.M. Please send us a copy of the book!

The parent(s) and their child read the book together and note several sections that they want to discuss. On a scheduled evening, two or three families gather around a table in the classroom or library, talk about their responses to the book, and bring up the sections they had noted.

As mentioned earlier, parents of intermediate students often stop reading with their children. Grand Discussions give them a chance to sit beside their children and read with them again. Families find a variety of engaging ways to read the text. Sometimes the parent reads one page and the child reads the next. Sometimes they take turns reading chapters. Sometimes younger brothers and sisters sit with them to listen. When families come to school for the Grand Discussion, a student might arrive with one parent or two, and sometimes with siblings and even grandparents.

The discussions that center around these books become models of rich conversations about reading. As families come in or leave, we hear parents make connections with other adult readers. Soon they are sharing books with each other, usually passed along in a child's bookbag brought to school.

Through Grand Discussions, parents and children get to know each other as readers, families share reading preferences with other families, and a network of conversations extends beyond the event itself. Parents tell us how much they enjoyed reading with their child again. Not everyone participates in the Grand Discussions, but those families that do develop a deeper understanding of the importance of conversations that surround the books we read.

Letting Parents In On Classroom Discussions

Often we explain certain classroom strategies to parents so they can reinforce these strategies as they read with their children at home. For example, after several read-aloud mini-lessons in which Franki's class discussed strategies for reading and understanding books that take several days to read, she sent home information so parents could support the learning at home. Her aim was to share some strategies that would help move parents beyond merely supporting their children in decoding and provide them with specific ways to help their young readers construct meaning (see the appendix).

> *Here are some helpful strategies to encourage your child to use before he or she begins to read a book:*
>
> * *Use the cover, the back of the book, the author blurb, the table of contents, and other book features to predict what may happen in the book.*
> * *Make sure the book is an appropriate match for your reading strategies and interest. Read the first page or two and ask yourself if you are able to understand the story so far.*
>
> *Here are some strategies you can encourage your child to use while reading:*
> * *Read back. Each day when you begin to read, reread the page or two that you finished reading yesterday. This will help you remember what is happening in the story.*
> * *Go back and reread a sentence that you don't understand.*
> * *Stop and talk about parts in the story that make you angry, surprise you, remind you of something that has happened to you, or remind you of another book.*
> * *Listen for clues that tell you what may happen next.*
> * *Stop and think for a minute about what you have just read.*

When we help parents support their children at home, they share observations about their child's reading with us. We hear stories of our students reading to their younger siblings. Often parents overhear our students using some of the same language we use at school to encourage them to stop to talk, go back in the text, and preview.

Throughout the year, Franki asks parents to write to her about their child's growth in reading, using letters like the one that follows.

Dear Parents,

We have been working to improve reading skills this fall. I would love to know of any changes that you have noticed in your child's reading this year so far. (How does he or she choose books? Does he or she talk about books differently? Is there more excitement about reading? What changes do you see in the understanding of books read?) Any feedback you can give will help me to plan for the remainder of the year. Please use the space below to tell me of any changes you've noticed.

Thank you!

The following response, from Andy's mother, helped Franki see that many of her classroom conversations were making it home:

I have definitely seen an increased interest in Andy's desire to read this year. He often stays up "too late" at night because he is engrossed in a book. Often when you are reading a book to the class, he begs me to get it from the library so we can find out what happens before you finish it in class.

Your book recommendations and author/series exposure at school have definitely had an impact as well. He now has favorite authors and series.

Your lessons have had an impact on me as well. I often spend a few minutes reading the jacket cover, author bio, and chapter titles to my children before rushing on to the first page of the book.

Clearly, Andy's mother is reinforcing the strategies that Franki is supporting at school. And she sounds excited about the new ways she has found to support her child's reading.

Hannah's mother emailed her response. Although she was responding to different aspects of her child's reading, Franki could clearly see the connection between school and home conversations:

It's funny that you should ask about reading—just last week I was thinking to myself what a change I've seen in Hannah's reading since the beginning of the year. Last Sunday, I took the three kids to Little Professor to pick out a book for their Valentine's Day gift. Hannah of course was able to find two for the price of one of the boys' books! When we got home, she was in such a quandary because there were SO MANY books that she wanted to read, and she just couldn't wait to get to all of them! This was good to hear because in the past, she has had a hard time deciding on ANY book to read. She has always enjoyed read-ing, but has never had a line-up!

Hannah has learned the value of having a stack of "next read" books, and her mother has enthusiastically encouraged her advance planning.

Lifetime Conversations About Books

Sometimes we realize that the conversations that began in our reading workshops and extended to the homes of our students last for years. Franki recently received an email from a parent of a student who had moved to another city. Kristin had been a student in Franki's third-grade classroom a few years ago. The following excerpt from Kristin's mother's message validates the conversations Franki had in her classroom, the links she made to conversations at home, and the critical involvement of a caring parent:

*Kristin's reading is still improving. She discovered a book that I had purchased for her years ago (*The Happy Hollisters*) and fell in love with it. I had read the books when I was her age . . . we went to an antique store and found other Hollister books . . . walked out of there with eight more of the Hollister books for $5 each. We were thrilled!*

And we were thrilled to hear about Kristin's bargain shopping as well as the fact that conversations that had started in the third grade were con-tinuing years later!

Parents are critical partners in helping children to read. When teach-ers help parents understand the kind of supports transitional readers need, they will help promote the same kind of thinking we do at school.

When we create opportunities for literary talk at home, we not only help our students through the transitional stage of reading, but also hope to have them begin to develop talk about books that will last a lifetime. We want them to become part of a reading community that reaches well beyond the classroom walls.

Epilogue

I have come to believe that all of us, as we write, or read, or draw . . .

As we hold the pages of a book tilted so the little one can see . . .

As we choose and wrap a book as a gift for a child . . .

As we provide privacy and a comfortable chair, or a favorite book on a table beside a guest room bed . . .

As we sift through memories, sort them out, and see their meaning . . .

And as we look back, and say to a child, "I remember—"

We do, in fact, hold the knowledge of the centuries.

And we all become Givers.

LOIS LOWRY, LOOKING BACK

We come to the end of this book with a sense of urgency to continue the conversation about the needs of early and transitional readers. We hope this book will be a starting point for further discussions about transitional readers and what teachers, parents, and learning communities can do to foster their independence.

In a time of test scores and accountability, teachers are being forced to spend precious classroom time in ways that do not necessarily foster lifelong reading. We worry that in the name of accountability we are increasingly pressed to find time for the things we know our transitional readers need.

Classrooms have changed to ensure that all children learn to read in the primary grades. However, it is just as important that thoughtful reading instruction continue throughout childhood. The best K–2 reading program does not mean that reading instruction is no longer necessary as students progress through the grades. We hope that teachers, parents, administrators, and politicians begin to realize that students continue to need high-quality reading instruction beyond the second grade.

Children beyond the second grade aren't just "reading to learn." Although reading to learn is important, children at this age will continue to need new skills and strategies as text becomes more sophisticated. In fact, we would argue that children at all levels of reading are learning to read and reading to learn.

Our time with children is limited, and we need to think hard about the ways we spend it with them. If we spend this time in ways we know will benefit them over a lifetime, we can be assured that our classrooms will be filled with children who are well on their way to independence—children who sit in their favorite spots around the room; children so engaged in reading that they do not seem to notice that the world is going on around them. With thoughtful instruction, we know that children will come to consider reading as something meaningful and purposeful.

Appendix

Small-Group Processing Sheet

Date:

Name   **Most Critical Need**

Temporary Reading Groups

Group Members **Reason** **Text/Book**

Before You Read

What do you know/predict from looking at the cover?

What do you know after reading the blurb about the book?

What do you know after looking at the table of contents?

What do you know after reading the first page?

_____'s Reading Log

Author	Title of Book	Date Began/ Date Finished	Pages

Looking at My Reading

Look at your Reading Log. Then answer the following questions about your reading.

What types of books have you read?

Have you tried any books that were too hard? Which ones?

Were most of the books on your reading list too hard, too easy, or just right?

How do you know when a book is just right for you?

How do you decide which books to read?

How have you changed in the way you choose books?

Is there a book that you know of that you'd like to read soon?

What is one of your favorite books on your reading log? Why?

Reading Log Tally

How many books have you read that are

	Tally	Total
realistic fiction?		
fantasy?		
science fiction?		
mystery?		
biography?		
nonfiction?		
adventure?		
historical fiction?		
poetry?		

Looking over your reading log, what do you notice about the genres you have read so far this year?

What else do you notice about your reading? (length of books, authors, completing a book, etc.)

Using your log and this survey, what is a goal you have for your reading?

Looking at Our Reading

I read with/interviewed _____ about his/her reading. We found out that we are the same in some ways and different in some ways. Here is what we learned.

We are the same because: **We are different because:**

Family Homework

Due Date:

Interview the people in your family about their reading. After your interview, write about each reader in your family. These questions may get your interview started:

- **What kinds of books do you like?**

- **What kinds of books are your least favorite?**

- **When do you read?**

- **Why do you read?**

- **Where do you like to read?**

- **How do you choose books?**

- **What is the title of the best book you have ever read?**

Use these questions to begin, but let each person tell you as much as he or she can about him- or herself as a reader.

Beyond Leveled Books: Supporting Early and Transitional Readers in Grades K–5. 2nd ed. Karen Szymusiak, Franki Sibberson, and Lisa Koch. Copyright © 2008. Stenhouse Publishers.

Family Homework

"Books I Read When I Was Young"

Interview any adults in your family. You should interview as many as you can. Have them answer the following questions.

What are three books that you remember from your childhood that have lived with you—those books that are your all-time favorite childhood books? Why do they stand out for you?

Reading at Home

Talking about books and reading is an important part of your child's learning. Below are some questions to help you get started in conversations about books and reading. It is important that your child read daily at home. The questions below will support the things we are doing in school.

- **Why did you choose this book?**

- **What do you think will happen next? Which part of the text makes you think that?**

- **Does this book remind you of anything that has ever happened to you?**

- **What have you been wondering as you read this?**

- **Does this book make you think of anything else you have read?**

- **Were there any words or phrases in your reading that you really liked? Which ones?**

- **What has been your favorite part of the book so far? Why?**

- **Was there a part of the book that surprised you? Why?**

- **Would you like to read another book by this same author? Why or why not?**

- **Can you think of someone else you know who would like this book? Why?**

- **Is this book too hard, too easy, or just right for you? How do you know?**

- **Were there any places in the book that had you confused? Did you reread to help you understand?**

Beyond Leveled Books: Supporting Early and Transitional Readers in Grades K–5, 2nd ed. Karen Szymusiak, Franki Sibberson, and Lisa Koch. Copyright © 2008. Stenhouse Publishers.

Helping Your Child Choose Appropriate Books

Reading at home should be a positive experience for both you and your child. Providing time to read and having books available are keys to your child's reading success. Your child can learn a great deal about reading from hearing you read aloud as well as from reading to you. You can support your child by providing opportunities to read alone and with others.

To help your child choose a book that is just right, encourage him or her to

- read the back of the book and ask, "Does it sound interesting?"

- look at the table of contents and ask, "Can I predict what may happen in the book?"

- talk to someone who has read the book and ask, "Would you recommend it?"

- flip through the book, looking at the print, pictures, and organization, and ask, "Does it look like a book that will keep my interest?"

- read the blurb about the author and ask, "Does it tell anything new about the book?"

- read the first page and ask, "Is it written in a way that is interesting to me?" and "Are there too many words that I don't understand?"

Many readers choose books because

- someone has recommended it;

- they have enjoyed other books by this author;

- it is about a topic of interest.

Books to Build a Home Library

Title   **Reason for Recommendation**

Homework Assignment: Sharing Reading at Home

We read this piece in school this week. For homework, share it with one or more members of your family. Discuss the piece. Share the things we talked about in our classroom. After your discussion, write down things about the discussion that you want to share with the class tomorrow.

Supporting Reading at Home

Here are some helpful strategies to encourage your child to use before he or she begins to read a book:

- Use the cover, the back of the book, the author blurb, the table of contents, and other book features to predict what may happen in the book.

- Make sure the book is an appropriate match for your reading strategies and interest. Read the first page or two and ask yourself if you are able to understand the story so far.

Here are some strategies you can encourage your child to use while reading:

- Read back. Each day when you begin to read, reread the page or two that you finished reading yesterday. This will help you remember what is happening in the story.

- Go back and reread a sentence that you don't understand.

- Stop and talk about parts in the story that make you angry, surprise you, remind you of something that has happened to you, or remind you of another book.

- Listen for clues that tell you what may happen next.

- Stop and think for a minute about what you have just read.

Beyond Leveled Books: Supporting Early and Transitional Readers in Grades K–5, 2nd ed. Karen Szymusiak, Franki Sibberson, and Lisa Koch.
Copyright © 2008. Stenhouse Publishers.

Bibliography

Children's Books

Ada, Alma Flor. 1994. *Dear Peter Rabbit*. New York: Atheneum.

———. 1998. *Yours Truly, Goldilocks*. New York: Atheneum.

Adler, David A. 1997. *Cam Jansen and the Mystery of the Babe Ruth Baseball*. New York: Dell.

Ahlberg, Allan. 2007. *Previously*. Cambridge, MA: Candlewick.

Applegate, Katherine. 2007. *Home of the Brave*. New York: Feiwel & Friends.

Aston, Diana Hutts. 2007. *A Seed Is Sleepy*. San Francisco: Chronicle Books.

Auch, Mary Jane, and Herm Auch. 2003. *Souperchicken*. New York: Holiday House.

Avi. 1995. *Poppy*. New York: Avon.

Aylesworth, Jim. 1988. *The Gingerbread Man*. New York: Scholastic.

Banks, Lynne Reid. 1995. *Indian in the Cupboard*. New York: Avon Books.

Bardoe, Cheryl. 2006. *Gregor Mendel: The Friar Who Grew Peas*. New York: Abrams Books for Young Readers.

Barton, Bryon. 1993. *The Little Red Hen*. New York: HarperCollins.

———. 2001. *My Car*. New York: Greenwillow Books.

Beaumont, Karen. 2006. *Move Over, Rover!* Orlando, FL: Harcourt.

Benton, Jim. 2003. *Lunch Walks Among Us*. (Franny K. Stein, Mad Scientist series). New York: Simon & Schuster.

Bingham, Caroline. 2007. *Buzz*. New York: Dorling Kindersley.

Bloom, Becky. 1999. *Wolf*. New York: Orchard Books.

Blume, Judy. 1972. *Tales of a Fourth Grade Nothing.* New York: Dutton.

———. 1985. *The Pain and the Great One.* New York: Dell.

Bogart, Jo Ellen. 1999. *Jeremiah Learns to Read.* New York: Orchard Books.

Borden, Louise. 1998. *The Little Ships.* New York: Margaret K. McElderry Books.

———. 1999. *Good Luck, Mrs. K.!* New York: Margaret K. McElderry Books.

———. 2000. *Sleds on Boston Common: A Story from the American Revolution.* New York: Margaret K. McElderry Books.

———. 2001. *The Day Eddie Met the Author.* New York: Margaret K. McElderry Books.

———. 2005. *The Journey That Saved Curious George.* Boston: Houghton Mifflin.

Bottner, Barbara. 2002. *Charlene Loves to Make Noise.* Philadelphia: Running Press.

Bradby, Marie. 1995. *More Than Anything Else.* New York: Orchard Books.

Brett, Jan. 1992. *Trouble with Trolls.* New York: Putnam.

———. 1999. *Gingerbread Baby.* New York: Putnam.

Brinckloe, Julie. 1985. *Fireflies!* New York: Aladdin.

Brisson, Pat. 1998. *The Summer My Father Was Ten.* Honesdale, PA: Boyds Mills.

Brown, Lisa. 2006. *How to Be.* New York: HarperCollins.

Bryant, Jen. 2004. *The Trial.* New York: Alfred A. Knopf.

Buehner, Caralyn. 2007. *Goldilocks and the Three Bears.* New York: Dial Books for Young Readers.

Bunting, Eve. 1989. *The Wednesday Surprise.* New York: Clarion Books.

———. 2007. *Hurry! Hurry!* Orlando, FL: Harcourt.

Burleigh, Robert. 1998. *Home Run: The Story of Babe Ruth.* San Diego: Silver Whistle.

Campbell, Rod. 1982. *Dear Zoo.* New York: Four Winds.

Carle, Eric. 1981. *The Very Hungry Caterpillar.* New York: Philomel Books.

Carroll, Lewis. 2000. *Alice's Adventures in Wonderland.* New York: Aladdin.

Child, Lauren. 2000. *I Will Never Not Ever Eat a Tomato.* Cambridge, MA: Candlewick.

———. 2001. *I Am Not Sleepy and I Will Not Go to Bed.* Cambridge, MA: Candlewick.

———. 2003. *I Am Too Absolutely Small for School.* Cambridge, MA: Candlewick.

———. 2005a. *But Excuse Me That Is My Book.* New York: Dial Books for Young Readers.

———. 2005b. *Can You Maybe Turn the Light On?* New York: Dial Books for Young Readers.

———. 2005c. *I Absolutely Must Do Coloring Now or Painting or Drawing.* New York: Dial Books for Young Readers.

———. 2006a. *I've Won, No I've Won, No I've Won.* New York: Grosset & Dunlap.

———. 2006b. *My Wobbly Tooth Must Not Ever Never Fall Out.* New York: Grosset & Dunlap.

———. 2006c. *The Princess and the Pea.* New York: Hyperion Books for Children.

———. 2006d. *Snow Is My Favorite and My Best.* New York: Dial Books for Young Readers.

———. 2006e. *We Honestly Can Look After Your Dog.* New York: Grosset & Dunlap.

———. 2006f. *Whoops! But It Wasn't Me.* New York: Grosset & Dunlap.

———. 2007a. *Boo! Made You Jump.* New York: Grosset & Dunlap.

———. 2007b. *Say Cheese!* New York: Dial Books for Young Readers.

———. 2007c. *I'm Really Ever So Not Well.* New York: Grosset & Dunlap.

———. 2007d. *Sizzles Is Completely Not Here.* New York: Grosset & Dunlap.

———. 2007e. *This Is Actually My Party.* New York: Grosset & Dunlap.

———. 2007f. *You Can Be My Friend.* New York: Grosset & Dunlap.

———. 2008a. *But I Am an Alligator.* New York: Grosset & Dunlap.

———. 2008b. *I Can Do Anything That's Everything All on My Own.* New York: Grosset & Dunlap.

Chodos-Irvine, Margaret. 2003. *Ella Sarah Gets Dressed.* San Diego: Harcourt.

———. 2006. *Best Best Friends.* Orlando, FL: Harcourt.

Christopher, Matt. 1978. *Soccer Halfback.* Boston: Little, Brown.

Cleary, Beverly. 1954. *Henry and Ribsy.* New York: Avon Books.

———. 1965. *The Mouse and the Motorcycle.* New York: Avon Books.

———. 1994. *Dear Mr. Henshaw.* New York: Avon Books.

Coles, Robert. 1995. *The Story of Ruby Bridges.* New York: Scholastic.

Conly, Jane Leslie. 1986. *Racso and the Rats of NIMH.* New York: Harper & Row.

Cook, Sally, and James Charlton. 2007. *Hey Batta Batta Swing! The Wild Old Days of Baseball.* New York: Margaret K. McElderry Books.

Cooney, Barbara. 1996. *Eleanor.* New York: Penguin.

Corey, Shana. 2000. *You Forgot Your Skirt, Amelia Bloomer.* New York: Scholastic.

Cowley, Joy. 1988. *Dan, the Flying Man.* DeSoto, TX: Wright Group/McGraw Hill.

———. 1988. *Mrs. Wishy-Washy.* DeSoto, TX: Wright Group/McGraw Hill.

Creech, Sharon. 2001. *Love That Dog.* New York: HarperCollins.

———. 2004. *Heartbeat.* New York: HarperCollins.

Cronin, Doreen. 2000a. *Click, Clack, Moo: Cows That Type.* New York: Simon & Schuster Books for Young Readers.

———. 2000b. *Giggle, Giggle, Quack.* New York: Simon & Schuster Books for Young Readers.

———. 2004. *Duck for President.* New York: Simon & Schuster Books for Young Readers.

———. 2006. *Dooby Dooby Moo.* New York: Atheneum Books for Young Readers.

———. 2007. *Bounce.* New York: Atheneum Books for Young Readers.

Crutcher, Chris. 1993. *Staying Fat for Sarah Byrnes.* New York: Greenwillow Books.

Dale, Penny. 2006. *Ten in the Bed*. Cambridge, MA: Candlewick.

Deedy, Carmen Agra. 1991. *Agatha's Feather Bed*. Atlanta: Peachtree.

dePaola, Tomie. 1999. *26 Fairmount Avenue*. New York: Putnam.

Dewdney, Anna. 2005. *Llama, Llama Red Pajama*. New York: Viking.

———. 2007. *Llama, Llama Mad at Mama*. New York: Viking.

DiCamillo, Kate. 2003. *The Tale of Despereaux: Being the Story of a Mouse, a Princess, Some Soup, and a Spool of Thread*. Cambridge, MA: Candlewick.

———. 2005. *Mercy Watson to the Rescue*. Cambridge, MA: Candlewick.

Dodd, Emma. 2001. *Dog's Colorful Day: A Messy Story About Colors and Counting*. New York: Dutton Children's Books.

Dooling, Michael. 2004. *Young Thomas Edison*. New York: Holiday House.

Doyle, Roddy. 2000. *The Giggler Treatment*. New York: Arthur A. Levine Books.

Dubowski, Cathy East. 1990. *The Story of Squanto: First Friend to the Pilgrims*. New York: Dell.

Dunrea, Olivier. 2002. *Gossie and Gertie*. Boston: Houghton Mifflin.

———. 2006. *Hanne's Quest*. New York: Philomel Books.

Elder, Joshua. 2006. *Mail Order Ninja*. Los Angeles: Tokyopop.

Ernst, Lisa Campbell. 2000. *Goldilocks Returns*. New York: Simon & Schuster.

Falconer, Ian. 2000. *Olivia*. New York: Atheneum Books for Young Readers.

———. 2001. *Olivia Saves the Circus*. New York: Atheneum Books for Young Readers.

———. 2002a. *Olivia's Opposites*. New York: Atheneum Books for Young Readers.

———. 2002b. *Olivia Counts*. New York: Atheneum Books for Young Readers.

———. 2003. *Olivia and the Missing Toy*. New York: Atheneum Books for Young Readers.

———. 2006. *Olivia Forms a Band*. New York: Atheneum Books for Young Readers.

———. 2007. *Olivia Helps with Christmas*. New York: Atheneum Books for Young Readers.

Faller, Regis. 2006. *The Adventures of Polo*. New Milford, CT: Roaring Brook Press.

Feiffer, Jules. 1999. *Bark, George*. New York: HarperCollins.

Fitzgerald, Ella. 2003. *A Tisket, A Tasket*. New York: Philomel Books.

Fleischman, Paul. 1999. *Weslandia*. Cambridge, MA: Candlewick.

Fleming, Denise. 2006. *The Cow Who Clucked*. New York: Henry Holt.

Fletcher, Ralph. 1995. *Fig Pudding*. New York: Bantam Doubleday Dell.

———. 1997. *Twilight Comes Twice*. New York: Clarion Books.

———. 1998. *Flying Solo*. New York: Clarion Books.

Foley, Greg. 2007. *Thank You Bear*. New York: Viking.

Forbes, Esther. 1976. *Johnny Tremain*. New York: Buccaneer.

Fox, Mem. 1984. *Wilfrid Gordon McDonald Partridge*. Brooklyn, NY: Kane/Miller.

———. 1993. *Time for Bed*. San Diego: Harcourt Brace Jovanovich.

———. 2004. *Where Is the Green Sheep?* New York: Harcourt.

Frazier, Craig. 2005a. *Stanley Mows the Lawn*. San Francisco: Chronicle Books.

————. 2005b. *Stanley Goes for a Drive*. San Francisco: Chronicle Books.

————. 2006. *Stanley Goes Fishing*. San Francisco: Chronicle Books.

Frost, Helen. 2004. *Spinning Through the Universe*. New York: Farrar, Straus and Giroux.

Gannett, Ruth Stiles. 1948. *My Father's Dragon*. New York: Yearling.

Garcia, Emma. 2007. *Tip Tip Dig Dig*. London: Boxer.

Gardiner, John Reynolds. 1980. *Stone Fox*. New York: HarperCollins.

George, Jean Craighead. 1988. *My Side of the Mountain*. New York: Dutton.

George, Kristine O'Connell. 1999. *Little Dog Poems*. New York: Clarion Books.

Giblin, James Cross. 2000. *The Amazing Life of Benjamin Franklin*. New York: Scholastic.

Gownley, Jim. 2003. *Amelia Rules!* New York: Simon & Schuster.

Graves, Donald. 1996. *Baseball, Snakes, and Summer Squash*. Honesdale, PA; Wordsong/Boyds Mills.

Gravett, Emily. 2007. *Orange Pear Apple Bear*. New York: Simon & Schuster.

Guarino, Deborah. 1989. *Is Your Mama a Llama?* New York: Scholastic.

Haddix, Margaret Peterson. 2007. *Dexter the Tough*. New York: Simon & Schuster.

Halls, Kelly Milner. 2004. *Albino Animals*. Plain City, OH: Darby Creek.

Harris, Robie H. 2007. *Maybe a Bear Ate It!* New York: Orchard Books.

Harrison, Kenny. 2002. *How I Became the Champion of the Universe*. Berkeley, CA: Tricycle.

Hatkoff, Isabella, Craig Hatcoff, and Dr. Paula Kahumbu. 2006. *Owen and Mzee: The True Story of a Remarkable Friendship*. New York: Scholastic.

Henkes, Kevin. 1997. *Sun and Spoon*. New York: Greenwillow Books.

————. 2004. *Kitten's First Full Moon*. New York: Greenwillow Books.

————. 2006. *Lilly's Big Day*. New York: Greenwillow Books.

————. 2007. *A Good Day*. New York: Greenwillow Books.

Hester, Nigel. 1991. *The Living House*. New York: F. Watts.

Himmelman, John. 2006. *Chickens to the Rescue*. New York: Holt.

Holm, Jennifer, and Matthew Holm. 2005. *Babymouse: Our Hero*. New York: Random House.

————. 2006. *Babymouse: Heartbreaker*. New York: Random House.

Hopkinson, Deborah. 1999. *Maria's Comet*. New York: Atheneum.

Horacek, Peter. 2007. *Butterfly, Butterfly: A Book of Colors*. Cambridge, MA: Candlewick.

Hornsey, Chris. 2007. *Why Do I Have to Eat Off the Floor?* New York: Walker & Company.

Howe, James. 1991. *Pinky and Rex and the Spelling Bee*. New York: Atheneum.

————. 1997. *Pinky and Rex and the New Neighbors*. New York: Atheneum.

Jackson, Donna M. 2003. *Hero Dogs: Courageous Canines in Action*. Boston: Little, Brown.

Jacques, Brian. 1998. *Mossflower*. New York: Philomel Books.

Jeffers, Oliver. 2006. *The Incredible Book-Eating Boy*. New York: Philomel Books.

Jenkins, Emily. 2007. *Love You When You Whine*. New York: Farrar, Straus and Giroux.

Jenkins, Steve. 2007a. *Dogs and Cats*. Boston: Houghton Mifflin.

———. 2007b. *Living Color*. Boston: Houghton Mifflin.

Keats, Ezra Jack. 1999. *Over in the Meadow*. New York: Puffin.

Kindersley, Barnabas, and Anabel Kindersley. 1995. *Children Just Like Me*. London: Dorling Kindersley.

Kipling, Rudyard. 1997. *Rikki Tikki Tavi*. New York: Morrow Junior Books.

Kirk, Daniel. 2001. *Bus Stop, Bus Go!* New York: Putnam.

Klise, Kate. 2001. *Trial by Journal*. New York: HarperCollins.

Knudsen, Michelle. 2006. *The Library Lion*. Cambridge, MA: Candlewick.

Konigsburg, E. L. 1996. *A View from Saturday*. New York: Atheneum.

Laminack, Lester. 1998. *The Sunsets of Miss Olivia Wiggins*. Atlanta: Peachtree.

———. 2006. *Jake's 100th Day of School*. Atlanta: Peachtree.

Langstaff, John. 1991. *Oh, A-Hunting We Will Go*. New York: Aladdin.

L'Engle, Madeline. 1963. *A Wrinkle in Time*. New York: Farrar, Straus and Giroux.

Lester, Helen. 1988a. *Tacky the Penguin*. Boston: Houghton Mifflin.

———. 1988b. *Tacky in Trouble*. Boston: Houghton Mifflin.

———. 1988c. *Tacky and the Winter Games*. Boston: Houghton Mifflin.

———. 1994. *Three Cheers for Tacky*. Boston: Houghton Mifflin.

———. 2000. *Tacky and the Emperor*. Boston: Houghton Mifflin.

———. 2002. *Tackylocks and the Three Bears*. Boston: Houghton Mifflin.

Lewis, C. S. 1950. *The Lion, the Witch, and the Wardrobe*. New York: Macmillan.

Livingston, Myra Cohn. 2007. *Calendar*. New York: Holiday House.

Long, Loren, and Phil Bildner. 2007. *Game One*. New York: Simon & Schuster.

Lopshire, Robert. 1960. *Put Me in the Zoo*. New York: Beginner Books.

Lowry, Lois. 1981. *Anastasia Again*. Boston: Houghton Mifflin.

———. 1993. *The Giver*. Boston: Houghton Mifflin.

———. 1998. *Looking Back: A Book of Memories*. Boston: Houghton Mifflin.

Lum, Kate. 1998. *What! Cried Granny: An Almost Bedtime Story*. New York: Putnam.

Lyon, George Ella. 1999. *Book*. New York: DK Ink.

MacLachlan, Patricia. 1985. *Sarah, Plain and Tall*. New York: HarperCollins.

———. 1994. *All the Places to Love*. New York: HarperCollins.

Marshall, Rita. 1992. *I Hate to Read*. Mankato, WI: Creative Education.

Martin, Ann M. 2001. *Belle Teal*. New York: Scholastic.

Martin, Bill. 1992. *Brown Bear, Brown Bear, What Do You See?* New York: Holt.

Martin, Bill, and John Archambault. 1989. *Chicka Chicka Boom Boom*. New York: Simon & Schuster.

Marx, Trish. 2000. *One Boy from Kosovo*. New York: HarperCollins.

Masurel, Claire. 2001. *A Cat and a Dog*. New York: North-South Books.

Matthews, Tina. 2007. *Out of the Egg*. Boston: Houghton Mifflin.

McGill, Alice. 1999. *Molly Bannaky*. Boston: Houghton Mifflin.

McLerran, Alice. 1991. *Roxaboxen*. New York: Lothrop, Lee & Shepard.

Menchin, Scott. 2007. *Taking a Bath with the Dog and Other Things That Make Me Happy*. Cambridge, MA: Candlewick.

Mills, Claudia. 1997. *Gus and Grandpa*. New York: Farrar, Straus and Giroux.

Miranda, Anne. 1997. *To Market, To Market*. San Diego: Harcourt Brace.

Mora, Pat. 1987. *Tomas and the Library Lady*. New York: Knopf.

Murphy, Mary. 2000. *Here Comes Spring and Summer and Autumn and Winter*. New York: Dorling Kindersley.

Naylor, Phyllis Reynolds. 1991. *Shiloh*. New York: Dell.

Nesbit, E. 2006. *Jack and the Beanstalk*. Cambridge, MA: Candlewick.

Neubecker, Robert. 2004. *Wow! City!* New York: Hyperion.

———. 2006. *Wow! America!* New York: Hyperion.

———. 2007. *Wow! School!* New York: Hyperion.

Newman, Jeff. 2006. *Hippo! No, Rhino*. New York: Little, Brown.

Norton, Mary. 1953. *The Borrowers*. New York: Harcourt, Brace & World.

O'Brien, Robert C. 1971. *Mrs. Frisby and the Rats of NIMH*. New York: Atheneum.

O'Connor, Jane. 2007. *Ready, Set, Skip!* New York: Viking.

Osborne, Mary Pope. 1992. *Dinosaurs Before Dark*. New York: Random House.

Parish, Peggy. 1999. *Amelia Bedelia*. New York: HarperFestival.

Park, Barbara. 1982. *Operation: Dump the Chump*. New York: Knopf.

———. 1995. *Mick Harte Was Here*. New York: Knopf.

———. 2000. *Junie B. Jones Has a Peep in Her Pocket*. New York: Random House.

———. 2006. *Junie B., First Grader: Aloha Ha Ha*. New York: Random House.

Paterson, Katherine. 1977. *Bridge to Terabithia*. New York: T. Y. Crowell.

———. 1999. "Back from IBBY." *The Horn Book Magazine*. Jan/Feb.

Paul, Ann Whitford. 1999. *All by Herself*. San Diego: Browndeer Press/ Harcourt Brace.

Pawagi, Manjusha. 1999. *The Girl Who Hated Books*. Hillsboro, OR: Beyond Words.

Peek, Merle. 1985. *Mary Wore Her Red Dress*. New York: Clarion Books.

Pham, Leuyen. 2005. *Big Sister, Little Sister*. New York: Hyperion Books for Children.

Pinto, Sara. 2008. *Apples and Oranges: Going Bananas with Pairs*. New York: Bloomsbury Children's Books.

Polacco, Patricia. 1996. *Aunt Chip and the Great Triple Creek Dam Affair*. New York: Philomel Books.

———. 1998a. *Chicken Sunday*. New York: Philomel Books.

———. 1998b. *Thank You, Mr. Falker*. New York: Philomel Books.

Portis, Antoinette. 2007. *Not a Box*. New York: HarperCollins.

Preller, James. 1998. *A Jigsaw Jones Mystery: The Case of the Christmas Snowman*. New York: Scholastic.

Pullman, Philip. 2005. *Aladdin and the Enchanted Lamp*. New York: Arthur A. Levine Books.

Rankin, Laura. 2007. *Ruthie and the (Not So) Teeny Tiny Lie*. New York: Bloomsbury.

Rappaport, Doreen, and Lyndall Callan. 2000. *Dirt on Their Skirts*. New York: Dial.

Rawls, Wilson. 1984. *Where the Red Fern Grows.* New York: Bantam.

Rockwell, Thomas. 1973. *How to Eat Fried Worms.* New York: Dell.

Rosen, Michael. 1993. *Poems for the Very Young.* Boston: Houghton Mifflin.

Rosenthal, Amy Krouse. 2007. *The OK Book.* New York: HarperCollins.

Ross, Pat. 1999. *Meet M and M.* New York: Puffin.

Ryan, Pam Nunoz. 2002. *When Marian Sang.* New York: Scholastic.

Rylant, Cynthia. 1985. *The Relatives Came.* New York: Bradbury.

———. 1987. *Henry and Mudge: The First Book.* New York: Bradbury.

———. 1988. *Every Living Thing.* New York: Aladdin.

———. 1992. *Henry and Mudge and the Long Weekend.* New York: Bradbury.

———. 1997a. *Mr. Putter and Tabby Fly the Plane.* San Diego: Harcourt Brace.

———. 1997b. *Poppleton and Friends.* New York: Blue Sky.

———. 1998. *The Van Gogh Cafe.* New York: Scholastic.

———. 2007. *Walt Disney's Cinderella.* New York: Disney.

Sachar, Louis. 1998. *Holes.* New York: Farrar, Straus and Giroux.

Sakai, Komako. 2006. *Emily's Balloon.* San Francisco: Chronicle Books.

Schade, Susan. 2006. *Travels of Thelonious: The Fog Mound.* New York: Simon & Schuster.

Schwartz, David M. 2007. *Where in the Wild.* Berkeley, CA: Tricycle.

Scieszka, Jon. 1999. *The True Story of the Three Little Pigs!* New York: Viking.

Seeger, Laura Vaccaro. 2004. *Lemons Are Not Red.* New Milford, CT: Roaring Brook.

———. 2007. *First the Egg.* New Milford, CT: Roaring Brook.

Selden, George. 1960. *The Cricket in Times Square.* New York: Ariel Books.

Selznick, Brian. 2007. *The Invention of Hugo Cabret.* New York: Scholastic.

Sendak, Maurice. 1963. *Where the Wild Things Are.* New York: HarperCollins.

Senisi, Ellen B. 1999. *Reading Grows.* Morton Grove, IL: Albert Whitman.

Shannon, David. 1998. *No, David!* New York: Blue Sky.

———. 1999. *David Goes to School.* New York: Blue Sky.

———. 2002. *David Gets in Trouble.* New York: Blue Sky.

Sharmat, Marjorie Weinman. 1972. *Nate the Great.* New York: Dell.

Shea, Bob. 2007. *New Socks.* New York: Little Brown.

Sherry, Kevin. 2007. *I'm the Biggest Thing in the Ocean.* New York: Dial Books.

Simon, Seymour. 1993. *Weather.* New York: Morrow Junior Books.

Singer, Marilyn. 2006. *What Stinks?* Plain City, OH: Darby Creek.

Sinnott, Susan. 1999. *Welcome to Kirsten's World, 1854.* Middleton, WI: Pleasant Company.

Siy, Alexandra. 2007. *Sneeze!* Watertown, MA: Charlesbridge.

Slavin, Bill. 2005. *Transformed: How Everyday Things Are Made.* Tonawanda, NY: Kids Can Press.

Slobodkina, Esphyr. 1968. *Caps for Sale.* New York: Scholastic.

Smee, Nicola. 2006. *Clip-Clop!* New York: Boxer Books.

Smith, Doris Buchanan. 1973. *A Taste of Blackberries.* New York: Crowell.

Smith, Lane. 2006. *John, Paul, George & Ben.* New York: Hyperion.

Spinelli, Eileen. 2001. *In My New Yellow Shirt.* New York: Holt.

———. 2007. *Where I Live.* New York: Dial Books for Young Readers.

Spinelli, Jerry. 2007. *Eggs*. New York: Little, Brown.

Spyri, Johanna. 1995. *Heidi*. New York: Puffin.

Stewart, David. 2005. *You Wouldn't Want to Explore with Sir Francis Drake: A Pirate You'd Rather Not Know*. New York: Franklin Watts.

Stewart, Sarah. 1995. *The Library*. New York: Farrar, Straus and Giroux.

———. 1997. *The Gardener*. New York: Farrar, Straus and Giroux.

Sturges, Philemon. 1999. *The Little Red Hen (Makes a Pizza)*. New York: Dutton Children's.

———. 2007. *How Do You Make a Baby Smile?* New York: HarperCollins.

Tafuri, Nancy. 2007. *Whose Chick Are You?* New York: HarperCollins.

Tankard, Jeremy. 2007. *Grumpy Bird*. New York: Scholastic.

Tesar, Jenny E. and Bruce Glassman. 1998. *Kidbits*. Farmington Hills, MI: Blackbirch.

Testa, Maria. 2002. *Becoming Joe DiMaggio*. Cambridge, MA: Candlewick.

———. 2003. *Almost Forever*. Cambridge, MA: Candlewick.

Thimmesh, Catherine. 2000. *Girls Think of Everything: Stories of Ingenious Inventions by Women*. Boston: Houghton Mifflin.

Thomas, Jan. 2007. *What Will Fat Cat Sit On?* New York: Harcourt.

Time for Kids. *Time for Kids Almanac*. 2006. New York: Time for Kids.

Tolhurst, Marilyn. 1990. *Somebody and the Three Blairs*. New York: Orchard Books.

Van Draanen, Wendelin. 2004. *Shredderman: Secret Identity*. New York: Knopf.

Walsh, Melanie. 2006. *Do Lions Live on Lily Pads?* New York: Houghton Mifflin.

Ward, Cindy. 1988. *Cookie's Week*. New York: Putnam.

Watt, Melanie. 2006. *Scaredy Squirrel*. Tonawanda, NY: Kids Can Press.

———. 2007. *Scaredy Squirrel Makes a Friend*. Tonawanda, NY: Kids Can Press.

Weatherford, Carole Boston. 2007. *Jesse Owens: Fastest Man Alive*. New York: Walker & Company.

Webb, Steve. 2003. *Tanka Tanka Skunk!* New York: Orchard Books.

Weiss, M. Jerry, and Bernice E. Cullinan, eds. 1980. *Books I Read When I Was Young: The Favorite Books of Famous People*. New York: HarperCollins.

Wells, Rosemary. 1999. *Rachel Field's Hitty: Her First Hundred Years*. New York: Simon & Schuster.

West, Jerry. 1953. *The Happy Hollisters*. Garden City, NY: Garden City Books.

Westcott, Nadine Bernard. 1988. *The Lady with the Alligator Purse*. Boston: Trumpet.

Wilder, Laura Ingalls. 1971. *Little House in the Big Woods*. New York: HarperTrophy.

Wiles, Deborah. 2001. *Love, Ruby Lavender*. San Diego: Harcourt.

Willems, Mo. 2003. *Don't Let the Pigeon Drive the Bus!* New York: Hyperion Books for Children.

———. 2004a. *Knuffle Bunny*. New York: Hyperion Books for Children.

———. 2004b. *The Pigeon Finds a Hot Dog!* New York: Hyperion Books for Children.

———. 2006. *Don't Let the Pigeon Stay Up Late!* New York: Hyperion Books for Children.

Williams, Marcia. 2005. *Hooray for Inventors!* Cambridge, MA: Candlewick.

Williams, Suzanne. 1997. *Library Lil.* New York: Dial.

Williams, Vera B. 2001. *Amber Was Brave, Essie Was Smart.* New York: Greenwillow Books.

Wilson, Karma. 2006. *Sleepyhead.* New York: Margaret K. McElderry Books.

Winter, Jeanette. 2005. *The Librarian of Basra.* Orlando, FL: Harcourt.

Wisniewski, David. 1999. *Tough Cookie.* New York: Lothrop, Lee & Shepard.

Wood, Audrey. 1984. *The Napping House.* San Diego: Harcourt Brace Jovanovich.

———. 1992. *Silly Sally.* San Diego: Harcourt Brace Jovanovich.

———. 2005. *The Deep Blue Sea: A Book of Colors.* New York: Blue Sky.

Woodruff, Elvira. 1999. *The Memory Coat.* New York: Scholastic.

Woodson, Jacqueline. 2003. *Locomotion.* New York: G. P. Putnam's Sons.

Yaccarino, Dan. 2002. *Unlovable.* New York: Henry Holt.

Yo! I Know. 2006. New York: World Almanac Books.

Yolen, Jane. 1983. *Commander Toad and the Big Black Hole.* New York: Putnam.

———. 2003. *Hoptoad.* San Diego: Harcourt.

Yolen, Jane, and Heidi Elizabet Yolen Stemple. 1999. *The Mary Celeste: An Unsolved Mystery from History.* New York: Simon & Schuster.

Yolen, Jane, and Andrew Fusek Peters. 2007. *Here's a Little Poem.* Cambridge, MA: Candlewick.

Zane, Alexander. 2005. *The Wheels on the Race Car.* New York: Orchard Books.

Zion, Gene. 1956. *Harry the Dirty Dog.* New York: Scholastic.

Series Books

Abbott, Tony. The Secrets of Droon.

Adler, David A. Cam Jansen.

Allard, Harry. The Stupids.

Ardagh, Philip. Further Adventures of Eddie Dickens.

Arnold, Tedd. Fly Guy.

Avi. Tales from Dimwood Forest.

Baker, Keith. Mr. and Mrs. Green.

Barrows, Annie. Ivy & Bean.

Barry, Dave, and Ridley Pearson. Peter and the Starcatchers.

Benton, Jim. Franny K. Stein, Mad Scientist.

Black, Holly, and Toni DiTerlizzi. Spiderwick Chronicles.

Blyton, Enid. The Secret Seven.

Brown, Jeff. Flat Stanley.

Brown, Marc. Arthur.

Buckley, Michael. Sisters Grimm.

Burch, Robert. Ida Early.

Byng, Georgian. Molly Moon.

Cazet, Denys. Minnie and Moo.
Child, Lauren. Charlie and Lola.
Christelow, Eileen. Five Little Monkeys.
Cleary, Beverly. The Mouse and the Motorcycle.
Clements, Andrew. Jake Drake.
Collins, Suzanne. The Underland Chronicles.
Cosby, Bill. Little Bill.
Cronin, Doreen, and Betsy Lewin. Duck.
Dadey, Debbie. Bailey School Kids.
————. Triplet Trouble.
De Campi, Alex. Kat & Mouse.
Delton, Judy. Pee Wee Scouts.
DiCamillo, Kate, Mercy Watson.
Doyle, Roddy. The Giggler Treatment.
Draper, Sharon. Ziggy and the Black Dinosaurs.
DuPrau, Jeanne. Books of Ember.
Edwards, Michelle. The Jackson Friends.
Elder, Joshua. Mail Order Ninja.
Etra, Jonathan. Aliens.
Falconer, Ian. Olivia.
Frazier, Craig. Stanley.
Friedman, Laurie. Mallory.
Gownley, Jimmy. Amelia Rules!
Greenburg, Dan. Zack Files.
Greenburg, J. C. Andrew Lost.
Gutman, Dan. My Weird School.
Haddix, Margaret Peterson. Among the Hidden.
Harper, Charise Mericle. Just Grace.
Haywood, Carolyn. Betsy.
Higginson, Hadley. Keeker.
Hills, Tad. Duck and Goose.
Holm, Jennifer, and Matthew Holm. Babymouse.
Howe, James. Pinky and Rex.
Hunter, Erin. Warriors.
Jacques, Brian. Redwall.
Kamaiko, Leah. Annie Bananie.
Keane, Dave. Joe Sherlock, Kid Detective.
Keene, Carolyn. Nancy Drew.
Kerrin, Jessica Scott. Martin Bridge.
Kline, Suzy. Horrible Harry.
Kormon, Gordon. Survivor.
Lester, Helen. Tacky.
Levy, Elizabeth. Invisible Inc.
————. Something Queer.
Lindgren, Astrid Ericson. Pippi Longstocking.
Lobel, Arnold. Frog and Toad.

Long, Loren, and Phil Bildner. Barnstormers.
MacDonald, Betty. Mrs. Piggle Wiggle.
McCarty, Peter. Hondo & Fabian.
McDonald, Megan. Beezy.
————. Judy Moody.
————. Stink.
McMullan, Kate. Dragon Slayers' Academy.
Naylor, Phyllis Reynolds. Shiloh.
Nimmo, Jenny. Charlie Bone.
O'Connor, Jane, and Robin Preiss Glasser. Fancy Nancy.
Osborne, Mary Pope. Magic Tree House.
Parish, Peggy. Amelia Bedelia.
Park, Barbara. Junie B. Jones.
Pennypacker, Sara. Clementine.
Pilkey, Dav. Captain Underpants.
Pleasant Company. American Girls.
Preller, James. Jigsaw Jones.
Ross, Pat. M and M.
Roy, Ron. A to Z Mysteries.
Rylant, Cynthia. Henry and Mudge.
————. Mr. Putter and Tabby.
————. Poppleton.
Sachar, Louis. Marvin Redpost.
Sage, Angie. Septimus Heap.
Scieszka, Jon. Time Warp Trio.
Sendak, Maurice. Little Bear.
Shannon, David. David.
Sharmat, Marjorie Weinman. Nate the Great.
Smith, Jeff. Bones.
Snicket, Lemony. A Series of Unfortunate Events.
Stilton, Geronimo. Geronimo Stilton.
Sweet, J. H. The Fairy Chronicles.
Telgemeier, Raina. The Baby-Sitter Club.
Thaler, Mike. Funny Firsts.
Van Draanen, Wendelin. Shredderman.
Watt, Melanie. Scaredy Squirrel.
Wesley, Valerie Wilson. Willimena Rules!
Wilder, Laura Ingalls. Little House.
Willems, Mo. Elephant and Piggie.
————. Pigeon.
Willner-Pardo, Gina. Spider Storch.
Winkler, Henry, and Lin Oliver. Hank Zipzer.
Wojciechowski, Susan. Bean.
Yolen, Jane. Commander Toad.

Professional References and Adult Resources

Allen, Janet. 2000. *Yellow Brick Roads: Shared and Guided Paths to Independent Reading 4–12*. Portland, ME: Stenhouse.

Allington, Richard L. 2001. *What Really Matters for Struggling Readers: Designing Research-Based Programs*. New York: Longman.

Anthony, Laurie. 1999. *Have a Great One! A Homeless Man's Story*. Kearney, NE: Morris.

Atwell, Nancie. 1998. *In the Middle: Writing, Reading, and Learning with Adolescents*. 2nd ed. Portsmouth, NH: Boynton Cook.

Beers, Kylene. 2002. *When Kids Can't Read, What Teachers Can Do: A Guide for Teachers, 6–12*. Portsmouth, NH: Heinemann.

Bender, Sue. 1989. *Plain and Simple: A Woman's Journey to the Amish*. New York: Harper & Row.

Booth, David. 2002. *Even Hockey Players Read: Boys, Literacy and Learning*. Markham, Ontario: Pembroke.

Chevalier, Tracy. 1999. *Girl with a Pearl Earring*. New York: Dutton.

Collins, Kathy. 2004. *Growing Readers: Units of Study in the Primary Classroom*. Portland, ME: Stenhouse.

Daniels, Harvey. 1994. *Literature Circles: Voice and Choice in the Student-Centered Classroom*. Portland, ME: Stenhouse.

Fountas, Irene, and Gay Su Pinnell. 1996. *Guided Reading: Good First Teaching for All Children*. Portsmouth, NH: Heinemann.

———. 1999. *Matching Books to Readers: Using Leveled Books in Guided Reading, K–3*. Portsmouth, NH: Heinemann.

———. 2001. *Guiding Readers and Writers (Grades 3–6): Teaching Comprehension, Genre, and Content Literacy*. Portsmouth, NH: Heinemann.

Gaines, Ernest J. 1993. *A Lesson Before Dying*. New York: Vintage.

Hahn, Mary Lee. 2002. *Reconsidering Read-Aloud*. Portland, ME: Stenhouse.

Harvey, Stephanie. 1998. *Nonfiction Matters: Reading, Writing, and Research in Grades 3–8*. Portland, ME: Stenhouse.

Harvey, Stephanie, and Anne Goudvis. 2007. *Strategies That Work: Teaching Comprehension for Understanding and Engagement*. 2nd ed. Portland, ME: Stenhouse.

Harwayne, Shelley. 2000. *Lifetime Guarantees: Toward Ambitious Literacy Teaching*. Portsmouth, NH: Heinemann.

Hindley, Joanne. 1996. *In the Company of Children*. Portland, ME: Stenhouse.

Hosseini, Khaled. 2007. *A Thousand Splendid Suns*. New York: Riverhead Books.

Huck, Charlotte, and Barbara Zulandt Kiefer. 1973. *Children's Literature in the Elementary School*. New York: McGraw-Hill.

Johnston, Peter. 2004. *Choice Words: How Our Language Affects Children's Learning*. Portland, ME: Stenhouse.

Keene, Ellin, and Susan Zimmermann. 2007. *Mosaic of Thought: The Power of Comprehension Strategy Instruction*. 2nd ed. Portsmouth, NH: Heinemann.

Kingsolver, Barbara. 1998. *The Poisonwood Bible*. New York: HarperFlamingo.

Letts, Billie. 1998. *The Honk and Holler Opening Soon*. New York: Warner Books.

Mermelstein, Leah. 2007. *Don't Forget to Share: The Crucial Last Step in the Writing Workshop*. Portsmouth, NH: Heinemann.

Palmer, Parker. 1998. *The Courage to Teach: Exploring the Inner Landscape of a Teacher's Life*. San Francisco: Jossey-Bass.

Pogrow, Stanley. 2000. "Beyond the Good Start Mentality." *Education Week* 19 (32): 44–47.

Prensky, Marc. 2001. "Digital Natives, Digital Immigrants." *On the Horizon* 9 (5). Available online at http://www.marcprensky.com/writing.

Quindlen, Anna. 1998. *How Reading Changed My Life*. New York: Ballantine.

Routman, Regie. 1994. *Invitations: Changing as Teachers and Learners, K–12*. Portsmouth, NH: Heinemann.

———. 2000. *Conversations: Strategies for Teaching, Learning, and Evaluating*. Portsmouth, NH: Heinemann.

Short, Kathy. 1997. *Literature as a Way of Knowing*. Portland, ME: Stenhouse.

Sibberson, Franki, and Karen Szymusiak. 2008. *Day-to-Day Assessment in the Reading Workshop*. New York: Scholastic.

Smith, Nila Banton. 2002. *American Reading Instruction*. Newark, Delaware: International Reading Association.

Szymusiak, Karen, and Franki Sibberson. 2001. *Beyond Leveled Books: Supporting Transitional Readers in Grades 2–5*. Portland, ME: Stenhouse.

Taberski, Sharon. 2000. *On Solid Ground: Strategies for Teaching Reading K–3*. Portsmouth, NH: Heinemann.

Thompson, Terry. 2008. *Adventures in Graphica: Using Comics and Graphic Novels to Teach Comprehension, 2–6*. Portland, ME: Stenhouse.

Titus, Diana. 1991. "Bookends: A Program for Pairs." *Teaching K–8* 21: 60-61.

Index

Page numbers followed by an *f* or *t* indicate figures or tables.